THE LOGIC OF
COLLECTIVE ACTION

Public Goods
and the
Theory of Groups

MANCUR OLSON

Harvard University Press

Cambridge • Massachusetts

Library of Congress Catalog Card Number 65–19826

SBN 674–53750–5

Printed in the United States of America

FOR ALISON

Preface, 1971

Since both the hardcover and paperback editions of this book are being reprinted at about the same time, this is a good occasion to consider making changes. It would be possible to amend the argument of the book, to add several ideas that have occurred to me since it was written, and to consider related work others have recently done. But I have decided against any such major revision. There has been no change in my views to justify rewriting the present text. Some of the ideas I would add to any new edition have already appeared in articles. It would take too long to deal adequately with what others have written. Accordingly, what I have done instead is to prepare a short Appendix. It provides any interested reader a guide to the articles I have done on the subject of this book and discusses an intriguing idea for further work that commentators on the book have proposed. This Appendix begins on page 169.

Though the memory of most favors fades in a short time, that has not been the case with my gratitude to the critics who helped me when the book was being written. I often have occasion to see that the reaction to the book would have been less generous (or more reserved) had early drafts not been criticized so well. The critic who was most helpful of all was Thomas Schelling of Harvard University. Though neither he nor my other critics are responsible for the faults of the book, much of whatever use it has had is due particularly to his criticisms. Edward C. Banfield and Otto Eckstein also criticized this study most helpfully when it was a draft of a Ph.D. thesis at Harvard. When the undertaking was in the prospectus stage, I benefited greatly from the criticisms of Samuel Beer, John Kenneth Galbraith, Carl Kaysen, and Talcott Parsons. As I began to revise the thesis for publication, I received uncommonly helpful comments from Alan Holmans, Dale Jorgenson, John Kain, Douglas Keare, Richard Lester, and George von Furstenberg. Also, at various stages in the process of making this book, William Baumol, David Bayley, Arthur Benavie, James Buchanan, Edward Claiborn, Aldrich Finegan, Louis Fourt, Gerald Garvey, Mohammed Guessous, W. E. Hamilton, Wolfram Hanrieder, Stanley Kelley, Roland McKean, Richard Musgrave, Robert Reichardt, Jerome Rothenberg, Craig Stubblebine, Gordon Tullock, Alan Williams, and Richard Zeckhauser made notable and constructive criticisms. Finally, I hope the dedication to my wife indicates how much I appreciate her help and encouragement. In addition to all of the other things she has done for me and for our three children, she helped with both the style and substance of this book.

I am also thankful that Professor F. A. von Hayek took the initiative in arranging for the translation of this book into German and in contributing a foreword to the German translation.

My work on this book was generously supported by the Social Science Research Council, the Shinner Foundation, and the Center for International Studies at Princeton University. I am also thankful to the Brookings Institution, whose hospitality greatly furthered my work on this and on a previous book.

Mancur Olson

Department of Economics
University of Maryland
College Park, Maryland

CONTENTS

THE LOGIC OF
COLLECTIVE ACTION

Introduction

It is often taken for granted, at least where economic objectives are involved, that groups of individuals with common interests usually attempt to further those common interests. Groups of individuals with common interests are expected to act on behalf of their common interests much as single individuals are often expected to act on behalf of their personal interests. This opinion about group behavior is frequently found not only in popular discussions but also in scholarly writings. Many economists of diverse methodological and ideological traditions have implicitly or explicitly accepted it. This view has, for example, been important in many theories of labor unions, in Marxian theories of class action, in concepts of "countervailing power," and in various discussions of economic institutions. It has, in addition, occupied a prominent place in political science, at least in the United States, where the study of pressure groups has been dominated by a celebrated "group theory" based on the idea that groups will act when necessary to further their common or group goals. Finally, it has played a significant role in many well-known sociological studies.

The view that groups act to serve their interests presumably is based upon the assumption that the individuals in groups act out of self-interest. If the individuals in a group altruistically disregarded their personal welfare, it would not be very likely that collectively they would seek some selfish common or group objective. Such altruism, is, however, considered exceptional, and self-interested behavior is usually thought to be the rule, at least when economic issues are at stake; no one is surprised when individual businessmen seek higher profits, when individual workers seek higher wages, or when individual consumers seek lower prices. The idea that groups tend to act in support of their group interests is supposed to follow logically from this widely accepted premise of rational, self-interested behavior. In other words, if the members of some group have a common interest or objective, and if they would all be better off if tnat objective were achieved, it has been thought to follow logically that the individuals in that group would, if they were rational and self-interested, act to achieve that objective.

But it is *not* in fact true that the idea that groups will act in their self-interest follows logically from the premise of rational and self-interested behavior. It does *not* follow, because all of the individuals in a group would gain if they achieved their group objective, that they would act to achieve that objective, even if they were all rational and self-interested. Indeed, unless the number of individuals in a group is quite small, or unless there is coercion or some other special device to make individuals act in their common interest, *rational, self-interested individuals will not act to achieve their common or group interests.* In other words, even if all of the individuals in a large group are rational and self-interested, and would gain if, as a group, they acted to achieve their common interest or objective, they will still not voluntarily act to achieve that common or group interest. The notion that groups of individuals will act to achieve their common or group interests, far from being a logical implication of the assumption that the individuals in a group will rationally further their individual interests, is in fact inconsistent with that assumption. This inconsistency will be explained in the following chapter.

If the members of a large group rationally seek to maximize their personal welfare, they will *not* act to advance their common or group objectives unless there is coercion to force them to do so, or unless some separate incentive, distinct from the achievement of the common or group interest, is offered to the members of the group individually on the condition that they help bear the costs or burdens involved in the achievement of the group objectives. Nor will such large groups form organizations to further their common goals in the absence of the coercion or the separate incentives just mentioned. These points hold true even when there is unanimous agreement in a group about the common good and the methods of achieving it.

The widespread view, common throughout the social sciences, that groups tend to further their interests, is accordingly unjustified, at least when it is based, as it usually is, on the (sometimes implicit) assumption that groups act in their self-interest because individuals do. There is paradoxically the logical possibility that groups composed of either altruistic individuals or irrational individuals may sometimes act in their common or group interests. But, as later, empirical parts of this study will attempt to show, this logical possibility is usually of no practical importance. Thus the customary view that groups of individuals with common interests tend to further those common interests appears to have little if any merit.

None of the statements made above fully applies to small groups, for the situation in small groups is much more complicated. In small groups there may very well be some voluntary action in support of the common purposes of the individuals in the group, but in most cases this action will cease before it reaches the optimal level for the members of the group as a whole. In the sharing of the costs of efforts to achieve a common goal in small groups, there is however a surprising tendency for the "exploitation" of the *great* by the *small*.

The proofs of all of the logical statements that have been made above are contained in Chapter I, which develops a logical or theoretical explanation of certain aspects of group and organizational behavior. Chapter II examines the implications of this analysis for groups of different size, and illustrates the conclusion that in many cases small groups are more efficient and viable than large ones. Chapter III considers the implications of the argument for labor unions, and draws the conclusion that some form of compulsory membership is, in most circumstances, indispensable to union survival. The fourth chapter uses the approach developed in this study to examine Marx's theory of social classes and to analyze the theories of the state developed by some other economists. The fifth analyzes the "group theory" used by many political scientists in the light of the logic elaborated in this study, and argues that that theory as usually understood is logically inconsistent. The final chapter develops a new theory of pressure groups which is consistent with the logical relationships outlined in the first chapter, and which suggests that the membership and power of large pressure-group organizations does not derive from their lobbying achievements, but is rather a by-product of their other activities.

Though I am an economist, and the tools of analysis used in this book are drawn from economic theory, the conclusions of the study are as relevant to the sociologist and the political scientist as they are to the economist. I have, therefore, avoided using the diagrammatic-mathematical language of economics whenever feasible. Unfortunately, many noneconomists will find one or two brief parts of the first chapter expressed in an obscure and uncongenial way, but all of the rest of the book should be perfectly clear, whatever the reader's disciplinary background.

I

A Theory of Groups and Organizations

A. THE PURPOSE OF ORGANIZATION

Since most (though by no means all) of the action taken by or on behalf of groups of individuals is taken through organizations, it will be helpful to consider organizations in a general or theoretical way.[1] The logical place to begin any systematic study of organizations is with their purpose. But there are all types and shapes and sizes of organizations, even of economic organizations, and there is then some question whether there is any single purpose that would be characteristic of organizations generally. One purpose that is nonetheless characteristic of most organizations, and surely of practically all organizations with an important economic aspect, is the furtherance of the interests of their members. That would seem obvious, at least from the economist's perspective. To be sure, some organizations may out of ignorance fail to further their members' interests, and others may be enticed into serving only the ends of the leadership.[2]

1. Economists have for the most part neglected to develop theories of organizations, but there are a few works from an economic point of view on the subject. See, for example, three papers by Jacob Marschak, "Elements for a Theory of Teams," *Management Science,* I (January 1955), 127–137, "Towards an Economic Theory of Organization and Information," in *Decision Processes,* ed. R. M. Thrall, C. H. Combs, and R. L. Davis (New York: John Wiley, 1954), pp. 187–220, and "Efficient and Viable Organization Forms," in *Modern Organization Theory,* ed. Mason Haire (New York: John Wiley, 1959), pp. 307–320; two papers by R. Radner, "Application of Linear Programming to Team Decision Problems," *Management Science,* V (January 1959), 143–150, and "Team Decision Problems," *Annals of Mathematical Statistics,* XXXIII (September 1962), 857–881; C. B. McGuire, "Some Team Models of a Sales Organization," *Management Science,* VII (January 1961), 101–130; Oskar Morgenstern, *Prolegomena to a Theory of Organization* (Santa Monica, Calif.: RAND Research Memorandum 734, 1951); James G. March and Herbert A. Simon, *Organizations* (New York: John Wiley, 1958); Kenneth Boulding, *The Organizational Revolution* (New York: Harper, 1953).

2. Max Weber called attention to the case where an organization continues to exist for some time after it has become meaningless because some official is making a living out of it. See his *Theory of Social and Economic Organization,* trans. Talcott Parsons and A. M. Henderson (New York: Oxford University Press, 1947), p. 318.

But organizations often perish if they do nothing to further the interests of their members, and this factor must severely limit the number of organizations that fail to serve their members.

The idea that organizations or associations exist to further the interests of their members is hardly novel, nor peculiar to economics; it goes back at least to Aristotle, who wrote, "Men journey together with a view to particular advantage, and by way of providing some particular thing needed for the purposes of life, and similarly the political association seems to have come together originally, and to continue in existence, for the sake of the *general* advantages it brings." [3] More recently Professor Leon Festinger, a social psychologist, pointed out that "the attraction of group membership is not so much in sheer belonging, but rather in attaining something by means of this membership." [4] The late Harold Laski, a political scientist, took it for granted that "associations exist to fulfill purposes which a group of men have in common." [5]

The kinds of organizations that are the focus of this study are *expected* to further the interests of their members. [6] Labor unions are expected to strive for higher wages and better working conditions for their members; farm organizations are expected to strive for favorable legislation for their members; cartels are expected to strive for higher prices for participating firms; the corporation is expected to further the interests of its stockholders; [7] and the state is expected

3. *Ethics* viii.9.1160a.
4. Leon Festinger, "Group Attraction and Membership," in *Group Dynamics,* ed. Dorwin Cartwright and Alvin Zander (Evanston, Ill.: Row, Peterson, 1953), p. 93.
5. *A Grammar of Politics,* 4th ed. (London: George Allen & Unwin, 1939), p. 67.
6. Philanthropic and religious organizations are not necessarily expected to serve only the interests of their members; such organizations have other purposes that are considered more important, however much their members "need" to belong, or are improved or helped by belonging. But the complexity of such organizations need not be debated at length here, because this study will focus on organizations with a significant economic aspect. The emphasis here will have something in common with what Max Weber called the "associative group"; he called a group associative if "the orientation of social action with it rests on a rationally motivated agreement." Weber contrasted his "associative group" with the "communal group" which was centered on personal affection, erotic relationships, etc., like the family. (See Weber, pp. 136–139, and Grace Coyle, *Social Process in Organized Groups,* New York: Richard Smith, Inc., 1930, pp. 7–9.) The logic of the theory developed here can be extended to cover communal, religious, and philanthropic organizations, but the theory is not particularly useful in studying such groups. See my pp. 61n17, 159–162.
7. That is, its members. This study does not follow the terminological usage of those organization theorists who describe employees as "members" of the organization for which they work. Here it is more convenient to follow the language of everyday

to further the common interests of its citizens (though in this nationalistic age the state often has interests and ambitions apart from those of its citizens).

Notice that the interests that all of these diverse types of organizations are expected to further are for the most part *common* interests: the union members' common interest in higher wages, the farmers' common interest in favorable legislation, the cartel members' common interest in higher prices, the stockholders' common interest in higher dividends and stock prices, the citizens' common interest in good government. It is not an accident that the diverse types of organizations listed are all supposed to work primarily for the *common* interests of their members. Purely personal or individual interests can be advanced, and usually advanced most efficiently, by individual, unorganized action. There is obviously no purpose in having an organization when individual, unorganized action can serve the interests of the individual as well as or better than an organization; there would, for example, be no point in forming an organization simply to play solitaire. But when a number of individuals have a common or collective interest—when they share a single purpose or objective—individual, unorganized action (as we shall soon see) will either not be able to advance that common interest at all, or will not be able to advance that interest adequately. Organizations can therefore perform a function when there are common or group interests, and though organizations often also serve purely personal, individual interests, their characteristic and primary function is to advance the common interests of groups of individuals.

The assumption that organizations typically exist to further the common interests of groups of people is implicit in most of the literature about organizations, and two of the writers already cited make this assumption explicit: Harold Laski emphasized that organizations exist to achieve purposes or interests which "a group of men have in common," and Aristotle apparently had a similar notion in mind when he argued that political associations are created and maintained because of the "general advantages" they bring. R. M.

---

usage instead, and to distinguish the members of, say, a union from the employees of that union. Similarly, the members of the union will be considered employees of the corporation for which they work, whereas the members of the corporation are the common stockholders.

MacIver also made this point explicitly when he said that "every organization presupposes an interest which its members all share." [8]

Even when unorganized groups are discussed, at least in treatments of "pressure groups" and "group theory," the word "group" is used in such a way that it means "a number of individuals with a common interest." It would of course be reasonable to label even a number of people selected at random (and thus without any common interest or unifying characteristic) as a "group"; but most discussions of group behavior seem to deal mainly with groups that do have common interests. As Arthur Bentley, the founder of the "group theory" of modern political science, put it, "there is no group without its interest." [9] The social psychologist Raymond Cattell was equally explicit, and stated that "every group has its interest." [10] This is also the way the word "group" will be used here.

Just as those who belong to an organization or a group can be presumed to have a common interest,[11] so they obviously also have purely individual interests, different from those of the others in the organization or group. All of the members of a labor union, for example, have a common interest in higher wages, but at the same time each worker has a unique interest in his personal income, which depends not only on the rate of wages but also on the length of time that he works.

8. R. M. MacIver, "Interests," *Encyclopaedia of the Social Sciences,* VII (New York: Macmillan, 1932), 147.

9. Arthur Bentley, *The Process of Government* (Evanston, Ill.: Principia Press, 1949), p. 211. David B. Truman takes a similar approach; see his *The Governmental Process* (New York: Alfred A. Knopf, 1958), pp. 33–35. See also Sidney Verba, *Small Groups and Political Behavior* (Princeton, N.J.: Princeton University Press, 1961), pp. 12–13.

10. Raymond Cattell, "Concepts and Methods in the Measurement of Group Syntality," in *Small Groups,* ed. A. Paul Hare, Edgard F. Borgatta, and Robert F. Bales (New York: Alfred A. Knopf, 1955), p. 115.

11. Any organization or group will of course usually be divided into subgroups or factions that are opposed to one another. This fact does not weaken the assumption made here that organizations exist to serve the common interests of members, for the assumption does not imply that intragroup conflict is neglected. The opposing groups within an organization ordinarily have some interest in common (if not, why would they maintain the organization?), and the members of any subgroup or faction also have a separate common interest of their own. They will indeed often have a common purpose in defeating some other subgroup or faction. The approach used here does not neglect the conflict within groups and organizations, then, because it considers each organization as a unit only to the extent that it does in fact attempt to serve a common interest, and considers the various subgroups as the relevant units with common interests to analyze the factional strife.

B. PUBLIC GOODS AND LARGE GROUPS

The combination of individual interests and common interests in an organization suggests an analogy with a competitive market. The firms in a perfectly competitive industry, for example, have a common interest in a higher price for the industry's product. Since a uniform price must prevail in such a market, a firm cannot expect a higher price for itself unless all of the other firms in the industry also have this higher price. But a firm in a competitive market also has an interest in selling as much as it can, until the cost of producing another unit exceeds the price of that unit. In this there is no common interest; each firm's interest is directly opposed to that of every other firm, for the more other firms sell, the lower the price and income for any given firm. In short, while all firms have a common interest in a higher price, they have antagonistic interests where output is concerned. This can be illustrated with a simple supply-and-demand model. For the sake of a simple argument, assume that a perfectly competitive industry is momentarily in a disequilibrium position, with price exceeding marginal cost for all firms at their present output. Suppose, too, that all of the adjustments will be made by the firms already in the industry rather than by new entrants, and that the industry is on an inelastic portion of its demand curve. Since price exceeds marginal cost for all firms, output will increase. But as all firms increase production, the price falls; indeed, since the industry demand curve is by assumption inelastic, the total revenue of the industry will decline. Apparently each firm finds that with price exceeding marginal cost, it pays to increase its output, but the result is that each firm gets a smaller profit. Some economists in an earlier day may have questioned this result,[12] but the fact that profit-maximizing firms in a perfectly competitive industry can act contrary to their interests as a group is now widely understood and accepted.[13] A group of profit-maximizing firms can act to reduce their aggregate profits because in perfect competition each firm is, by definition, so small that it can ignore the effect of its output on price. Each firm finds it to its advantage to increase output to the point where mar-

12. See J. M. Clark, *The Economics of Overhead Costs* (Chicago: University of Chicago Press, 1923), p. 417, and Frank H. Knight, *Risk, Uncertainty and Profit* (Boston: Houghton Mifflin, 1921), p. 193.

13. Edward H. Chamberlin, *Monopolistic Competition,* 6th ed. (Cambridge, Mass.: Harvard University Press, 1950), p. 4.

ginal cost equals price and to ignore the effects of its extra output on the position of the industry. It is true that the net result is that all firms are worse off, but this does not mean that every firm has not maximized its profits. If a firm, foreseeing the fall in price resulting from the increase in industry output, were to restrict its own output, it would lose more than ever, for its price would fall quite as much in any case and it would have a smaller output as well. A firm in a perfectly competitive market gets only a small part of the benefit (or a small share of the industry's extra revenue) resulting from a reduction in that firm's output.

For these reasons it is now generally understood that if the firms in an industry are maximizing profits, the profits for the industry as a whole will be less than they might otherwise be.[14] And almost everyone would agree that this theoretical conclusion fits the facts for markets characterized by pure competition. The important point is that this is true because, though all the firms have a common interest in a higher price for the industry's product, it is in the interest of each firm that the other firms pay the cost—in terms of the necessary reduction in output—needed to obtain a higher price.

About the only thing that keeps prices from falling in accordance with the process just described in perfectly competitive markets is outside intervention. Government price supports, tariffs, cartel agreements, and the like may keep the firms in a competitive market from acting contrary to their interests. Such aid or intervention is quite common. It is then important to ask how it comes about. How does a competitive industry obtain government assistance in maintaining the price of its product?

Consider a hypothetical, competitive industry, and suppose that most of the producers in that industry desire a tariff, a price-support program, or some other government intervention to increase the price for their product. To obtain any such assistance from the government, the producers in this industry will presumably have to organize a lobbying organization; they will have to become an active pressure group.[15] This lobbying organization may have to conduct a con-

14. For a fuller discussion of this question see Mancur Olson, Jr., and David McFarland, "The Restoration of Pure Monopoly and the Concept of the Industry," *Quarterly Journal of Economics,* LXXVI (November 1962), 613–631.

15. Robert Michels contends in his classic study that "democracy is inconceivable without organization," and that "the principle of organization is an absolutely essential condition for the political struggle of the masses." See his *Political Parties,*

siderable campaign. If significant resistance is encountered, a great amount of money will be required.[16] Public relations experts will be needed to influence the newspapers, and some advertising may be necessary. Professional organizers will probably be needed to organize "spontaneous grass roots" meetings among the distressed producers in the industry, and to get those in the industry to write letters to their congressmen.[17] The campaign for the government assistance will take the time of some of the producers in the industry, as well as their money.

There is a striking parallel between the problem the perfectly competitive industry faces as it strives to obtain government assistance, and the problem it faces in the marketplace when the firms increase output and bring about a fall in price. *Just as it was not rational for a particular producer to restrict his output in order that there might be a higher price for the product of his industry, so it would not be rational for him to sacrifice his time and money to support a lobbying organization to obtain government assistance for the industry. In neither case would it be in the interest of the individual producer to assume any of the costs himself. A lobbying organization, or indeed a labor union or any other organization, working in the interest of a large group of firms or workers in some industry, would get no assistance from the rational, self-interested individuals in that industry.* This would be true even if everyone in the industry were absolutely convinced that the proposed program was in their interest (though in fact some might think otherwise and make the organization's task yet more difficult).[18]

Although the lobbying organization is only one example of the logical analogy between the organization and the market, it is of

trans. Eden and Cedar Paul (New York: Dover Publications, 1959), pp. 21–22. See also Robert A. Brady, *Business as a System of Power* (New York: Columbia University Press, 1943), p. 193.

16. Alexander Heard, *The Costs of Democracy* (Chapel Hill: University of North Carolina Press, 1960), especially note 1, pp. 95–96. For example, in 1947 the National Association of Manufacturers spent over $4.6 million, and over a somewhat longer period the American Medical Association spent as much on a campaign against compulsory health insurance.

17. "If the full truth were ever known . . . lobbying, in all its ramifications, would prove to be a billion dollar industry." U.S. Congress, House, Select Committee on Lobbying Activities, *Report,* 81st Cong., 2nd Sess. (1950), as quoted in the *Congressional Quarterly Almanac,* 81st Cong., 2nd Sess., VI, 764–765.

18. For a logically possible but practically meaningless exception to the conclusion of this paragraph, see footnote 68 in this chapter.

some practical importance. There are many powerful and well-financed lobbies with mass support in existence now, but these lobbying organizations do not get that support because of their legislative achievements. The most powerful lobbying organizations now obtain their funds and their following for other reasons, as later parts of this study will show.

Some critics may argue that the rational person will, indeed, support a large organization, like a lobbying organization, that works in his interest, because he knows that if he does not, others will not do so either, and then the organization will fail, and he will be without the benefit that the organization could have provided. This argument shows the need for the analogy with the perfectly competitive market. For it would be quite as reasonable to argue that prices will never fall below the levels a monopoly would have charged in a perfectly competitive market, because if one firm increased its output, other firms would also, and the price would fall; but each firm could foresee this, so it would not start a chain of price-destroying increases in output. In fact, it does not work out this way in a competitive market; nor in a large organization. When the number of firms involved is large, no one will notice the effect on price if one firm increases its output, and so no one will change his plans because of it. Similarly, in a large organization, the loss of one dues payer will not noticeably increase the burden for any other one dues payer, and so a rational person would not believe that if he were to withdraw from an organization he would drive others to do so.

The foregoing argument must at the least have some relevance to economic organizations that are mainly means through which individuals attempt to obtain the same things they obtain through their activities in the market. Labor unions, for example, are organizations through which workers strive to get the same things they get with their individual efforts in the market—higher wages, better working conditions, and the like. It would be strange indeed if the workers did not confront some of the same problems in the union that they meet in the market, since their efforts in both places have some of the same purposes.

However similar the purposes may be, critics may object that attitudes in organizations are not at all like those in markets. In organizations, an emotional or ideological element is often also involved. Does this make the argument offered here practically irrelevant?

A most important type of organization—the national state—will serve to test this objection. Patriotism is probably the strongest non-economic motive for organizational allegiance in modern times. This age is sometimes called the age of nationalism. Many nations draw additional strength and unity from some powerful ideology, such as democracy or communism, as well as from a common religion, language, or cultural inheritance. The state not only has many such powerful sources of support; it also is very important economically. Almost any government is economically beneficial to its citizens, in that the law and order it provides is a prerequisite of all civilized economic activity. But despite the force of patriotism, the appeal of the national ideology, the bond of a common culture, and the indispensability of the system of law and order, no major state in modern history has been able to support itself through voluntary dues or contributions. Philanthropic contributions are not even a significant source of revenue for most countries. Taxes, *compulsory* payments by definition, are needed. Indeed, as the old saying indicates, their necessity is as certain as death itself.

If the state, with all of the emotional resources at its command, cannot finance its most basic and vital activities without resort to compulsion, it would seem that large private organizations might also have difficulty in getting the individuals in the groups whose interests they attempt to advance to make the necessary contributions voluntarily.[19]

The reason the state cannot survive on voluntary dues or payments,

19. Sociologists as well as economists have observed that ideological motives alone are not sufficient to bring forth the continuing effort of large masses of people. Max Weber provides a notable example:

"All economic activity in a market economy is undertaken and carried through by individuals for their own ideal or material interests. This is naturally just as true when economic activity is oriented to the patterns of order of corporate groups . . .

"Even if an economic system were organized on a socialistic basis, there would be no fundamental difference in this respect . . . The structure of interests and the relevant situation might change; there would be other means of pursuing interests, but this fundamental factor would remain just as relevant as before. It is of course true that economic action which is oriented on purely ideological grounds to the interest of others does exist. But it is even more certain that the mass of men do not act in this way, and it is an induction from experience that they cannot do so and never will . . .

"In a market economy the interest in the maximization of income is necessarily the driving force of all economic activity." (Weber, pp. 319–320.)

Talcott Parsons and Neil Smelser go even further in postulating that "performance" throughout society is proportional to the "rewards" and "sanctions" involved. See their *Economy and Society* (Glencoe, Ill.: Free Press, 1954), pp. 50–69.

but must rely on taxation, is that the most fundamental services a nation-state provides are, in one important respect,[20] like the higher price in a competitive market: they must be available to everyone if they are available to anyone. The basic and most elementary goods or services provided by government, like defense and police protection, and the system of law and order generally, are such that they go to everyone or practically everyone in the nation. It would obviously not be feasible, if indeed it were possible, to deny the protection provided by the military services, the police, and the courts to those who did not voluntarily pay their share of the costs of government, and taxation is accordingly necessary. The common or collective benefits provided by governments are usually called "public goods" by economists, and the concept of public goods is one of the oldest and most important ideas in the study of public finance. A common, collective, or public good is here defined as any good such that, if any person X_i in a group $X_1, \ldots, X_i, \ldots, X_n$ consumes it, it cannot feasibly be withheld from the others in that group.[21] In

20. See, however, section E of this chapter, on "exclusive" and "inclusive" groups.

21. This simple definition focuses upon two points that are important in the present context. The first point is that most collective goods can only be defined with respect to some specific group. One collective good goes to one group of people, another collective good to another group; one may benefit the whole world, another only two specific people. Moreover, some goods are collective goods to those in one group and at the same time private goods to those in another, because some individuals can be kept from consuming them and others can't. Take for example the parade that is a collective good to all those who live in tall buildings overlooking the parade route, but which appears to be a private good to those who can see it only by buying tickets for a seat in the stands along the way. The second point is that once the relevant group has been defined, the definition used here, like Musgrave's, distinguishes collective good in terms of infeasibility of excluding potential consumers of the good. This approach is used because collective goods produced by organizations of all kinds seem to be such that exclusion is normally not feasible. To be sure, for some collective goods it is physically possible to practice exclusion. But, as Head has shown, it is not necessary that exclusion be technically impossible; it is only necessary that it be infeasible or uneconomic. Head has also shown most clearly that nonexcludability is only one of two basic elements in the traditional understanding of public goods. The other, he points out, is "jointness of supply." A good has "jointness" if making it available to one individual means that it can be easily or freely supplied to others as well. The polar case of jointness would be Samuelson's pure public good, which is a good such that additional consumption of it by one individual does not diminish the amount available to others. By the definition used here, jointness is not a necessary attribute of a public good. As later parts of this chapter will show, at least one type of collective good considered here exhibits no jointness whatever, and few if any would have the degree of jointness needed to qualify as pure public goods. Nonetheless, most of the collective goods to be studied here do display a large measure of jointness. On the definition and importance of public goods, see John G. Head,

other words, those who do not purchase or pay for any of the public or collective good cannot be excluded or kept from sharing in the consumption of the good, as they can where noncollective goods are concerned.

Students of public finance have, however, neglected the fact that *the achievement of any common goal or the satisfaction of any common interest means that a public or collective good has been provided for that group.*[22] The very fact that a goal or purpose is *common* to a group means that no one in the group is excluded from the benefit or satisfaction brought about by its achievement. As the opening paragraphs of this chapter indicated, almost all groups and organizations have the purpose of serving the common interests of their members. As R. M. MacIver puts it, "Persons . . . have common interests in the degree to which they participate in a cause . . . which indivisibly embraces them all."[23] It is of the essence of an organization that it provides an inseparable, generalized benefit. It follows that the provision of public or collective goods is the fundamental function of organizations generally. A state is first of all an organization that provides public goods for its members, the citizens; and other types of organizations similarly provide collective goods for their members.

And just as a state cannot support itself by voluntary contributions, or by selling its basic services on the market, neither can other large organizations support themselves without providing some sanction,

---

"Public Goods and Public Policy," *Public Finance,* vol. XVII, no. 3 (1962), 197–219; Richard Musgrave, *The Theory of Public Finance* (New York: McGraw-Hill, 1959); Paul A. Samuelson, "The Pure Theory of Public Expenditure," "Diagrammatic Exposition of A Theory of Public Expenditure," and "Aspects of Public Expenditure Theories," in *Review of Economics and Statistics,* XXXVI (November 1954), 387–390, XXXVII (November 1955), 350–356, and XL (November 1958), 332–338. For somewhat different opinions about the usefulness of the concept of public goods, see Julius Margolis, "A Comment on the Pure Theory of Public Expenditure," *Review of Economics and Statistics,* XXXVII (November 1955), 347–349, and Gerhard Colm, "Theory of Public Expenditures," *Annals of the American Academy of Political and Social Science,* CLXXXIII (January 1936), 1–11.

22. There is no necessity that a public good to one group in a society is necessarily in the interest of the society as a whole. Just as a tariff could be a public good to the industry that sought it, so the removal of the tariff could be a public good to those who consumed the industry's product. This is equally true when the public-good concept is applied only to governments; for a military expenditure, or a tariff, or an immigration restriction that is a public good to one country could be a "public bad" to another country, and harmful to world society as a whole.

23. R. M. MacIver in *Encyclopaedia of the Social Sciences,* VII, 147.

or some attraction distinct from the public good itself, that will lead individuals to help bear the burdens of maintaining the organization. The individual member of the typical large organization is in a position analogous to that of the firm in a perfectly competitive market, or the taxpayer in the state: his own efforts will not have a noticeable effect on the situation of his organization, and he can enjoy any improvements brought about by others whether or not he has worked in support of his organization.

There is no suggestion here that states or other organizations provide *only* public or collective goods. Governments often provide noncollective goods like electric power, for example, and they usually sell such goods on the market much as private firms would do. Moreover, as later parts of this study will argue, large organizations that are not able to make membership compulsory *must also* provide some noncollective goods in order to give potential members an incentive to join. Still, collective goods are the characteristic organizational goods, for ordinary noncollective goods can always be provided by individual action, and only where common purposes or collective goods are concerned is organization or group action ever indispensable.[24]

C. THE TRADITIONAL THEORY OF GROUPS

There is a traditional theory of group behavior that implicitly assumes that private groups and associations operate according to principles entirely different from those that govern the relationships among firms in the maketplace or between taxpayers and the state. This "group theory" appears to be one of the principal concerns of many political scientists in the United States, as well as a major preoccupation of many sociologists and social psychologists.[25] This traditional theory of groups, like most other theories, has been developed by different writers with varying views, and there is accordingly an inevitable injustice in any attempt to give a common

24. It does not, however, follow that organized or coordinated group action is *always* necessary to obtain a collective good. See section D of this chapter, "Small Groups."

25. For a discussion of the importance of "groups" of various sorts and sizes for the theory of politics, see Verba, *Small Groups and Political Behavior;* Truman, *Governmental Process;* and Bentley, *Process of Government.* For examples of the type of research and theory about groups in social psychology and sociology, see *Group Dynamics,* ed. Cartwright and Zander, and *Small Groups,* ed. Hare, Borgatta, and Bales.

treatment to these different views. Still, the various exponents of the traditional understanding of groups do have a common relationship to the approach developed in the present study. It is therefore appropriate to speak here in a loose way of a single traditional theory, provided that a distinction is drawn between the two basic variants of this theory: the casual variant and the formal variant.

In its most casual form, the traditional view is that private organizations and groups are ubiquitous, and that this ubiquity is due to a fundamental human propensity to form and join associations. As the famous Italian political philosopher Gaetano Mosca puts it, men have an "instinct" for "herding together and fighting with other herds." This "instinct" also "underlies the formation of all the divisions and subdivisions . . . that arise within a given society and occasion moral and, sometimes, physical conflicts." [26] Aristotle may have had some similar gregarious faculty in mind when he said that man was by nature a political animal.[27] The ubiquitous and inevitable character of group affiliation was emphasized in Germany by Georg Simmel, in one of the classics of sociological literature,[28] and in America by Arthur Bentley, in one of the best-known works on political science.[29] This universal joining tendency or propensity is often thought to have reached its highest intensity in the United States.[30]

The formal variant of the traditional view also emphasizes the universality of groups, but does not begin with any "instinct" or "tendency" to join groups. Instead it attempts to explain the associations and group affiliations of the present day as an aspect of the evolution of modern, industrial societies out of the "primitive" societies that preceded them. It begins with the fact that "primary groups" [31]—groups so small that each of the members has face-to-face

26. *The Ruling Class* (New York: McGraw-Hill, 1939), p. 163.

27. *Politics* i.2.9.1253a. Many others have also emphasized the human propensity towards groups; see Coyle, *Social Process in Organized Groups;* Robert Lowie, *Social Organization* (New York: Rinehart & Co., 1948); Truman, especially pp. 14–43.

28. Georg Simmel, *Conflict and the Web of Group Affiliations,* trans. Kurt Wolff and Reinhard Bendix (Glencoe, Ill.: Free Press, 1950).

29. Bentley, *Process of Government.*

30. Alexis de Tocqueville, *Democracy in America* (New York: New American Library, 1956), p. 198; James Bryce, *The American Commonwealth,* 4th ed. (New York: Macmillan, 1910), pp. 281–282; Charles A. Beard and Mary R. Beard, *The Rise of American Civilization,* rev. ed. (New York: Macmillan, 1949), pp. 761–762; and Daniel Bell, *The End of Ideology* (Glencoe, Ill.: Free Press, 1960), esp. p. 30.

31. Charles H. Cooley, *Social Organization* (New York: Charles Scribner's Sons,

relationships with the others—like family and kinship groups are predominant in primitive societies. As Talcott Parsons contends, "it is well-known that in many primitive societies there is a sense in which kinship 'dominates' the social structure; there are few concrete structures in which participation is independent of kinship status."[32] Only small family or kinship type units represent the interests of the individual. R. M. MacIver describes it this way in the *Encyclopaedia of the Social Sciences:* "Under more simple conditions of society the social expression of interests was mainly through caste or class groups, age groups, kin groups, neighborhood groups, and other unorganized or loosely organized solidarities."[33] Under "primitive" conditions the small, family-type units account for all or almost all human "interaction."

But, these social theorists contend, as society develops, there is structural differentiation: new associations emerge to take on some of the functions that the family had previously undertaken. "As the social functions performed by the family institution in our society have declined, some of these secondary groups, such as labor unions, have achieved a rate of interaction that equals or surpasses that of certain of the primary groups."[34] In Parsons' words, "It is clear that in the more 'advanced' societies a far greater part is played by non-kinship structures like states, churches, the larger business firms, universities and professional societies . . . The process by which non-kinship units become of prime importance in the social structure inevitably entails 'loss of function' on the part of some or even all of the kinship units."[35] If this is true, and if, as MacIver claims, "the most marked structural distinction between a primitive society and a civilized society is the paucity of specific associations in the one

1909), p. 23; George C. Homans, *The Human Group* (New York: Harcourt, Brace, 1950), p. 1; Verba, pp. 11–16.

32. Talcott Parsons and Robert F. Bales, *Family* (Glencoe, Ill.: Free Press, 1955), p. 9; see also Talcott Parsons, Robert F. Bales, and Edward A. Shils, *Working Papers in the Theory of Action* (Glencoe, Ill.: Free Press, 1953).

33. MacIver in *Encyclopaedia of the Social Sciences,* VII, 144–148, esp. 147. See also Truman, p. 25.

34. Truman, pp. 35–36; see also Eliot Chapple and Carlton Coon, *Principles of Anthropology* (New York: Henry Holt, 1942), pp. 443–462.

35. Parsons and Bales, p. 9. See also Bernard Barber, "Participation and Mass Apathy in Associations," in *Studies in Leadership,* ed. Alvin W. Gouldner (New York: Harper, 1950), pp. 477–505, and Neil J. Smelser, *Social Change in the Industrial Revolution* (London: Routledge & Kegan Paul, 1959).

and their multiplicity in the other," [36] then it would seem that the large association in the modern society is in some sense an equivalent of the small group in the primitive society, and that the large, modern association and the small, primitive group must be explained in terms of the same fundamental source or cause.[37]

What then is the fundamental source which accounts alike for the small primary groups in primitive societies and the large voluntary association of modern times? This the advocates of the formal variant of the theory have left implicit and unclear. It could be the supposed "instinct" or "tendency" to form and join associations, which is the hallmark of the casual variant of the traditional view; this predilection for forming and joining groups would then manifest itself in small family and kinship groups in primitive societies and in large voluntary associations in modern societies. This interpretation would however probably be unfair to many of the theorists who subscribe to the formal variant of the traditional theory, for many of them doubtless would not subscribe to any theory of "instincts" or "propensities." They are no doubt aware that no explanation whatever is offered when the membership of associations or groups is said to be due to an "instinct" to belong; this merely adds a word, not an explanation. Any human action can be ascribed to an instinct or propensity for that kind of action, but this adds nothing to our knowledge. If instincts or propensities to join groups are ruled out as meaningless, what then could be the source of the ubiquitous groups and associations, large and small, posited by the traditional theory? Probably some of the traditional theorists were thinking in "functional" terms—that is of the functions that groups or associations of different types and sizes can perform. In primitive societies small primary groups prevailed because they were best suited (or at

36. MacIver in *Encyclopaedia of the Social Sciences*, VII, 144–148, esp. 147. See also Louis Wirth, "Urbanism as a Way of Life," *American Journal of Sociology*, XLIV (July 1938), 20; Walter Firey, "Coalition and Schism in a Regional Conservation Program," *Human Organization*, XV (Winter 1957), 17–20; Herbert Goldhamer, "Social Clubs," in *Development of Collective Enterprise*, ed. Seba Eldridge (Lawrence: University of Kansas Press, 1943), p. 163.

37. For a different interpretation of the voluntary association see Oliver Garceau, *The Political Life of the American Medical Association* (Cambridge, Mass.: Harvard University Press, 1941), p. 3: "With the advent of political intervention and control, particularly over the economy, it became evident that the formation of policy could not be confined to ballot or legislature. To fill the gap the voluntary group was resorted to, not only by the individual who felt himself alone, but by the government which felt itself ignorant."

least sufficient) to perform certain functions for the people of these societies; in modern societies, by contrast, large associations are supposed to predominate because in modern conditions they alone are capable of performing (or are better able to perform) certain useful functions for the people of these societies. The large voluntary association, for example, could then be explained by the fact that it peformed a function—that is, satisfied a demand, furthered an interest, or met a need—for some large number of people that small groups could not perform (or perform so well) in modern circumstances. This demand or interest provides an incentive for the formation and maintenance of the voluntary association.

It is characteristic of the traditional theory in all its forms that it assumes that participation in voluntary associations is virtually universal, and that small groups and large organizations tend to attract members for the same reasons. The casual variant of the theory assumed a propensity to belong to groups without drawing any distinctions between groups of different size. Though the more sophisticated variant may be credited with drawing a distinction between those functions that can best be served by small groups and those that can best be served by large associations, it nonetheless assumes that, when there is a need for a large association, a large association will tend to emerge and attract members, just as a small group will when there is a need for a small group. Thus in so far as the traditional theory draws any distinction at all between small and large groups, it is apparently with respect to the scale of the functions they perform, not the extent they succeed in performing these functions or their capacity to attract members. It assumes that small and large groups differ in degree, but not in kind.

But is this true? Is it really the case that small, primary groups and large associations attract members in the same way, that they are about equally effective in performing their functions, or that they differ only in size but not in their basic character? This traditional theory is called into question by the empirical research which shows that the average person does *not* in fact typically belong to large voluntary associations and that the allegation that the typical American is a "joiner" is largely a myth.[38] It is therefore worth

---

38. Murray Hausknecht, *The Joiners—A Sociological Description of Voluntary Association Membership in the United States* (New York: Bedminster Press, 1962); Mirra Komaravsky, "The Voluntary Associations of Urban Dwellers," *American*

asking if it is really true that there is no relation between the size of a group and its coherence, or effectiveness, or appeal to potential members; and whether there is any relation between the size of a group and the individual incentives to contribute toward the achievement of group goals. These are questions which must be answered before the traditional theory of groups can be properly assessed. What needs to be known, in the words of the German sociologist Georg Simmel, is "the bearing which the number of sociated individuals has upon the form of social life." [39]

One obstacle, it would seem, to any argument that large and small groups operate according to fundamentally different principles, is the fact, emphasized earlier, that any group or organization, large or small, works for some collective benefit that by its very nature will benefit all of the members of the group in question. Though all of the members of the group therefore have a common interest in obtaining this collective benefit, they have no common interest in paying the cost of providing that collective good. Each would prefer that the others pay the entire cost, and ordinarily would get any benefit provided whether he had borne part of the cost or not. If this is a fundamental characteristic of all groups or organizations with an economic purpose, it would seem unlikely that large organizations would be much different from small ones, and unlikely that there is any more reason that a collective service would be provided for a small group than a large one. Still, one cannot help but feel intuitively that sufficiently small groups would sometimes provide themselves with public goods.

This question cannot be answered satisfactorily without a study of the costs and benefits of alternative courses of action open to individuals in groups of different sizes. The next section of this chapter contains such a study. The nature of this question is such that some of the tools of economic analysis must be used. The following section contains a small amount of mathematics which, though extremely rudimentary, might naturally still be unclear to readers who have never studied that subject. Some points in the following section,

Sociological Review, XI (December 1946), 686–698; Floyd Dotson, "Patterns of Voluntary Membership Among Working Class Families," *American Sociological Review*, XVI (October 1951), 687; John C. Scott, Jr., "Membership and Participation in Voluntary Associations," *American Sociological Review*, XXII (June 1957), 315.

39. Georg Simmel, *The Sociology of Georg Simmel*, trans. Kurt H. Wolff (Glencoe, Ill.: Free Press [1950]), p. 87.

moreover, refer to oligopolistic groups in the marketplace, and the references to oligopoly may interest only the economist. Accordingly, some of the highlights of the following section are explained in an intuitively plausible, though loose and imprecise, way in the "non-technical summary" of section D, for the convenience of those who might wish to skip the bulk of the following section.

D. SMALL GROUPS

The difficulty of analyzing the relationship between group size and the behavior of the individual in the group is due partly to the fact that each individual in a group may place a different value upon the collective good wanted by his group. Each group wanting a collective good, moreover, faces a different cost function. One thing that will hold true in every case, however, is that the total cost function will be rising, for collective goods are surely like non-collective goods in that the more of the good taken, the higher total costs will be. It will, no doubt, also be true in virtually all cases that there will be significant initial or fixed costs. Sometimes a group must set up a formal organization before it can obtain a collective good, and the cost of establishing an organization entails that the first unit of a collective good obtained will be relatively expensive. And even when no organization or coordination is required, the lumpiness or other technical characteristics of the public goods themselves will ensure that the first unit of a collective good will be disproportionately expensive. Any organization will surely also find that as its demands increase beyond a certain point, and come to be regarded as "excessive," the resistance and the cost of additional units of the collective good rise disproportionately. In short, cost (C) will be a function of the rate or level (T) at which the collective good is obtained $(C = f(T))$, and the average cost curves will have the conventional U shape.

One point is immediately evident. If there is some quantity of a collective good that can be obtained at a cost sufficiently low in relation to its benefit that some one person in the relevant group would gain from providing that good all by himself, then there is some presumption that the collective good will be provided. The total gain would then be so large in relation to the total cost that some one individual's share would exceed the total cost.

An individual will get some share of the total gain to the group, a share that depends upon the number in the group and upon how much the individual will benefit from that good in relation to the others in the group. The total gain to the group will depend upon the rate or level at which the collective good is obtained (T), and the "size" of the group (S_g), which depends not only upon the number of individuals in the group, but also on the value of a unit of the collective good to each individual in the group. This could be illustrated most simply by considering a group of property owners lobbying for a property tax rebate. The total gain to the group would depend upon the "size" (S_g) of the group, that is, the total assessed valuation of all the group property, and the rate or level (T) of tax rebate per dollar of assessed valuation of property. The gain to an individual member of the group would depend upon the "fraction" (F_i) of the group gain he got.

The group gain (S_gT) could also be called V_g, for "value" to the group, and the gain to the individual V_i, for "value" to the individual. The "fraction" (F_i) would then equal V_i/V_g, and the gain to the individual would be F_iS_gT. The advantage (A_i) that any individual i would get from obtaining any amount of the collective or group good would be the gain to the individual (V_i) minus the cost (C).

What a group does will depend on what the individuals in that group do, and what the individuals do depends on the relative advantages to them of alternative courses of action. So the first thing to do, now that the relevant variables have been isolated, is to consider the individual gain or loss from buying different amounts of the collective good. This will depend on the way the advantage to the individual ($A_i = V_i - C$) changes with changes in T, that is, on

$$dA_i/dT = dV_i/dT - dC/dT.$$

For a maximum, $dA_i/dT = 0$.[40] Since $V_i = F_iS_gT$, and F_i and S_g are, for now, assumed constant,[41]

$$d(F_iS_gT)/dT - dC/dT = 0$$
$$F_iS_g - dC/dT = 0.$$

40. The second-order conditions for a maximum must also be satisfied; that is, $d^2A_i/dT^2 < 0$.

41. In cases where F_i and S_g are not constant, the maximum is given when:

$$d(F_iS_gT)/dT - dC/dT = 0$$
$$F_iS_g + F_iT(dS_g/dT) + S_gT(dF_i/dT) - dC/dT = 0.$$

This indicates the amount of the collective good that an individual acting independently would buy, if he were to buy any. This result can be given a general, common-sense meaning. Since the optimum point is found when

$$dA_i/dT = dV_i/dT - dC/dT = 0$$

and since $dV_i/dT = F_i(dV_g/dT)$

$$F_i(dV_g/dT) - dC/dT = 0$$
$$F_i(dV_g/dT) = dC/dT.$$

This means that the optimal amount of a collective good for an individual to obtain, if he should obtain any, is found when the rate of gain to the group, multiplied by the fraction of the group gain the individual gets, equals the rate of increase of the total cost of the collective good. In other words, the rate of gain to the group (dV_g/dT) must exceed the rate of increase in cost (dC/dT) by the same multiple that the group gain exceeds the gain to the individual concerned $(1/F_i = V_g/V_i)$.[42]

But what matters most is *not* how much of the collective good will be provided if some is provided, but rather whether *any* of the collective good will be provided. And it is clear that, at the optimum point for the individual acting independently, the collective or group good will presumably be provided if $F_i > C/V_g$.

For if

$$F_i > C/V_g$$
$$V_i/V_g > C/V_g$$

then

$$V_i > C.$$

Thus, if $F_i > C/V_g$, the gain to an individual from seeing that the collective good is provided will exceed the cost. This means there is a presumption that the collective good will be provided if the cost of the collective good is, at the optimal point for any individual in the group, so small in relation to the gain of the group as a whole

---

42. The same point could be made by focusing attention on the individual's cost and benefit functions alone, and neglecting the gains to the group. But this would divert attention from the main purpose of the analysis, which is studying the relation between the size of the group and the likelihood that it will be provided with a collective good.

from that collective good, that the total gain exceeds the total cost by as much as or more than the gain to the group exceeds the gain to the individual.

In summary, then, the rule is that there is a presumption that a collective good will be provided if, when the gains to the group from the collective good are *increasing* at $1/F_i$ times the *rate* of increase in the total cost of providing that good (that is, when $dV_g/dT = 1/F_i(dC/dT)$), the total benefit to the group is a larger multiple of the cost of that good than the gains to the group are of the gains to the individual in question (that is, $V_g/C > V_g/V_i$).

The degree of generality of the basic idea in the foregoing model can be illustrated by applying it to a group of firms in a market. Consider an industry producing a homogeneous product, and assume that the firms in the industry *independently* seek to maximize profits. For simplicity, suppose also that marginal costs of production are zero. In order to avoid adding any new notational symbols, and to bring out the applicability of the foregoing analysis, assume that T now stands for price, that S_g now stands for the physical volume of the group's or industry's sales, and S_i for the size or physical volume of the sales of firm i. F_i still indicates the "fraction" of the total accounted for by the individual firm or member of the group. It indicates now the fraction of the total group or industry sales going to firm i at any given moment: $F_i = S_i/S_g$. The price, T, will affect the amount sold by the industry to an extent given by the elasticity of demand, E. The elasticity $E = -T/S_g(dS_g/dT)$, and from this a convenient expression for the slope of the demand curve, dS_g/dT, follows: $dS_g/dT = -ES_g/T$. With no production costs, the optimum output for a firm will be given when:

$$dA_i/dT = d(S_iT)/dT = 0$$
$$S_i + T(dS_i/dT) = 0$$
$$F_iS_g + T(dS_i/dT) = 0.$$

Here, where it is assumed that the firm acts independently, i.e., expects no reaction from other firms, $dS_i = dS_g$, so

$$F_iS_g + T(dS_g/dT) = 0$$

and since $dS_g/dT = -ES_g/T$,

$$F_iS_g - T(ES_g/T) = 0$$
$$S_g(F_i - E) = 0.$$

This can happen only when $F_i = E$. Only when the elasticity of demand for the industry is less than or equal to the fraction of the industry's output supplied by a particular firm will that firm have any incentive to restrict its output. A firm that is deciding whether or not to restrict its output in order to bring about a higher price will measure the cost or loss of the foregone output against the gains it gets from the "collective good"—the higher price. The elasticity of demand is a measure of this. If F_i is equal to E it means that the elasticity of demand for the industry is the same as the proportion of the output of the industry shared by the firm in question; if the elasticity of demand is, say, 1/4, it means that a 1 per cent reduction in output will bring a 4 per cent increase in price, which makes it obvious that if a given firm has one fourth of the total industry output it should stop increasing, or restrict, its own output. If there were, say, a thousand firms of equal size in an industry, the elasticity of demand for the industry's product would have to be 1/1000 or less before there would be any restriction of output. Thus there are no profits in equilibrium in any industry with a really large number of firms. A profit-maximizing firm will start restricting its output, that is, will start acting in a way consistent with the interests of the industry as a whole, when the rate at which the gain to the group increases, as more T (a higher price) is provided, is $1/F_i$ times as great as the rate at which the total cost of output restriction increases. This is the same criterion for group-oriented behavior used in the more general case explained earlier.

This analysis of a market is identical with that offered by Cournot.[43] This should not be surprising, for Cournot's theory is essentially a special case of a more general theory of the relationship between the interests of the member of a group and of the interests of the group as a whole. The Cournot theory can be regarded as a special case of the analysis developed here. The Cournot solution thus boils down to the common-sense statement that a firm will act to keep up the price of the product its industry sells only when the total cost of keeping up the price is not more than its share of the industry's gain from the higher price. The Cournot theory is, like the analysis of group action outside the market, a theory that asks

43. Augustin Cournot, *Researches into the Mathematical Principles of the Theory of Wealth,* trans. Nathaniel T. Bacon (New York: Macmillan, 1897), especially chap. vii, pp. 79–90.

when it is in the interest of an individual unit in a group to act in the interest of the group as a whole.

The Cournot case is in one respect simpler than the group situation outside the marketplace that is the main concern of this study. When a group seeks an ordinary collective good, rather than a higher price through output restriction, it finds, as the opening paragraph of this section argued, that the first unit of the collective good obtained will be more expensive per unit than some subsequent units of the good. This is because of the lumpiness and other technical characteristics of collective goods, and because it may sometimes be necessary to create an organization to obtain the collective good. This calls to attention the fact that there are two distinct questions that an individual in a nonmarket group must consider. One is whether the total benefit he would get from providing some amount of the collective good would exceed the total cost of that amount of the good. The other question is how much of the collective good he should provide, if some should be provided, and the answer here depends of course on the relationship between marginal, rather than total, costs and benefits.

There are similarly also two distinct questions that must be answered about the group as a whole. It is not enough to know whether a small group will provide itself with a collective good; it is also necessary to determine whether the amount of the collective good that a small group will obtain, if it obtains any, will tend to be Pareto-optimal for the group as a whole. That is, will the group gain be maximized? The optimal amount of a collective good for a group as a whole to obtain, if it should obtain any, would be given when the gain to the group was increasing at the same rate as the cost of the collective good, i.e., when $dV_g/dT = dC/dT$. Since, as shown earlier, each individual in the group would have an incentive to provide more of the collective good until $F_i(dV_g/dT = dC/dT$, and since $\Sigma F_i = 1$, it would at first glance appear that the sum of what the individual members acting independently would provide would add up to the group optimum. It would also seem that each individual in the group would then bear a fraction, F_i, of the total burden or cost, so that the burden of providing the public good would be shared in the "right" way in the sense that the cost would be shared in the same proportion as the benefits.

But this is not so. Normally, the provision of the collective good will be strikingly suboptimal and the distribution of the burden will be highly arbitrary. This is because the amount of the collective good that the individual obtains for himself will automatically also go to others. It follows from the very definition of a collective good that an individual cannot exclude the others in the group from the benefits of that amount of the public good that he provides for himself.[44] This means that no one in the group will have an incentive independently to provide any of the collective good once the amount that would be purchased by the individual in the group with the largest F_i was available. This suggests that, just as there is a tendency for large groups to fail to provide themselves with any collective good at all, so *there is a tendency in small groups toward a suboptimal provision of collective goods.* The suboptimality will be the more serious the smaller the F_i of the "largest" individual in the group. *Since the larger the number in the group, other things equal, the smaller the F_i's will be, the more individuals in the group, the more serious the suboptimality will be.* Clearly then groups with larger numbers of members will generally perform less efficiently than groups with smaller numbers of members.

It is not, however, sufficient to consider only the number of individuals or units in a group, for the F_i of any member of the group will depend not only on how many members there are in the group, but also on the "size" (S_i) of the individual member, that is, the extent to which he will be benefited by a given level of provision of the collective good. An owner of vast estates will save more from a given reduction in property taxes than the man with only a modest cottage, and other things equal will have a larger F_i.[45] A group com-

44. In the rest of this section it is convenient and helpful to assume that every member of the group receives the same amount of the public good. This is in fact the case whenever the collective good is a "pure public good" in Samuelson's sense. This assumption is, however, more stringent than is usually necessary. A public good may be consumed in unequal amounts by different individuals, yet be a full public good in the sense that one individual's consumption does not in any way diminish that of another. And even when additional consumption by one individual does lead to marginal reductions in the amount available to others, the qualitative conclusions that there will be suboptimality and disproportionate burden sharing still hold.

45. Differences in size can also have some importance in market situations. The large firm in a market will get a larger fraction of the total benefit from any higher price than a small firm, and will therefore have more incentive to restrict output. This suggests that the competition of a few large firms among the many small ones, contrary to some opinions, can lead to a serious misallocation of resources. For a different view on this subject, see Willard D. Arant, "The Competition of the Few among the Many," *Quarterly Journal of Economics*, LXX (August 1956), 327–345.

posed of members of unequal S_i, and, therefore, unequal F_i, will show less of a tendency toward suboptimality (and be more likely to provide itself with some amount of a collective good) than an otherwise identical group composed of members of equal size.

Since no one has an incentive to provide any more of the collective good, once the member with the largest F_i has obtained the amount he wants, it is also true that the distribution of the burden of providing the public good in a small group will *not* be in proportion to the benefits conferred by the collective good. The member with the largest F_i will bear a disproportionate share of the burden.[46] Where small groups with common interests are concerned, then, *there is a systematic tendency for "exploitation"* [47] *of the great by the small!*

The behavior of small groups interested in collective goods can sometimes be quite complex—much more complex than the preceding paragraphs would suggest.[48] There are certain institutional

46. The discussion in the text is much too brief and simple to do full justice even to some of the most common situations. In what is perhaps the most common case, where the collective good is *not* a money payment to each member of some group, and not something that each individual in the group can sell for money, the individuals in the group must compare the additional cost of another unit of the collective good with the additional "utility" they would get from an additional unit of that good. They could not, as the argument in the text assumes, merely compare a money cost with a money return, and indifference curves would accordingly also have to be used in the analysis. The marginal rate of substitution would be affected not only by the fact that the taste for additional units of the collective good would diminish as more of the good was consumed, but also by the income effects. The income effects would lead a group member that had sacrificed a disproportionate amount of his income to obtain the public good to value his income more highly than he would have done had he got the collective good free from others in the group. Conversely, those who had not borne any of the burden of providing the collective good they enjoyed would find their real incomes greater, and unless the collective good were an inferior good, this gain in real income tend would strengthen their demand for the collective good. These income effects would tend to keep the largest member of the group from bearing *all* of the burden of the collective good (as he would in the much too simple case considered in the text). I am thankful to Richard Zeckhauser for bringing the importance of income effects in this context to my attention.

47. The moral overtones of the word "exploitation" are unfortunate; no general moral conclusions can follow from a purely logical analysis. Since the word "exploitation" is, however, commonly used to describe situations where there is a disproportion between the benefits and sacrifices of different people, it would be pedantic to use a different word here.

48. For one thing, the argument in the text assumes independent behavior, and thus neglects the strategic interaction or bargaining that is possible in small groups. As later parts of this chapter will show, strategic interaction is usually much less important in nonmarket groups seeking collective goods than it is among groups of firms in the marketplace. And even when there is bargaining, it will often be

arrangements and behavioral assumptions that will not always lead to the suboptimality and disproportionality that the preceding paragraphs have described. Any adequate analysis of the tendency toward suboptimal provision of collective goods, and toward disproportionate sharing of the burdens of providing them, would be too long to fit comfortably into this study, which is concerned mainly with large groups, and brings in small groups mainly for purposes of comparison and contrast. The problem of small groups seeking collective goods is of some importance, both theoretically [49] and practically, and has not been adequately treated in the literature. It will accordingly be analyzed in more detail in forthcoming articles. The Nontechnical Summary of this section will list a few of the specific cases that this approach to small groups and organizations can be used to study.

The necessary conditions for the optimal provision of a collective good, through the voluntary and independent action of the members of a group, can, however, be stated very simply. The marginal cost of additional units of the collective good must be shared in exactly the same proportion as the additional benefits. Only if this is done will each member find that his own marginal costs and benefits are

---

the case that there will be a disparity of bargaining power that will lead to about the same results as are described in the text. When a group member with a large F_i bargains with a member with a small F_i, all he can do is threaten the smaller member by saying, in effect, "If you do not provide more of the collective good, I will provide less myself, and you will then be worse off than you are now." But when the large member restricts his purchase of the public good, he will suffer *more* than the smaller member, simply because his F_i is greater. The large member's threat is thus not apt to be credible. Another factor that works in the same direction is that the maximum amount of collective good provision that a successful bargain can extract from the small member is less than the amount a successful bargain can bring forth from the large member. This means that the large member may not gain enough even from successful bargaining to justify the risks or other costs of bargaining, while the small member by contrast finds that the gain from a successful bargain is large in relation to his costs of bargaining. The bargaining problem is of course more complex than this, but it is nonetheless clear that bargaining will usually lead toward the same results as the forces explained in the text.

49. Erik Lindahl's famous "voluntary theory of public exchange" can, I believe, usefully be amended and expanded with the aid of the analysis adumbrated in the text. I am thankful to Richard Musgrave for bringing to my attention the fact that Lindahl's theory and the approach used in this study must be closely related. He sees this relationship in a different way, however. For analyses of Lindahl's theory see Richard Musgrave, "The Voluntary Exchange Theory of Public Economy," *Quarterly Journal of Economics*, LIII (February 1939), 213–237; Leif Johansen, "Some Notes on the Lindahl Theory of Determination of Public Expenditures," *International Economic Review*, IV (September 1963), 346–358; John G. Head, "Lindahl's Theory of the Budget," *Finanzarchiv*, XXIII (October 1964), 421–454.

equal at the same time that the total marginal cost equals the total or aggregate marginal benefit. If marginal costs are shared in *any* other way, the amount of collective good provided will be *sub-optimal*.[50] It might seem at first glance that if some cost allocations lead to a suboptimal provision of a collective good, then some other cost allocations would lead to a supraoptimal supply of that good; but this is not so. In any group in which participation is voluntary, the member or members whose shares of the marginal cost exceed their shares of the additional benefits will stop contributing to the achievement of the collective good *before* the group optimum has been reached. And there is no conceivable cost-sharing arrangement in which *some* member does not have a marginal cost greater than his share of the marginal benefit, except the one in which every member of the group shares marginal costs in exactly the same proportion in which he shares incremental benefits.[51]

50. There is an illustration of this point in many farm tenancy agreements, where the landlord and tenant often share the produce of the crop in some prearranged proportion. The farm's output can then be regarded as a public good to the landlord and tenant. Often the tenant will provide *all* of the labor, machinery, and fertilizer, and the landlord will maintain *all* of the buildings, drainage, ditches, etc. As some agricultural economists have rightly pointed out, such arrangements are inefficient, for the tenant will use labor, machinery, and fertilizer only up to the point where the marginal cost of these factors of production equals the marginal return from his *share* of the crop. Similarly, the landlord will provide a suboptimal amount of the factors he provides. The only way in which this suboptimal provision of the factors can be prevented in a share-tenancy is by having the landlord and tenant share the costs of each of the (variable) factors of production in the *same* proportion in which they share the output. Perhaps this built-in inefficiency in most share-tenancy agreements helps account for the observation that in many areas where farmers do not own the land they farm, land reform is necessary to increase agricultural efficiency. See Earl O. Heady and E. W. Kehrberg, *Effect of Share and Cash Renting on Farming Efficiency* (Iowa Agricultural Experiment Station Bulletin 386), and Earl O. Heady, *Economics of Agricultural Production and Resource Use* (New York: Prentice-Hall, 1952), esp. pp. 592 and 620.

51. A similar argument could sometimes be used to help explain the common observation that there is "public squalor" midst "private splendor," that is, a suboptimal supply of public goods. Such an argument would be relevant at least in those situations where proposed Pareto-optimal public expenditures benefit a group of people smaller than the group that would be taxed to pay for these expenditures. The point that even Pareto-optimal public expenditures usually benefit groups of people smaller than the group taxed to pay for these expenditures was suggested to me by Julius Margolis' useful paper on "The Structure of Government and Public Investment," in *American Economic Review: Papers and Proceedings*, LIV (May 1964), 236–247. See my "Discussion" of Margolis' paper (and others) in the same issue of the *American Economic Review* (pp. 250–251) for a suggestion of a way in which a model of the kind developed in this study can be used to explain private

Though there is a tendency for even the smallest groups to provide suboptimal amounts of a collective good (unless they arrange marginal cost-sharing of the kind just described), the more important point to remember is that some sufficiently small groups can pro-

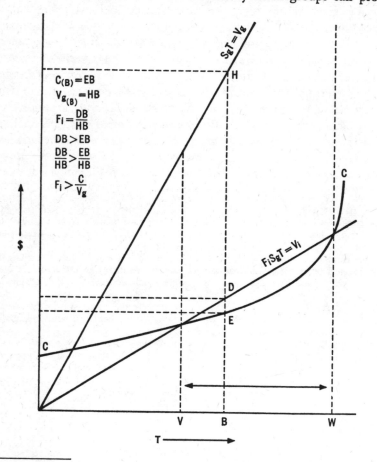

affluence and public squalor. It is interesting that John Head (*Finanzarchiv*, XXIII, 453–454) and Leif Johansen (*International Economic Review*, IV, 353), though they started out at different points from mine and used instead Lindahl's approach, still had arrived at conclusions on this point that are not altogether different from mine. For interesting arguments that point to forces that could lead to supra-optimal levels of government expenditure, see two other papers in the issue of the *American Economic Review* cited above, namely "Fiscal Institutions and Efficiency in Collective Outlay" (pp. 227–235) by James M. Buchanan, and "Divergencies between Individual and Total Costs within Government" (pp. 243–249) by Roland N. McKean.

vide themselves with some amount of a collective good through the voluntary and rational action of one or more of their members. In this they are distinguished from really large groups. There are two things to determine in finding out whether there is any presumption that a given group will voluntarily provide itself with a collective good. First, the optimal amount of the collective good for each *individual* to buy, if he is to buy any, must be discovered; this is given when $F_i(dV_g/dT) = dC/dT$.[52] Second, it must be determined whether any member or members of the group would find at that individual optimum that the benefit to the group from the collective good exceeded the total cost by more than it exceeded the member's own benefit from that collective good; that is, whether $F_i > C/V_g$. The argument may be stated yet more simply by saying that, *if at any level of purchase of the collective good, the gain to the group exceeds the total cost by more than it exceeds the gain to any individual, then there is a presumption that the collective good will be provided, for then the gain to the individual exceeds the total cost of providing the collective good to the group.* This is illustrated in the accompanying figure, where an individual would presumably be better off for having provided the collective good, whether he provided amount V or amount W or any amount in between. If any amount of the collective good between V and W is obtained, even if it is not the optimal amount for the individual, F_i will exceed C/V_g.

Nontechnical summary of Section D

The technical part of this section has shown that certain small groups can provide themselves with collective goods without relying on coercion or any positive inducements apart from the collective good itself.[53] This is because in some small groups each of the mem-

---

52. If F_i is not a constant, this individual optimum is given when:
$$F_i(dV_g/dT) + V_g(dF_i/dT) = dC/dT.$$

53. I am indebted to Professor John Rawls of the Department of Philosophy at Harvard University for reminding me of the fact that the philosopher David Hume sensed that small groups could achieve common purposes but large groups could not. Hume's argument is however somewhat different from my own. In *A Treatise of Human Nature,* Everyman edition (London: J. M. Dent, 1952), II, 239, Hume wrote: "There is no quality in human nature which causes more fatal errors in our conduct, than that which leads us to prefer whatever is present to the distant and remote, and makes us desire objects more according to their situation than their intrinsic value. Two neighbours may agree to drain a meadow, which they possess

bers, or at least one of them, will find that his personal gain from having the collective good exceeds the total cost of providing some amount of that collective good; there are members who would be better off if the collective good were provided, even if they had to pay the entire cost of providing it themselves, than they would be if it were not provided. In such situations there is a presumption that the collective good will be provided. Such a situation will exist only when the benefit to the group from having the collective good exceeds the total cost by more than it exceeds the gain to one or more individuals in the group. Thus, in a very small group, where each member gets a substantial proportion of the total gain simply because there are few others in the group, a collective good can often be provided by the voluntary, self-interested action of the members of the group. In smaller groups marked by considerable degrees of inequality—that is, in groups of members of unequal "size" or extent of interest in the collective good—there is the greatest likelihood that a collective good will be provided; for the greater the interest in the collective good of any single member, the greater the likelihood that that member will get such a significant proportion of the total benefit from the collective good that he will gain from seeing that the good is provided, even if he has to pay all of the cost himself.

Even in the smallest groups, however, the collective good will not ordinarily be provided on an optimal scale. That is to say, the members of the group will not provide as much of the good as it would be in their common interest to provide. Only certain special

in common: because it is easy for them to know each other's mind; and each must perceive, that the immediate consequence of his failing in his part, is the abandoning of the whole project. But it is very difficult, and indeed impossible, that a thousand persons should agree in any such action; it being difficult for them to concert so complicated a design, and still more difficult to execute it; while each seeks a pretext to free himself of the trouble and expense, and would lay the whole burden on others. Political society easily remedies both these inconveniences. Magistrates find an immediate interest in the interest of any considerable part of their subjects. They need consult nobody but themselves to form any scheme for promoting that interest. And as the failure of any one piece in the execution is connected, though not immediately, with the failure of the whole, they prevent that failure, because they find no interest in it, either immediate or remote. Thus, bridges are built, harbours opened, ramparts raised, canals formed, fleets equipped, and armies disciplined, everywhere, by the care of government, which, though composed of men subject to all human infirmities, becomes, by one of the finest and most subtle inventions imaginable, a composition which is in some measure exempted from all these infirmities."

institutional arrangements will give the individual members an incentive to purchase the amounts of the collective good that would add up to the amount that would be in the best interest of the group as a whole. This tendency toward suboptimality is due to the fact that a collective good is, by definition, such that other individuals in the group cannot be kept from consuming it once any individual in the group has provided it for himself. Since an individual member thus gets only part of the benefit of any expenditure he makes to obtain more of the collective good, he will discontinue his purchase of the collective good before the optimal amount for the group as a whole has been obtained. In addition, the amounts of the collective good that a member of the group receives free from other members will further reduce his incentive to provide more of that good at his own expense. Accordingly, *the larger the group, the farther it will fall short of providing an optimal amount of a collective good.*

This suboptimality or inefficiency will be somewhat less serious in groups composed of members of greatly different size or interest in the collective good. In such unequal groups, on the other hand, there is a tendency toward an arbitrary sharing of the burden of providing the collective good. The largest member, the member who would on his own provide the largest amount of the collective good, bears a disproportionate share of the burden of providing the collective good. The smaller member by definition gets a smaller fraction of the benefit of any amount of the collective good he provides than a larger member, and therefore has less incentive to provide additional amounts of the collective good. Once a smaller member has the amount of the collective good he gets free from the largest member, he has more than he would have purchased for himself, and has no incentive to obtain any of the collective good at his own expense. In small groups with common interests there is accordingly *a surprising tendency for the "exploitation" of the great by the small.*

The argument that small groups providing themselves with collective goods tend to provide suboptimal quantities of these goods, and that the burdens of providing them are borne in an arbitrary and disproportionate way, does not hold in all logically possible situations. Certain institutional or procedural arrangements can lead to different outcomes. The subject cannot be analyzed adequately in any brief discussion. For this reason, and because the main focus of this book is on large groups, many of the complexities of small-group behavior have been neglected in this study. An argument of the kind just outlined could, however, fit some important practical situations rather well, and may serve the purpose of suggesting that a more detailed analysis of the kind outlined above could help to explain the apparent tendency for large countries to bear disproportionate shares of the burdens of multinational organizations, like the United Nations and NATO, and could help to explain some of the popularity of neutralism among smaller countries. Such an analysis would also tend to explain the continual complaints that international organizations and alliances are not given adequate (optimal) amounts of resources.[54] It would also suggest that neighboring local governments in metropolitan areas that provide collective goods (like commuter roads and education) that benefit individuals in two or more local government jurisdictions would tend to provide inadequate amounts of these services, and that the largest local government (e.g., the one representing the central city) would bear disproportionate shares of the burdens of providing them.[55] An analysis of the foregoing type might, finally, provide some additional insight into the phenomenon of price leadership, and particularly the possible disadvantages involved in being the largest firm in an industry.

The most important single point about small groups in the present context, however, is that they may very well be able to provide themselves with a collective good simply because of the attraction of the collective good to the individual members. In this, small groups differ from larger ones. The larger a group is, the farther it will fall short of obtaining an optimal supply of any collective good, and the less likely that it will act to obtain even a minimal amount of such a good. In short, the larger the group, the less it will further its common interests.

E. "EXCLUSIVE" AND "INCLUSIVE" GROUPS

The movement in and out of the group must no longer be ignored. This is an important matter; for industries or market groups differ

54. Some of the complexities of behavior in small groups are treated in Mancur Olson, Jr., and Richard Zeckhauser, "An Economic Theory of Alliances," *Review of Economics and Statistics,* XLVIII (August 1966), 266–279, and in "Collective Goods, Comparative Advantage, and Alliance Efficiency," in *Issues of Defense Economics* (A Conference of the Universities-National Bureau-Committee for Economics Research), Roland McKean, ed., (New York: National Bureau of Economic Research, 1967), pp. 25–48. [Footnote added in 1970.]

55. I am indebted to Alan Williams of York University in England, whose study of local government brought the importance of these sorts of spillovers among local governments to my attention.

fundamentally from nonmarket groups in their attitudes toward movement in and out of the group. The firm in an industry wants to keep new firms from coming in to share the market and wants as many as possible of those firms already in the industry to leave the industry. It wants the group of firms in the industry to shrink until there is preferably only one firm in the group: its ideal is a monopoly. Thus the firms in a given market are competitors or rivals. In nonmarket groups or organizations seeking a collective good the opposite is true. Usually the larger the number available to share the benefits and costs the better. An increase in the size of the group does not bring competition to anyone, but may lead to lower costs for those already in the group. The truth of this view is evident from everyday observation. Whereas firms in a market lament any increase in competition, associations that supply collective goods in nonmarket situations almost always welcome new members. Indeed, such organizations sometimes attempt to make membership compulsory.

Why is there this difference between the market and nonmarket groups which previous sections of this chapter have shown to have striking similarities? If the businessman in the market, and the member of the lobbying organization, are alike in that each of them finds that the benefits of any effort made to achieve group goals would accrue mostly to other members of the group, then why are they so much different where entry and exit from the group are concerned? The answer is that in a market situation the "collective good"—the higher price—is such that if one firm sells more at that price, other firms must sell less, so that the benefit it provides is fixed in supply; but in nonmarket situations the benefit from a collective good is *not* fixed in supply. Only so many units of a product can be sold in any given market without driving down the price, but any number of people can join a lobbying organization without necessarily reducing the benefits for others.[56] Usually in a market situation what one firm captures another firm cannot obtain; essentially in a nonmarket situation what one consumes another may also enjoy. If a firm in a market situation prospers, it becomes a more formidable rival; but if an individual in a nonmarket group prospers, he may

56. In a social club that gives members status because it is "exclusive," the collective good in question is like a supracompetitive price in a market, not like the normal nonmarket situation. If the top "400" were to become the top "4000," the benefits to the entrants would be offset by the losses of old members, who would have traded an exalted social connection for one that might be only respectable.

well then have an incentive to pay a larger share of the cost of the collective good.

Because of the fixed and thus limited amount of the benefit that can be derived from the "collective good"—the higher price—in the market situation, which leads the members of a market group to attempt to reduce the size of their group, this sort of collective good will here be called an "exclusive collective good." [57] Because the supply of collective goods in nonmarket situations, by contrast, automatically expands when the group expands, this sort of public good should be called an "inclusive collective good." [58]

57. This usage of the idea of the collective good is, to be sure, in some respects over-broad, in that the collective-good concept is not needed to analyze market behavior; other theories are usually better for that purpose. But it is helpful in this particular context to treat a supracompetitive price as a special type of collective good. It is a useful expositional technique for bringing out parallels and contrasts between market and nonmarket situations with respect to the relationships between individual interests and group-oriented action. I hope that in the following pages it will also offer some insight into organizations that have functions both inside and outside the market, and into the extent of bargaining in market and nonmarket groups.

58. There are some interesting parallels between my concepts of "exclusive" and "inclusive" collective goods and some recent work by other economists. There is, first, a relationship between these concepts and John Head's previously cited article on "Public Goods and Public Policy" (*Public Finance*, XVII, 197–219). I did not understand all of the implications of my discussion of inclusive and collective goods until I had read all of Head's article. As I now see it, these concepts can be explained in terms of his distinction between the two defining characteristics of the traditional public good: infeasibility of exclusion and jointness of supply. My exclusive collective good is then a good such that, at least within some given group, exclusion is not feasible, but at the same time such that there is no jointness of supply whatever, so that the members of the group hope that others can be kept out of the group. My inclusive collective good is also such that exclusion is infeasible, at least within some given group, but it is however also characterized by at least some considerable degree of jointness in supply, and this accounts for the fact that additional members can enjoy the good with little or no reduction in the consumption of the old members. There is, second, a relationship between my inclusive-exclusive distinction and a paper by James M. Buchanan entitled "An Economic Theory of Clubs" (mime.). Buchanan's paper assumes that exclusion is possible, but that a (severely limited) degree of jointness in supply exists, and shows that on these assumptions the optimal number of users of a given public good is normally finite, will vary from case to case, and may sometimes be quite small. Buchanan's approach and my own are related in that both of us ask how the interests of a member of a group enjoying a collective good will be affected by increases or decreases in the number of people who consume the good. Both of us have been working on this problem independently, and until very recently in ignorance of each other's interest in this particular question. Buchanan generously suggests that I may have asked this question earlier than he did, but whereas I have barely touched upon the question merely to facilitate other parts of my general argument, he has developed an interesting and general model which shows the relevance of this question to a wide range of policy problems.

Whether a group behaves exclusively or inclusively, therefore, depends upon the nature of the objective the group seeks, not on any characteristics of the membership. Indeed, the same collection of firms or individuals might be an exclusive group in one context and an inclusive group in another. The firms in an industry would be an exclusive group when they sought a higher price in their industry by restricting output, but they would be an inclusive group, and would enlist all the support they could get, when they sought lower taxes, or a tariff, or any other change in government policy. The point that the exclusiveness or inclusiveness of a group depends on the objective at issue, rather than on any traits of the membership, is important, since many organizations operate both in the market to raise prices by restricting output, and also in the political and social systems to further other common interests. It might be interesting, if space permitted, to study such groups with the aid of the distinction between exclusive and inclusive collective goods. The logic of this distinction suggests that such groups would have ambivalent attitudes toward new entrants. And in fact they do. Labor unions, for example, sometimes advocate the "solidarity of the working class" and demand the closed shop, yet set up apprenticeship rules that limit new "working class" entrants into particular labor markets. Indeed, this ambivalence is a fundamental factor with which any adequate analysis of what unions seek to maximize must deal.[59]

A further difference between inclusive and exclusive groups is evident when formally organized, or even informally coordinated,

59. There is some uncertainty about what unions maximize. It is sometimes thought that unions do not maximize wage rates, since higher wages reduce the quantity of labor demanded by the employer and thereby also union membership. This reduction in membership is in turn contrary to the institutional interests of the union and harmful to the power and prestige of the union leaders. Yet some unions, such as the United Mine Workers, have in fact raised wages to a point they conceded would reduce employment in their industry. One possible explanation is that unions seek inclusive collective goods from government, as well as higher wages in the market. In this nonmarket capacity each union has an interest in acquiring new members, *outside* its "own" industry or craft as well as inside it. Higher wages do not hinder the expansion of a union in other industries or skill categories. Indeed, the higher the wages a union wins in any given labor market the greater the prestige of its leaders and the greater its appeal to workers in other labor markets, thus facilitating the growth of union membership outside its original clientele. This is something a union may be happy to do because this will help it fulfill its political, lobbying function. Interestingly, the CIO, and the catch-all District 50 of the UMW, may possibly have allowed the influence of John L. Lewis and the UMW to expand at some times when union wage levels limited employment in coal mining. I am thankful to one of my former students, John Beard, for stimulating ideas on this point.

behavior is attempted. When there is organized or coordinated effort in an inclusive group, as many as can be persuaded to help will be included in that effort.[60] Yet it will *not* (except in marginal cases, where the collective good is only just worth its cost) be essential that every individual in the group participate in the organization or agreement. In essence this is because the nonparticipant normally does not take the benefits of an inclusive good away from those who do cooperate. An inclusive collective good is by definition such that the benefit a noncooperator receives is not matched by corresponding losses to those who do cooperate.[61]

When a group seeks an exclusive collective good through an agreement or organization of the firms in the market—that is, if there is explicit or even tacit collusion in the market—the situation is much different. In such a case, though the hope is that the number of firms in the industry will be as small as possible, it is paradoxically almost always essential that there be 100 per cent participation of those who

60. Riker's interesting argument, in *The Theory of Political Coalitions,* that there will be a tendency toward minimum winning coalitions in many political contexts, does not in any way weaken the conclusion here that inclusive groups try to increase their membership. Nor does it weaken any of the conclusions in this book, for Riker's argument is relevant only to zero-sum situations, and no such situations are analyzed in this book. Any group seeking an inclusive collective good would not be in a zero-sum situation, since the benefit by definition increases in amount as more join the group, and as more of the collective good is provided. Even groups seeking exclusive collective goods do not fit Riker's model, for though the amount that can be sold at any given price is fixed, the amount the price will be raised and thus the gain to the group are variable. It is unfortunate that Riker's otherwise stimulating and useful book considers some phenomena, like military alliances, for which his zero-sum assumption is most inappropriate. See William H. Riker, *The Theory of Political Coalitions* (New Haven, Conn.: Yale University Press, 1962).

61. If the collective good were a "pure public good" in Samuelson's sense, the benefit the noncooperator receives would not only not lead to a corresponding loss to those who did cooperate; it would not lead to any loss whatever for them. The pure-public-good assumption seems, however, to be unnecessarily stringent for present purposes. It would surely often be true that after some point, additional consumers of a collective good would, however slightly, reduce the amount available to others. The argument in the text therefore does not require that inclusive collective goods be pure public goods. When an inclusive collective good is not a pure public good, however, those in the group enjoying the good would not welcome additional members who failed to pay adequate dues. Dues would not be adequate unless they were at least equal in value to the reduction in the consumption of the old members entailed by the consumption of the new entrant. As long as any significant degree of "jointness in supply" remains, however, the gains to new entrants will exceed the dues payment needed to ensure that the old members will be adequately compensated for any curtailment in their own consumption, so the group will remain truly "inclusive."

remain in the group. In essence this is because even one nonparticipant can usually take all the benefits brought about by the action of the collusive firms for himself. Unless the costs of the nonparticipating firm rise too rapidly with increases in output,[62] it can continually expand its output to take advantage of the higher price brought about by the collusive action until the collusive firms, if they foolishly continue to maintain the higher price, have reduced their output to zero, all for the benefit of the nonparticipating firm. The nonparticipating firm can deprive the collusive firms of all the benefits of their collusion because the benefit of any given supracompetitive price is fixed in amount; so whatever he takes the collusive firms lose. There is then an all-or-none quality about exclusive groups, in that there must often be either 100 per cent participation or else no collusion at all. This need for 100 per cent participation has the same effects in an industry that a constitutional provision that all decisions must be unanimous has in a voting system. Whenever unanimous participation is required, any single holdout has extraordinary bargaining power; he may be able to demand for himself most of the gain that would come from any group-oriented action.[63] Moreover, any one in the group can attempt to be a holdout, and demand a greater share of the gain in return for his (indispensable) support. This incentive to holdouts makes any group-oriented action less likely than it would otherwise be. It also implies that each member has a great incentive to bargain; he may gain all by a good bargain, or lose all in a bad one. This means much more bargaining is likely in any situation where 100 per cent participation is required than when some smaller percentage can undertake group-oriented activity.

It follows that the relationship among individuals in inclusive and

62. If marginal costs rise very steeply, and accordingly no firm has an incentive to increase output greatly in response to the higher price, a single holdout need not be fatal to a collusive agreement. But a holdout will still be costly, for he will tend to gain more from the collusion than a firm that colludes, and whatever he gains the collusive firms lose.

63. On the implications of a unanimity requirement, see the important book by James M. Buchanan and Gordon Tullock, *The Calculus of Consent: Logical Foundations of Constitutional Democracy* (Ann Arbor: University of Michigan Press, 1962), especially chap. viii, pp. 96–116. I believe that some complications in their useful and provocative study could be cleared up with the aid of some of the ideas developed in the present study; see for example my review of their book in the *American Economic Review,* LII (December 1962), 1217–1218.

exclusive groups usually is quite different, whenever groups are so small one member's action has a perceptible effect on any other member, so that individual relationships matter. The firms in the exclusive group want as few others in the group as possible, and therefore each firm warily watches other firms for fear they will attempt to drive it out of the industry. Each firm must, before it takes any action, consider whether it will provoke a "price war" or "cut-throat competition." This means that each firm in an exclusive group must be sensitive to the other firms in the group, and consider the reactions they may have to any action of its own. At the same time, any group-oriented behavior in an exclusive group will usually require 100 per cent participation, so each firm in an industry is not only a rival of every other firm, but also an indispensable collaborator in any collusive action. Therefore, whenever any collusion, however tacit, is in question, each firm in the industry may consider bargaining or holding out for a larger share of the gains. The firm that can best guess what reaction other firms will have to each move of its own will have a considerable advantage in this bargaining. This fact, together with the desire of the firms in an industry to keep the number in that industry as small as possible, makes each of the firms in any industry with a small number of firms very anxious about the reactions other firms will have to any action it takes. In other words, both the desire to limit the size of the group, and the usual need for 100 per cent participation in any kind of collusion, increase the intensity and complexity of oligopolistic reactions. The conclusion that industries with small numbers of firms will be characterized by oligopolistic interaction with mutual dependence recognized is of course familiar to every economist.

It is not however generally understood that in inclusive groups, even small ones, on the other hand, bargaining or strategic interaction is evidently much less common and important. This is partly because there is no desire to eliminate anyone from the inclusive group. It is also partly because nothing like unanimous participation is normally required, so that individuals in the inclusive group are not so likely to try to be holdouts in order to get a larger share of the gain. This tends to reduce the amount of bargaining (and also makes group-oriented action more likely). Though the problem is extremely complex, and some of the tools needed to determine exactly how much bargaining there will be in a given situation do not now exist, it nonetheless seems very likely that there is much less strategic interaction in inclusive groups, and that the hypothesis of independent behavior will frequently describe members of these groups reasonably well.

F. A TAXONOMY OF GROUPS

To be sure, there can also be many instances in inclusive or non-market groups in which individual members do take into account the reactions of other members to their actions when they decide what action to take—that is, instances in which there is the strategic interaction among members characteristic of oligopolistic industries in which mutual dependence is recognized. In groups of one size range at least, such strategic interaction must be relatively important. That is the size range where the group is not so small that one individual would find it profitable to purchase some of the collective good himself, but where the number in the group is nonetheless sufficiently small that each member's attempts or lack of attempts to obtain the collective good would bring about noticeable differences in the welfare of some, or all, of the others in the group. This can best be understood by assuming for a moment that an inclusive collective good is already being provided in such a group through a formal organization, and then asking what would happen if one member of the group were to cease paying his share of the cost of the good. If, in a reasonably small organization, a particular person stops paying for the collective good he enjoys, the costs will rise noticeably for each of the others in the group; accordingly, they may then refuse to continue making their contributions, and the collective good may no longer be provided. However, the first person could realize that this might be the result of his refusal to pay anything for the collective good, and that he would be worse off when the collective good is not provided than when it was provided and he met part of the cost. Accordingly he might continue making a contribution toward the purchase of the collective good. He might; or he might not. As in oligopoly in a market situation, the result is indeterminate. The rational member of such a group faces a strategic problem and while the Theory of Games and other types of analyses might prove very helpful, there seems to be no way at present of getting a general, valid, and determinate solution at the level of abstraction of this chapter.[64]

64. It is of incidental interest here to note also that oligopoly in the marketplace is in some respects akin to logrolling in the organization. If the "majority" that vari-

What is the range of this indeterminateness? In a small group in which a member gets such a large fraction of the total benefit that he would be better off if he paid the entire cost himself, rather than go without the good, there is some presumption that the collective good will be provided. In a group in which no one member got such a large benefit from the collective good that he had an interest in providing it even if he had to pay all of the cost, but in which the individual was still so important in terms of the whole group that his contribution or lack of contribution to the group objective had a noticeable effect on the costs or benefits of others in the group, the result is indeterminate.[65] By contrast, in a large group in which no single individual's contribution makes a perceptible difference to the group as a whole, or the burden or benefit of any single member of the group, it is certain that a collective good will *not* be provided unless there is coercion or some outside inducements that will lead the members of the large group to act in their common interest.[66]

---

ous interests in a legislature need is viewed as a collective good—something that a particular interest cannot obtain unless other interests also share it—then the parallel is quite close. The cost each special-interest legislator would like to avoid is the passage of the legislation desired by the other special-interest legislators, for if these interests gain from their legislation, often others, including his own constituents, may lose. But unless he is willing to vote for the legislation desired by the others, the particular special-interest legislator in question will not be able to get his own legislation passed. So his goal would be to work out a coalition with other special-interest legislators in which they would vote for exactly the legislation he wanted, and he in turn would give them as little in return as possible, by insisting that they moderate their legislative demands. But since every potential logroller has this same strategy, the result is indeterminate: the logs may be rolled or they may not. Every one of the interests will be better off if the logrolling is done than if it is not, but as individual interests strive for better legislative bargains the result of the competing strategies may be that no agreement is reached. This is quite similar to the situation oligopolistic groups are in, as they all desire a higher price and will all gain if they restrict output to get it, but they may not be able to agree on market shares.

65. The result is clearly indeterminate when F_i is less than C/V_g at every point and it is also true that the group is not so large that no one member's actions have a noticeable effect.

66. One friendly critic has suggested that even a large pre-existing organization could continue providing a collective good simply by conducting a kind of plebiscite among its members, with the understanding that if there were not a unanimous or nearly unanimous pledge to contribute toward providing the collective good, this good would no longer be provided. This argument, if I understand it correctly, is mistaken. In such a situation, an individual would know that if others provided the collective good he would get the benefits whether he made any contribution or not. He would therefore have no incentive to make a pledge unless a completely unanimous set of pledges was required, or for some other reason his one pledge would decide whether or not the good would be provided. But if a pledge were required

The last distinction, between the group so large it definitely cannot provide itself with a collective good, and the oligopoly-sized group which may provide itself with a collective good, is particularly important. It depends upon whether any two or more members of the group have a perceptible interdependence, that is, on whether the contribution or lack of contribution of any one individual in the group will have a perceptible effect on the burden or benefit of any other individual or individuals in the group. Whether a group will have the possibility of providing itself with a collective good without coercion or outside inducements therefore depends to a striking degree upon the number of individuals in the group, since the larger the group, the less the likelihood that the contribution of any one will be perceptible. It is not, however, strictly accurate to say that it depends solely on the number of individuals in the group. The relation between the size of the group and the significance of an individual member cannot be defined quite that simply. A group which has members with highly unequal degrees of interest in a collective good, and which wants a collective good that is (at some level of provision) extremely valuable in relation to its cost, will be more apt to provide itself with a collective good than other groups with the same number of members. The same situation prevails in the study of market structure, where again the number of firms an industry can have and still remain oligopolistic (and have the possibility of supracompetitive returns) varies somewhat from case to case. The standard for determining whether a group will have the capacity to act, without coercion or outside inducements, in its group interest is (as it should be) the same for market and non-market groups: it depends on whether the individual actions of any one or more members in a group are noticeable to any other individuals in the group.[67] This is most obviously, but not exclusively, a function of the number in the group.

---

of every single member, or if for any other reason any one member could decide whether or not the group would get a collective good, this one member could deprive all of the others in the group of great gains. He would therefore be in a position to bargain for bribes. But since any other members of the group might gain just as much from the same holdout strategy, there is no likelihood that the collective good would be provided. See again Buchanan and Tullock, pp. 96–116.

67. The noticeability of the actions of a single member of a group may be influenced by the arrangements the group itself sets up. A previously organized group, for example, might ensure that the contributions or lack of contributions of any member of the group, and the effect of each such member's course on the burden and benefit for others, would be advertised, thus ensuring that the group effort

It is now possible to specify when either informal coordination or formal organization will be necessary to obtain a collective good. The smallest type of group—the group in which one or more members get such a large fraction of the total benefit that they find it worthwhile to see that the collective good is provided, even if they have to pay the entire cost—may get along without any group agreement or organization. A group agreement might be set up to spread the costs more widely or to step up the level of provision of the collective good. But since there is an incentive for unilateral and individual action to obtain the collective good, neither a formal organization nor even an informal group agreement is indispensable to obtain a collective good. In any group larger than this, on the other hand, no collective good can be obtained without some group agreement, coordination, or organization. In the intermediate or oligopoly-sized group, where two or more members must act simultaneously before a collective good can be obtained, there must be at least tacit coordination or organization. Moreover, the larger a group is, the more agreement and organization it will need. The larger the group, the greater the number that will usually have to be included in the group agreement or organization. It may not be necessary that the entire group be organized, since some subset of the whole group may be able to provide the collective good. But to establish a group agreement or organization will nonetheless always tend to be more difficult the larger the size of the group, for the larger the group the more difficult it will be to locate and organize even a subset of the group, and those in the subset will have an incentive to continue bargaining with the others in the group until the burden is widely shared, thereby adding to the expense of bargaining. In short, costs of organization are an increasing function of the number of individuals in the group. (Though the more

would not collapse from imperfect knowledge. I therefore define "noticeability" in terms of the degree of knowledge, and the institutional arrangements, that actually exist in any given group, insetad of assuming a "natural noticeability" unaffected by any group advertising or other arrangements. This point, along with many other valuable comments, has been brought to my attention by Professor Jerome Rothenberg, who does, however, make much more of a group's assumed capacity to create "artificial noticeability" than I would want to do. I know of no practical example of a group or organization that has done much of anything, apart from improve information, to enhance the noticeability of an individual's actions in striving for a collective good.

members in the group the greater the total costs of organization, the costs of organization per person need not rise, for there are surely economies of scale in organization.) In certain cases a group will already be organized for some other purpose, and then these costs of organization are already being met. In such a case a group's capacity to provide itself with a collective good will be explained in part by whatever it was that originally enabled it to organize and maintain itself. This brings attention back again to the costs of organization and shows that these costs cannot be left out of the model, except for the smallest type of group in which unilateral action can provide a collective good. The costs of organization must be clearly distinguished from the type of cost that has previously been considered. The cost functions considered before involved only the direct resource costs of obtaining various levels of provision of a collective good. When there is no pre-existing organization of a group, and when the direct resource costs of a collective good it wants are more than any single individual could profitably bear, additional costs must be incurred to obtain an agreement about how the burden will be shared and to coordinate or organize the effort to obtain the collective good. These are the costs of communication among group members, the costs of any bargaining among them, and the costs of creating, staffing, and maintaining any formal group organization.

A group cannot get infinitesimally small quantities of a formal organization, or even of an informal group agreement; a group with a given number of members must have a certain minimal amount of organization or agreement if it is to have any at all. Thus there are significant initial or minimal costs of organization for each group. Any group that must organize to obtain a collective good, then, will find that it has a certain minimum organization cost that must be met, however little of the collective good it obtains. The greater the number in the group, the greater these minimal costs will be. When this minimal organizational cost is added to the other initial or minimal costs of a collective good, which arise from its previously mentioned technical characteristics, it is evident that the cost of the first unit of a collective good will be quite high in relation to the cost of some subsequent units. However immense the benefits of a collective good, the higher the absolute total costs of getting any amount of that good, the less likely it is that even a minimal amount of that good could be obtained without coercion or separate, outside incentives.

This means that there are now three separate but cumulative factors that keep larger groups from furthering their own interests. First, the larger the group, the smaller the fraction of the total group benefit any person acting in the group interest receives, and the less adequate the reward for any group-oriented action, and the farther the group falls short of getting an optimal supply of the collective good, even if it should get some. Second, since the larger the group, the smaller the share of the total benefit going to any individual, or to any (absolutely) small subset of members of the group, the less the likelihood that any small subset of the group, much less any single individual, will gain enough from getting the collective good to bear the burden of providing even a small amount of it; in other words, the larger the group the smaller the likelihood of oligopolistic interaction that might help obtain the good. Third, the larger the number of members in the group the greater the organization costs, and thus the higher the hurdle that must be jumped before any of the collective good at all can be obtained. For these reasons, the larger the group the farther it will fall short of providing an optimal supply of a collective good, and very large groups normally will not, in the absence of coercion or separate, outside incentives, provide themselves with even minimal amounts of a collective good.[68]

68. There is one logically conceivable, but surely empirically trivial, case in which a large group could be provided with a very small amount of a collective good without coercion or outside incentives. If some very small group enjoyed a collective good so inexpensive that any one of the members would benefit by making sure that it was provided, even if he had to pay all of the cost, and if millions of people then entered the group, with the cost of the good nonetheless remaining constant, the large group could be provided with a little of this collective good. This is because by hypothesis in this example the costs have remained unchanged, so that one person still has an incentive to see that the good is provided. Even in such a case as this, however, it would still not be quite right to say that the large group was acting in its group interest, since the output of the collective good would be incredibly suboptimal. The optimal level of provision of the public good would increase each time an individual entered the group, since the unit cost of the collective good by hypothesis is constant, while the benefit from an additional unit of it increases with every entrant. Yet the original provider would have no incentive to provide more as the group expanded, unless he formed an organization to share costs with the others in this (now large) group. But that would entail incurring the considerable costs of a large organization, and there would be no way these costs could be covered through the voluntary and rational action of the individuals in the group. Thus,

Now that all sizes of groups have been considered, it is possible to develop the classification of groups that is needed. In an article that was originally part of this study, but which has been published elsewhere,[69] this writer and his co-author argued that the concept of the group or industry can be given a precise theoretical meaning, and should be used, along with the concept of pure monopoly, in the study of market structure. In that article the situation in which there was only one firm in the industry was called pure monopoly. The situation where the firms are so few that the actions of one firm would have a noticeable effect on some one other firm or group of firms was called oligopoly; and the situation where no one firm had any noticeable effect on any other firm was called "atomistic competition." The category of atomistic competition was subdivided into pure competition and monopolistic competition within the large group, and oligopoly was also divided into two subdivisions according as the product was homogeneous or differentiated.

For inclusive or nonmarket groups the categories must be slightly different. The analog to pure monopoly (or pure monopsony) is obviously the single individual outside the market seeking some noncollective good, some good without external economies or diseconomies. In the size range that corresponds to oligopoly in market groups, there are two separate types of nonmarket groups: "privileged" groups and "intermediate" groups. A "privileged" group is a

---

if the total benefit from a collective good exceeded its costs by the thousandfold or millionfold, it is logically possible that a large group could provide itself with some amount of that collective good, but the level of provision of the collective good in such a case would be only a minute fraction of the optimal level. It is not easy to think of practical examples of groups that would fit this description, but one possible example is discussed on page 161, note 94. It would be easy to rule out even any such exceptional cases, however, simply by defining *all* groups that could provide themselves with some amount of a collective good as "small groups" (or by giving them other names), while putting all groups that could not provide themselves with a collective good in another class. But this easy route must be rejected, for that would make this part of the theory tautologous and thus incapable of refutation. Therefore the approach here has been to make the (surely reasonable) empirical hypothesis that the total costs of the collective goods wanted by large groups are large enough to exceed the value of the small fraction of the total benefit that an individual in a large group would get, so that he will not provide the good. There may be exceptions to this, as to any other empirical statement, and thus there may be instances in which large groups could provide themselves with (at most minute amounts of) collective goods through the voluntary and rational action of one of their members.

69. Olson and McFarland (note 14 above).

group such that each of its members, or at least some one of them, has an incentive to see that the collective good is provided, even if he has to bear the full burden of providing it himself. In such a group there is a presumption[70] that the collective good will be obtained, and it may be obtained without any group organization or coordination whatever. An "intermediate" group is a group in which no single member gets a share of the benefit sufficient to give him an incentive to provide the good himself, but which does not have so many members that no one member will notice whether any other member is or is not helping to provide the collective good. In such a group a collective good may, or equally well may not, be obtained, but no collective good may ever be obtained without some group coordination or organization.[71] The analog to atomistic competition in the nonmarket situation is the very large group, which will here be called the "latent" group. It is distinguished by the fact that, if one member does or does not help provide the collective good, no other one member will be significantly affected and therefore none has any reason to react. Thus an individual in a "latent" group, by definition, cannot make a noticeable contribution to any group effort, and since no one in the group will react if he makes no contribution, he has no incentive to contribute. Accordingly, large or "latent" groups have no incentive to act to obtain a collective good because, however valuable the collective good might be to the group as a whole, it does not offer the individual any incentive to pay dues

70. It is conceivable that a "privileged" group might not provide itself with a collective good, since there might be bargaining within the group and this bargaining might be unsuccessful. Imagine a privileged group in which *every* member of the group would gain so much from the collective good that he would be better off if he paid the full cost of providing the collective good than he would be if the good were not provided. It is still conceivable that each member of the group, knowing that each of the others would also be better off if they provided the good alone than they would be if no collective good were obtained, would refuse to contribute anything toward obtaining the collective good. Each could refuse to help provide the collective good on the mistaken assumption that the others would provide it without him. It does not seem very likely that all of the members of the group would go on making this mistake permanently, however.

71. "The character of the numerically intermediate structure, therefore, can be explained as a mixture of both: so that each of the features of both the small and large group appears in the intermediate group, as a fragmentary trait, now emerging, now disappearing or becoming latent. Thus, the intermediate structures objectively share the essential character of the smaller and larger structures—partially or alternately. This explains the subjective uncertainty regarding the decision to which of the two they belong." (Simmel, *Sociology of Georg Simmel,* pp. 116–117.)

to any organization working in the latent group's interest, or to bear in any other way any of the costs of the necessary collective action. Only a *separate and "selective" incentive* will stimulate a rational individual in a latent group to act in a group-oriented way. In such circumstances group action can be obtained only through an incentive that operates, not indiscriminately, like the collective good, upon the group as a whole, but rather *selectively* toward the individuals in the group. The incentive must be "selective" so that those who do not join the organization working for the group's interest, or in other ways contribute to the attainment of the group's interest, can be treated differently from those who do. These "selective incentives" can be either negative or positive, in that they can either coerce by punishing those who fail to bear an allocated share of the costs of the group action, or they can be positive inducements offered to those who act in the group interest.[72] A latent group that has been led to act in its group interest, either because of coercion of the individuals in the group or because of positive rewards to those individuals, will here be called a "mobilized" latent group.[73] Large groups are thus called "latent" groups because they have a latent power or capacity for action, but that potential power can be realized or "mobilized" only with the aid of "selective incentives."

The chances for group-oriented action are indeed different in each of the categories just explained. In some cases one may have some expectation that the collective or public good will be provided; in other cases one may be assured that (unless there are selective incentives) it will not; and still other cases could just as easily go either

72. Coercion is here defined to be a punishment that leaves an individual on a lower indifference curve than he would have been on had he borne his allocated share of the cost of the collective good and not been coerced. A positive inducement is defined to be any reward that leaves an individual who pays his allocated share of the cost of a collective good and receives the reward, on a higher indifference curve than he would have been had he borne none of the cost of the collective good and lost the reward. In other words, selective incentives are defined to be greater in value, in terms of each individual's preferences, than each individual's share of the cost of the collective good. Sanctions and inducements of smaller value will not be sufficient to mobilize a latent group. On some of the problems of distinguishing and defining coercion and positive incentives see Alfred Kuhn, *The Study of Society: A Unified Approach* (Homewood, Ill.: Richard D. Irwin, Inc. and the Dorsey Press, Inc., 1963), pp. 365–370.

73. Deutsch has also used the term "mobilization" in a somewhat similar context, but his use of the word is not the same. See Karl Deutsch, "Social Mobilization and Political Development," *American Political Science Review*, LV (September 1961), 493–514.

way. In any event, size is one of the determining factors in deciding whether or not it is possible that the voluntary, rational pursuit of individual interest will bring forth group-oriented behavior. Small groups will further their common interests better than large groups.

The question asked earlier in this chapter can now be answered. It now seems that small groups are not only quantitatively, but also qualitatively, different from large groups, and that the existence of large associations cannot be explained in terms of the same factors that explain the existence of small groups.

II

Group Size and Group Behavior

A. THE COHERENCE AND EFFECTIVENESS OF SMALL GROUPS

The greater effectiveness of relatively small groups—the "privileged" and "intermediate" groups—is evident from observation and experience as well as from theory. Consider, for example, meetings that involve too many people, and accordingly cannot make decisions promptly or carefully. Everyone would like to have the meeting end quickly, but few if any will be willing to let their pet concern be dropped to make this possible. And though all of those participating presumably have an interest in reaching sound decisions, this all too often fails to happen. When the number of participants is large, the typical participant will know that his own efforts will probably not make much difference to the outcome, and that he will be affected by the meeting's decision in much the same way no matter how much or how little effort he puts into studying the issues. Accordingly, the typical participant may not take the trouble to study the issues as carefully as he would have if he had been able to make the decision by himself. The decisions of the meeting are thus public goods to the participants (and perhaps others), and the contribution that each participant will make toward achieving or improving these public goods will become smaller as the meeting becomes larger. It is for these reasons, among others, that organizations so often turn to the small group; committees, subcommittees, and small leadership groups are created, and once created they tend to play a crucial role.

This observation is corroborated by some interesting research results. John James, among others, has done empirical work on this subject, with results that support the theory offered in this study, though his work was not done to prove any such theory. Professor James found that in a variety of institutions, public and private, national and local, "action taking" groups and subgroups tended to be much smaller than "non-action taking" groups and subgroups. In one sample he studied, the average size of the "action taking" sub-groups was 6.5 members, whereas the average size of the "non-action taking" subgroups was 14 members. These subgroups were in a large banking concern, whose secretary spontaneously offered the following opinion: "We have found," he wrote, "that committees should be small when you expect action and relatively large when you are looking for points of view, reactions, etc."[1] This is apparently not a situation restricted to banking. It is widely known that in the United States Congress and in the state legislatures, power resides to a remarkable, and what is to many an alarming degree, in the committees and subcommittees.[2] James found that U.S. Senate sub-committees at the time of his investigation had 5.4 members on the average, House subcommittees had 7.8, the Oregon state government, 4.7, and the Eugene, Oregon, municipal government, 5.3.[3] In short, the groups that actually do the work are quite small. A different study corroborates James's findings; Professor A. Paul Hare, in controlled experiments with groups of five and twelve boys, found that the performance of the groups of five was generally superior.[4] The sociologist Georg Simmel explicitly stated that smaller groups could act more decisively and use their resources more effectively than large groups: "Small, centripetally organized groups usually call on and use all their energies, while in large groups, forces remain much oftener potential."[5]

The fact that the partnership can be a workable institutional form when the number of partners is quite small, but is generally unsuccessful when the number of partners is very large, may provide

1. John James, "A Preliminary Study of the Size Determinant in Small Group Interaction," *American Sociological Review*, XVI (August 1951), 474–477.

2. Bertram M. Gross, *The Legislative Struggle* (New York: McGraw-Hill, 1953), pp. 265–337; see also Ernest S. Griffith, *Congress* (New York: New York University Press, 1951).

3. For a light-hearted and humorous, but nonetheless helpful, argument that the ideal committee or cabinet has only five members, see C. Northcote Parkinson, *Parkinson's Law* (Boston: Houghton Mifflin, 1957), pp. 33–34.

4. A. Paul Hare, "A Study of Interaction and Consensus in Different Sized Groups," *American Sociological Review*, XVII (June 1952), 261–268.

5. Georg Simmel, *The Sociology of George Simmel*, trans. Kurt H. Wolff (Glencoe, Ill.: Free Press [1950]), p. 92. In another place Simmel says that socialist societies, by which he appears to mean voluntary groups that share their incomes according to some principle of equity, must necessarily be small. "Up to this day, at least, socialistic or nearly socialistic societies have been possible only in very small groups and have always failed in larger ones" (p. 88).

another illustration of the advantages of smaller groups. When a partnership has many members, the individual partner observes that his own effort or contribution will not greatly affect the performance of the enterprise, and expects that he will get his prearranged share of the earnings whether or not he contributes as much as he could have done. The earnings of a partnership, in which each partner gets a prearranged percentage of the return, are a collective good to the partners, and when the number of partners increases, the incentive for each partner to work for the welfare of the enterprise lessens. This is to be sure only one of a number of reasons why partnerships tend to persist only when the number of partners is fairly small, but it is one that could be decisive in a really large partnership.[6]

The autonomy of management in the large modern corporation, with thousands of stockholders, and the subordination of management in the corporation owned by a small number of stockholders, may also illustrate the special difficulties of the large group. The fact that management tends to control the large corporation and is able, on occasion, to further its own interest at the expense of the stockholders, is surprising, since the common stockholders have the legal power to discharge the management at their pleasure, and since they have, as a group, also an incentive to do so, if the management is running the corporation partly or wholly in the interest of the managers. Why, then, do not the stockholders exercise their power? They do not because, in a large corporation, with thousands of stockholders, any effort the typical stockholder makes to oust the management will probably be unsuccessful; and even if the stockholder should be successful, most of the returns in the form of higher dividends and stock prices will go to the rest of the stockholders, since the typical stockholder owns only a trifling percentage of the outstanding stock. The income of the corporation is a collective good to the stockholders, and the stockholder who holds only a minute percentage of the total stock, like any member of a latent group, has no incentive to work in the group interest. Specifically, he has no incentive to challenge the management of the company, however inept or corrupt it might be. (This argument does not, however, entirely apply to the stockholder who wants the manager's position

---

6. The foregoing argument need not apply to partners that are *supposed* to be "sleeping partners," i.e., provide only capital. Nor does it take account of the fact that in many cases each partner is liable for the losses of the whole partnership.

and pelf for himself, for he is not working for a collective good; it is significant that most attempts to overthrow corporate management are started by those who want to take over the management themselves.) Corporations with a small number of stockholders, by contrast, are not only *de jure,* but also *de facto,* controlled by the stockholders, for in such cases the concepts of privileged or intermediate groups apply.[7]

There is also historical evidence for the theory presented here. George C. Homans, in one of the best-known books in American social science,[8] has pointed out that the small group has shown much more durability throughout history than the large group:

> At the level of . . . the small group, at the level, that is, of a social unit (no matter by what name we call it) each of whose members can have some firsthand knowledge of each of the others, human society, for many millennia longer than written history, has been able to cohere . . . They have tended to produce a surplus of the goods that make organization successful.
>
> . . . ancient Egypt and Mesopotamia were civilizations. So were classical India and China; so was Greco-Roman civilization, and so is our own Western civilization that grew out of medieval Christendom . . .
>
> The appalling fact is that, after flourishing for a span of time, every civilization but one has collapsed . . . formal organizations that articulated the whole have fallen to pieces . . . much of the technology has even been forgotten for lack of the large scale cooperation that could put it in effect . . . the civilization has slowly sunk to a Dark Age, a situation, much like the one from which it started on its upward path, in which the mutual hostility of small groups is the condition of the internal cohesion of each one . . . Society can fall thus far, but apparently no farther . . . One can read the dismal story, eloquently told, in the historians of civilization from Spengler to Toynbee. The one civilization that has not entirely gone to pieces is our Western Civilization, and we are desperately anxious about it.
>
> [But] At the level of the tribe or group, society has always found itself able to cohere.[9]

7. See Adolph A. Berle, Jr., and Gardiner C. Means, *The Modern Corporation and Private Property* (New York: Macmillan, 1932); J. A. Livingston, *The American Stockholder,* rev. ed. (New York: Collier Books, 1963); P. Sargent Florence, *Ownership, Control and Success of Large Companies* (London: Sweet & Maxwell, 1961); William Mennell, *Takeover* (London: Lawrence & Wishart, 1962).

8. George C. Homans, *The Human Group* (New York: Harcourt, Brace, 1950).

9. *Ibid.,* pp. 454–456. See also Neil W. Chamberlain, *General Theory of Economic Process* (New York: Harper, 1955), esp. pp. 347–348, and Sherman Krupp, *Pattern in Organization Analysis* (Philadelphia: Chilton, 1961), pp. 118–139 and 171–176.

Homans' claim that the smallest groups are the most durable is quite persuasive and certainly supports the theory offered here. But his deduction from these historical facts is not wholly consistent with the approach in this study. His book focuses on the following idea: "Let us put our case for the last time: At the level of the small group, society has always been able to cohere. We infer, therefore, that if civilization is to stand, it must retain . . . some of the features of the small group itself." [10] Homans' conclusion depends on the assumption that the techniques or methods of the small group are more effective. But this is not necessarily true; the small, or "privileged," group is in a more advantageous position from the beginning, for some or all of its members will have an incentive to see that it does not fail. This is not true of the large group; the large group does not automatically find that the incentives that face the group also face the individuals in the group. Therefore, it does not follow that, because the small group has historically been more effective, the very large group can prevent failure by copying its methods. The "privileged" group, and for that matter the "intermediate" group, are simply in a more advantageous position. [11]

B. PROBLEMS OF THE TRADITIONAL THEORIES

Homans' belief that the lessons of the small group should be applied to large groups has much in common with the assumption upon which much small-group research is based. There has been a vast amount of research into the small group in recent years, much of it based on the idea that the results of (experimentally convenient) research on small groups can be made directly applicable to larger groups merely by multiplying these results by a scale factor. [12] Some social psychologists, sociologists, and political scientists assume that the small group is so much like the large group, in matters other than size, that it must behave according to somewhat similar laws. But if the distinctions drawn here among the "privileged" group, the "inter-

10. Homans, p. 468.

11. The difference between latent groups and privileged or intermediate groups is only one of several factors accounting for the instability of many ancient empires and civilizations. I have pointed to another such factor myself in a forthcoming book.

12. Kurt Lewin, *Field Theory in Social Change* (New York: Harper, 1951), pp. 163–164; Harold H. Kelley and John W. Thibaut, *The Social Psychology of Groups* (New York: John Wiley, 1959), pp. 6, 191–192; Hare, "Study of Interaction and Consensus," pp. 261–268; Sidney Verba, *Small Groups and Political Behavior* (Princeton, N.J.: Princeton University Press, 1961), pp. 4, 14, 99–109, 245–248.

mediate" group, and the "latent" group have any meaning, this assumption is unwarranted, at least so long as the groups have a common, collective interest. For the small, privileged group can expect that its collective needs will probably be met one way or another, and the fairly small (or intermediate) group has a fair chance that voluntary action will solve its collective problems, but the large, latent group cannot act in accordance with its common interests so long as the members of the group are free to further their individual interests.

The distinctions developed in this study also suggest that the traditional explanation of voluntary associations explained in Chapter I needs amendment. The traditional theory emphasizes the (alleged) universality of participation in voluntary associations in modern societies and explains small groups and large organizations in terms of the same causes. In its most sophisticated form, the traditional theory argues that the prevalence of participation in the modern voluntary association is due to the "structural differentiation" of developing societies; that is, to the fact that as the small, primary groups of primitive society have declined or become more specialized, the functions that multitudes of these small groups used to perform are being taken over by large voluntary associations. But, if the meaningless notion of a universal "joiner instinct" is to be rejected, how is the membership in these new, large voluntary associations recruited? There are admittedly functions for large associations to perform, as small, primary groups become more specialized and decline. And the performance of these functions no doubt would bring benefits to large numbers of people. But will these benefits provide an incentive for any of the individuals affected to join, much less create, a large voluntary association to perform the function in question? The answer is that, however beneficial the functions large voluntary associations are expected to perform, there is no incentive for any individual in a latent group to join such an association.[13] However important a function may be, there is no presumption that a latent group will be able to organize and act to perform this function. Small primary groups by contrast presumably can act to perform functions that are beneficial to them. The traditional theory

---

13. There is no suggestion here, of course, that all groups are necessarily explained in terms of monetary or material interests. The argument does not require that individuals have only monetary or material wants. See note 17 below.

of voluntary associations is therefore mistaken to the extent that it implicitly assumes that latent groups will act to perform functional purposes the same way small groups will. The existence of such large organizations as do exist must moreover be explained by different factors from those that explain the existence of smaller groups. This suggests that the traditional theory is incomplete, and needs to be modified in the light of the logical relationships explained in this study. This contention is strengthened by the fact that the traditional theory of voluntary associations is not at all in harmony with the empirical evidence, which indicates that participation in large voluntary organizations is very much less than that theory would suggest.[14]

There is still another respect in which the analysis developed here can be used to modify the traditional analysis. This involves the question of group consensus. It is often assumed (though usually implicitly) in discussions of organizational or group cohesion that the crucial matter is the degree of consensus; if there are many serious disagreements, there will be no coordinated, voluntary effort, but if there is a high degree of agreement on what is wanted and how to get it there will almost certainly be effective group action.[15] The degree of consensus is sometimes discussed as though it were the *only* important determinant of group action or group cohesion. There is, of course, no question that a lack of consensus is inimical to the prospects for group action and group cohesion. But it does not follow that perfect consensus, both about the desire for the collective good and the most efficient means of getting it, will always bring about the achievement of the group goal. In a large,

14. Mirra Komaravsky, "The Voluntary Associations of Urban Dwellers," *American Sociological Review*, XI (December 1946), 686–698; Floyd Dotson, "Patterns of Voluntary Membership among Working Class Families," *American Sociological Review*, XVI (October 1951), 687; John C. Scott, Jr., "Membership and Participation in Voluntary Associations," *American Sociological Review*, XXII (June 1957), 315; and Murray Hausknecht, *The Joiners—A Sociological Description of Voluntary Association Membership in the United States* (New York: Bedminster Press, 1962).

15. See Hare, "Study of Interaction and Consensus"; Raymond Cattell, "Concepts and Methods in the Measurement of Group Syntality," in *Small Groups*, ed. A. Paul Hare, Edward F. Borgatta, and Robert F. Bales (New York: Alfred A. Knopf, 1955); Leon Festinger, *A Theory of Cognitive Dissonance* (Evanston, Ill.: Row, Peterson, 1957); Leon Festinger, Stanley Schachter, and Kurt Back, "The Operation of Group Standards," in *Group Dynamics*, ed. Dorwin Cartwright and Alvin Zander (Evanston, Ill.: Row, Peterson, 1953); David B. Truman, *The Governmental Process* (New York: Alfred A. Knopf, 1958).

latent group there will be no tendency for the group to organize to achieve its goals through the voluntary, rational action of the members of the group, even if there is perfect consensus. Indeed, *the assumption made in this work is that there is perfect consensus.* This is, to be sure, an unrealistic assumption, for perfection of consensus, as of other things, is at best very rare. But the results obtained under this assumption are, for that reason, all the stronger, for if voluntary, rational action cannot enable a large, latent group to organize for action to achieve its collective goals, even with perfect consensus, then *a fortiori* this conclusion should hold in the real world, where consensus is usually incomplete and often altogether absent. It is thus very important to distingiush between the obstacles to group-oriented action that are due to a lack of group consensus and those that are due to a lack of individual incentives.

C. SOCIAL INCENTIVES AND RATIONAL BEHAVIOR

Economic incentives are not, to be sure, the only incentives; people are sometimes also motivated by a desire to win prestige, respect, friendship, and other social and psychological objectives. Though the phrase "socio-economic status" often used in discussions of status suggests that there may be a correlation between economic position and social position, there is no doubt that the two are sometimes different. The possibility that, in a case where there was no economic incentive for an individual to contribute to the achievement of a group interest, there might nonetheless be a social incentive for him to make such a contribution, must therefore be considered. And it is obvious that this is a possibility. If a small group of people who had an interest in a collective good happened also to be personal friends, or belonged to the same social club, and some of the group left the burden of providing that collective good on others, they might, even if they gained economically by this course of action, lose socially by it, and the social loss might outweigh the economic gain. Their friends might use "social pressure" to encourage them to do their part toward achieving the group goal, or the social club might exclude them, and such steps might be effective, for everyday observation reveals that most people value the fellowship of their friends and associates, and value social status, personal prestige, and self-esteem.

The existence of these social incentives to group-oriented action does not, however, contradict or weaken the analysis of this study. If anything, it strengthens it, *for social status and social acceptance are individual, noncollective goods.* Social sanctions and social rewards are "selective incentives"; that is, they are among the kinds of incentives that may be used to mobilize a latent group. It is in the nature of social incentives that they can distinguish among individuals: the recalcitrant individual can be ostracized, and the cooperative individual can be invited into the center of the charmed circle. Some students of organizational theory have rightly emphasized that social incentives must be analyzed in much the same way as monetary incentives.[16] Still other types of incentives can be analyzed in much the same way.[17]

16. See especially Chester I. Barnard, *The Functions of the Executive* (Cambridge, Mass.: Harvard University Press, 1938), chap xi, "The Economy of Incentives," pp. 139–160, and the same author's *Organization and Management* (Cambridge, Mass.: Harvard University Press, 1948), chap. ix, "Functions and Pathology of Status Systems in Formal Organizations," pp. 207–244; Peter B. Clark and James Q. Wilson, "Incentive Systems: A Theory of Organizations," *Administrative Science Quarterly,* VI (September 1961), 129–166; and Herbert A. Simon, *Administrative Behavior* (New York: Macmillan, 1957), esp. pp. 115–117. I am indebted to Edward C. Banfield for helpful suggestions on social incentives and organization theory.

17. In addition to monetary and social incentives, there are also erotic incentives, psychological incentives, moral incentives, and so on. To the extent that any of these types of incentives leads a latent group to obtain a collective good, it could again only be because they are or can be used as "selective incentives," i.e., because they distinguish between those individuals who support action in the common interest and those who do not. Even in the case where moral attitudes determine whether or not a person will act in a group-oriented way, the crucial factor is that the moral reaction serves as a "selective incentive." If the sense of guilt, or the destruction of self-esteem, that occurs when a person feels he has forsaken his moral code, affected those who had contributed toward the achievement of a group good, as well as those who had not, the moral code could not help to mobilize a latent group. To repeat: the point is that moral attitudes could mobilize a latent group only to the extent they provided selective incentives. The adherence to a moral code that demands the sacrifices needed to obtain a collective good therefore need *not* contradict any of the analysis in this study; indeed, this analysis shows the need for such a moral code or for some other selective incentive.

At no point in this study, however, will any such moral force or incentive be used to explain any of the examples of group action that will be studied. There are three reasons for this. First, it is not possible to get empirical proof of the motivation behind any person's action; it is not possible definitely to say whether a given individual acted for moral reasons or for other reasons in some particular case. A reliance on moral explanations could thus make the theory untestable. Second, no such explanation is needed, since there will be sufficient explanations on other grounds for all the group action that will be considered. Third, most organized pressure groups are explicitly working for gains for themselves, not gains for other groups, and in such cases it is hardly plausible to ascribe group action to any moral code. Moral motives or incentives for group action have therefore been discussed, not to explain any

In general, social pressure and social incentives operate only in groups of smaller size, in the groups so small that the members can have face-to-face contact with one another. Though in an oligopolistic industry with only a handful of firms there may be strong resentment against the "chiseler" who cuts prices to increase his own sales at the expense of the group, in a perfectly competitive industry there is usually no such resentment; indeed, the man who succeeds in increasing his sales and output in a perfectly competitive industry is usually admired and set up as a good example by his competitors. Anyone who has observed a farming community, for instance, knows that the most productive farmer, who sells the most and thus does the most to lower the price, is usually the one with the highest status. There are perhaps two reasons for this difference in the attitudes of large and small groups. First, in the large, latent group, each member, by definition, is so small in relation to the total that his actions will not matter much one way or another; so it would seem pointless for one perfect competitor, or a member of some other latent group, to snub or abuse another for a selfish, antigroup action, because the recalcitrant's action would not be decisive in any event. Second, in any large group everyone cannot possibly know everyone else, and the group will *ipso facto* not be a friendship group; so a person will ordinarily not be affected socially if he fails to make sacrifices on behalf of his group's goals. To return to the case of the farmer, it is clear that one farmer cannot possibly know all the other farmers who sell the same commodity; he would not feel that the social group within which he measured his status had much to do with the group with which he shared the interest in the collective good. Accordingly, there is no presumption that social incentives will lead individuals in the latent group to obtain a collective good.

There is, however, one case in which social incentives may well be able to bring about group-oriented action in a latent group. This is

---

given example of group action, but rather to show that their existence need not contradict the theory offered here, and could if anything tend to support it.

The erotic and psychological incentives that must be important in family and friendship groups could logically be analyzed within the framework of the theory. On the other hand, "affective" groups such as family and friendship groups could normally be studied much more usefully with entirely different sorts of theories, since the analysis used in this study does not shed much light on these groups. On the special features of "affective" groups, see Verba (note 12, above), p. 6 and pp. 142–184.

the case of a "federal" group—a group divided into a number of small groups, each of which has a reason to join with the others to form a federation representing the large group as a whole. If the central or federated organization provides some service to the small constituent organizations, they may be induced to use their social incentives to get the individuals belonging to each small group to contribute toward the achievement of the collective goals of the whole group. Thus, organizations that use selective *social* incentives to mobilize a latent group interested in a collective good must be federations of smaller groups. The more important point, however, is that social incentives are important mainly only in the small group, and play a role in the large group only when the large group is a federation of smaller groups.

The groups small enough to be classified here as "privileged" and "intermediate" groups are thus twice blessed in that they have not only economic incentives, but also perhaps social incentives, that lead their members to work toward the achievement of the collective goods. The large, "latent" group, on the other hand, always contains more people than could possibly know each other, and is not likely (except when composed of federated small groups) to develop social pressures that would help it satisfy its interest in a collective good. There is, of course, much evidence for this skepticism about social pressures in a large group in the history of perfectly competitive industries in the United States. Now, if the conclusion that the strength of social pressures varies greatly between small and large groups has validity, it further weakens the traditional theory of voluntary organizations.[18]

18. There is, however, another kind of social pressure that may occasionally be operative. That is the social pressure that is generated, not primarily through person-to-person friendships, but through mass media. If the members of a latent group are somehow continuously bombarded with propaganda about the worthiness of the attempt to satisfy the common interest in question, they may perhaps in time develop social pressures not entirely unlike those that can be generated in a face-to-face group, and these social pressures may help the latent group to obtain the collective good. A group cannot finance such propaganda unless it is already organized, and it may not be able to organize until it has already been subjected to the propaganda; so this form of social pressure is probably not ordinarily sufficient by itself to enable a group to achieve its collective goals. It would, for example, seem unlikely that there would be much prospect of success in a program to persuade farmers through propaganda to further their interests by voluntarily restricting output, unless there were some captive source of funds to finance the effort. So this form of social pressure generated by mass media does not seem likely to be an important independent source

Some critics may protest that even if social pressure does not exist in the large or latent group, it does not follow that the completely selfish or profit-maximizing behavior, which the concept of latent groups apparently assumes, is necessarily significant either; people might even in the absence of social pressure act in a selfless way. But this criticism of the concept of the latent group is not relevant, for that concept does *not* necessarily assume the selfish, profit-maximizing behavior that economists usually find in the marketplace. The concept of the large or latent group offered here holds true whether behavior is selfish or unselfish, so long as it is strictly speaking "rational." Even if the member of a large group were to neglect his own interests entirely, he still would not rationally contribute toward the provision of any collective or public good, since his own contribution would not be perceptible. A farmer who placed the interests of other farmers above his own would not necessarily restrict his production to raise farm prices, since he would know that his sacrifice would not bring a noticeable benefit to anyone. Such a rational farmer, however unselfish, would not make such a futile and pointless sacrifice, but he would allocate his philanthropy in order to have a perceptible effect on someone. Selfless behavior that has no perceptible effect is sometimes not even considered praiseworthy. A man who tried to hold back a flood with a pail would probably be considered more of a crank than a saint, even by those he was trying to help. It is no doubt possible infinitesimally to lower the level of a river in flood with a pail, just as it is possible for a single farmer infinitesimally to raise prices by limiting his production, but in both cases the effect is imperceptible, and those who sacrifice themselves in the interest of imperceptible improvements may not even receive the praise normally due selfless behavior.

The argument about large, latent groups, then, does not necessarily imply self-interested behavior, though such behavior would be completely consistent with it.[19] The only requirement is that the behavior

of coordinated effort to bring about the satisfaction of a common interest. Moreover, as was emphasized earlier, the nation-state, with all the emotional loyalty it commands, cannot support itself without compulsion. Therefore it does not seem likely that many large private groups could support themselves solely through social pressure.

19. Organizations with primarily economic purposes, like labor unions, farm organizations, and other types of pressure groups, normally claim that they are serving the interests of the groups they represent, and do not contend that they are mainly philanthropic organizations out to help other groups. Thus it would be surprising if

of individuals in large groups or organizations of the kind considered should generally be rational, in the sense that their objectives, whether selfish or unselfish, should be pursued by means that are efficient and effective for achieving these objectives.

The foregoing arguments, theoretical and factual, in this and the previous chapter should at the least justify the separate treatment that large and small groups are given in this study. These arguments are not meant as attacks on any previous interpretations of group behavior, though it seems that some of the usual explanations of large voluntary associations may need elaboration because of the theories offered here. All that need be granted, to accept the main argument of this study, is that large or latent groups will *not* organize for coordinated action merely because, as a group, they have a reason for doing so, though this could be true of smaller groups.

Most of the rest of this study will deal with large organizations and will attempt to prove that most of the large economic organizations in the United States have had to develop special institutions to solve the membership problem posed by the large scale of their objectives.

---

most of the members of these "interest groups" should always neglect their own, individual interests. An essentially selfish group interest would not normally attract members who were completely selfless. Thus self-interested behavior may in fact be common in organizations of the kind under study. For intelligent arguments contending that self-interested behavior is general in politics, see James M. Buchanan and Gordon Tullock, *The Calculus of Consent* (Ann Arbor: University of Michigan Press, 1962), pp. 3–39. See also the interesting book by Anthony Downs, *An Economic Theory of Democracy* (New York: Harper, 1957), pp. 3–35.

III

The Labor Union and Economic Freedom

A. COERCION IN LABOR UNIONS

In this age of big business and big labor, most labor unions are large organizations. But it was not always so. The first labor unions were small, local organizations, and they remained small and local for some time. The American labor movement began as a series of small unions with local interests, each independent of the others. (This incidentally was also true in Great Britain.[1]) The development of viable national unions in the United States took over half a century after local unions had emerged; and, even after national unions had been established, it was some time before they superseded the local unions as the main manifestation of labor's strength. Many of the earlier national unions, such the Knights of Labor, failed. It was not only true that local unions were formed well before national unions; it was also significant that these first unions emerged, not in the larger factories, but in the smaller workplaces, so that the early unions were not nearly as large as some modern union locals. Unions are naturally supposed to have the greatest function to perform in the large factory, where there can be no personal relationships between employer and employee, and it is in such factories that many of the powerful unions are found today. Yet the early unions sprang up, not in the factories being spawned by the industrial revolution, but mainly in the building trades, in printing, in shoemaking, and in other industries characterized by small-scale production. The vast factories of the steel industry, the automobile industry, and the like were among the last workplaces organized. The usual explanation is that skilled workers are supposed to be the most amenable to organization, and they were perhaps more common in smaller firms. But this explanation at best cannot be the whole story, for the coal-mining industry has been dominated by unskilled workers, and yet

---

1. G. D. H. Cole, *A Short History of the British Working Class Movement, 1789–1947*, new ed. (London: George Allen & Unwin, 1948), pp. 35–43.

the small-scale firms of this industry were organized long before the great industrial giants.[2]

There may be many different factors that help to account for this historical pattern of labor-union growth, but that pattern may be explained at least partly by the fact that small groups can better provide themselves with collective goods than large groups. The higher wages, shorter hours, and better working conditions that unions demand are collective goods to the workers. The sacrifices required to create and maintain an effective union are moreover quite considerable, for a continuing organization must be supported, and the strike that is the union's major weapon requires that each worker normally forego his entire income until the employer comes to terms. Small unions may have a further advantage over larger unions stemming from the fact that they can be meaningful social and recreational units, and thus also offer noncollective social benefits that attract members. The social aspect seems to have been significant in a number of the earliest unions.[3] For these reasons it may be significant that in their earlier days, when they faced the resistance of inertia and an especially hostile environment, unions began as small and independent local units and remained so for some time.

Once a local union exists, there are, however, several forces that may drive it to organize all of its craft or industry, or to federate with other local unions in the same craft or industry. Market forces work against any organization that operates only in a part of a market. Employers often will not be able to survive if they pay higher wages than competing firms. Thus an existing union often has an interest in seeing that all firms in any given market are forced to pay union wage scales. When only part of an industry or skill group is organized, employers also have a ready source of strikebreakers. In addition, workers with a given skill who migrate from one community

2. See Lloyd Ulman, *The Rise of the National Trade Union* (Cambridge, Mass.: Harvard University Press, 1955); Robert Ozanne, "The Labor History and Labor Theory of John R. Commons: An Evaluation in the Light of Recent Trends and Criticism," in *Labor, Management, and Social Policy*, ed. Gerald G. Somers (Madison: University of Wisconsin Press, 1963), pp. 25–46; Norman J. Ware, *The Labor Movement in the United States, 1860–95* (New York: D. Appleton, 1929); Richard A. Lester, *Economics of Labor*, 2nd ed. (New York: Macmillan, 1964), pp. 55–116.

3. Foster Rhea Dulles, *Labor in America: A History* (New York: Thomas Y. Crowell, 1949), p. 23. G. D. H. Cole points out that the early English unions often met in inns or pubs, which suggests a significant social aspect. See his *Working Class Movement*, pp. 35 and 174.

to another have an interest in belonging to a national union that gives them access to employment in each new community. Finally, the political strength of a large union is obviously greater than that of a small one. The incentives to federate local unions and organize unorganized firms increase considerably as improvements in transportation and communication enlarge the market.[4]

The attempts to create large, national unions are accordingly understandable. But how can the success of some of these attempts to provide collective goods to large, latent groups be explained? By far the most important single factor enabling large, national unions to survive was that membership in those unions, and support of the strikes they called, was to a great degree compulsory.

The "union shop," the "closed shop," and other such instruments for making union membership compulsory are not, as some suppose, modern inventions. About sixty years ago Sidney and Beatrice Webb pointed out that the closed shop was even then a venerable institution in England. In words that fit contemporary America quite as well, they attacked the "strange delusion in the journalistic mind that this compulsory trade unionism . . . is a modern device." Compulsory union membership was something "any student of trade union annals knows to be . . . coeval with trade unionism itself," they said. "The trade clubs of handicraftsmen in the eighteenth century would have scouted the idea of allowing any man to work at their trade who is not a member of the club . . . It is, in fact, as impossible for a non-unionist plater or rivetter to get work in a Tyneside shipyard, as it is for him to take a house in Newcastle without paying the rates [property taxes]. This silent and unseen, but absolutely complete compulsion, is the ideal of every Trade Union."[5] Compulsory unionism has retained its "silent and unseen" character in Britain to the present, and the "right-to-work" question is hardly a live issue there.[6]

4. Ulman, *passim;* Lloyd G. Reynolds, *Labor Economics and Labor Relations,* 3rd ed. (Englewood Cliffs, N.J.: Prentice-Hall, 1959), pp. 140–142.

5. Sidney and Beatrice Webb, *Industrial Democracy* (London: Longmans, Green, 1902), pp. 214–215. John Head has called my attention to the fact that some of the English classical economists, presumably observing the difficulties of early English trade unions, recognized that unions needed compulsion, or at least powerful social sanctions, to perform their functions. See John Stuart Mill, *Principles of Political Economy,* Book V, chap. xi, section 12, and Henry Sidgwick, *The Principles of Political Economy* (London: Macmillan, 1883), pp. 355–360.

6. Allan Flanders, "Great Britain," in *Comparative Labor Movements,* ed. Walter

In the early years of the American labor movement, too, the closed shop was enforced whenever possible by the labor unions, though the specific contractual union-shop guarantees that now are typical did not normally exist then. For example, in 1667 in New York City the carters, predecessors of the teamsters, apparently obtained a closed shop.[7] And in 1805 the constitution of the New York Cordwainers (shoemakers) declared that no member could work for anyone who had any cordwainers in his employ who were not members of the union.[8] In printing the closed shop was fully developed by 1840.[9] "If all the available evidence is summed up," says one student of the question, "it may be said that practically every trade union prior to the civil war was in favor of excluding non-members from employment."[10]

In sum, compulsory unionism, far from being a modern innovation, goes back to the earliest days of organized labor, and existed even in the small, pre-national unions. Compulsory membership cannot, however, explain the creation or emergence of the first, small, local unions, as it can account for the viability of the later, larger, national unions that the local unions ultimately created. Compulsory membership implies some instrument or organization to *make* membership compulsory, that is, to enforce the rule that nonunion members may not work in a given workplace. It is not possible for unorganized workers to create a *large* union, even if they are aware of the need for coercion, since they have to organize first in order to have an organization that will enforce the union-shop policy. But

Galenson (New York: Prentice-Hall, 1952), pp. 24–26; W. E. J. McCarthy, *The Closed Shop in Britain* (Oxford: Basil Blackwell, 1964).

7. Jerome Toner, *The Closed Shop* (Washington, D.C.: American Council on Public Affairs, 1942), pp. 1–93, and esp. p. 60. Toner points out that the medieval guilds were essentially closed shops. The closed-shop practices of labor unions developed independently, however.

8. *Ibid.*, p. 64.

9. F. T. Stockton, *The Closed Shop in American Trade Unions,* Johns Hopkins University Studies in Historical and Political Science, series 29, no. 3 (Baltimore: Johns Hopkins Press, 1911), p. 23. See also John R. Commons and Associates, *History of Labour in the United States* (New York: Macmillan, 1946), I, 598.

10. Stockton, p. 68. For a different view about the prevalence of compulsory membership in the history of American unionism, see Philip D. Bradley, "Freedom of the Individual under Collectivized Labor Arrangements," in *The Public Stake in Union Power,* ed. Philip D. Bradley (Charlottesville: University of Virginia Press, 1959), pp. 153–156. But Bradley's curious, polemical essay shows such an unthinking bias against the closed shop, and such confused arguments, that there is no reason to give his conclusion any weight.

it is possible for a small union to emerge without compulsion, and then, if it so decides, to ensure its survival and increase its strength by making membership compulsory. Once a union exists, it may be able to expand in size, or combine with other unions, in order to represent large groups of workers, if it has compulsory membership. The early use of coercion in labor unions is not therefore in any way inconsistent with the hypothesis that unionism had to begin with small groups in small-scale firms.

In view of the importance of compulsory membership, and the fact that strikebreakers are *legally* free to cross picket lines and make any strike ineffective, it should not be surprising that violence has had a prominent place in the history of labor relations, especially in periods when there were attempts to create or expand large, national unions.[11] This violence has involved employers with mercenary gangs as well as workers. (Jay Gould boasted: "I can hire one half of the working class to kill the other half."[12]) As Daniel Bell points out, "Beginning with the railroad strikes of 1877 . . . almost every major strike for the next forty years was attended by an outbreak of violence." This he ascribes to the "Social Darwinism" in American thought, which accounted for an "integrated value system" that "sanctioned industry's resistance to unionism."[13] No doubt fanatical ideologues among employers and their friends accounted for some

11. "The threat of potential violence and intimidation through the device of the picket line are powerful factors—so powerful, in fact, that nowadays a firm rarely attempts any operations at all if a strike has been called, although it would be within its legal rights to do so. For all practical purposes the alternative of making a bargain with anyone other than the union has been removed." Quotation from Edward H. Chamberlin, "Can Union Power Be Curbed?" *Atlantic Monthly* (June 1959), p. 49. See also Robert V. Bruce, *1877: Year of Violence* (Indianapolis: Bobbs-Merrill, 1959); Stewart H. Holbrook, *The Rocky Mountain Revolution* (New York: Henry Holt, 1956). For a vigorous polemic that includes lurid and interesting accounts of the bloodiest strikes, as seen from the far left, see Louis Adamic, *Dynamite: The Story of Class Violence in America,* rev. ed. (New York: Viking Press, 1934).

12. Herbert Harris, *American Labor* (New Haven, Conn.: Yale University Press, 1939), p. 228.

13. Daniel Bell, *The End of Ideology* (Glencoe, Ill.: Free Press, 1960), pp. 195–197. In *Atchison, T. & S.F. Ry.* v. *Gee,* 139 Fed. 584 (C.C.S.D. Iowa, 1905), the court stated: "There is and can be no such thing as peaceful picketing, any more than there can be chaste vulgarity, or peaceful mobbing, or lawful lynching. When men want to converse or persuade, they do not organize a picket line." This is an extreme view—the Supreme Court has since legalized peaceful picketing—but one that has an element of truth in it, especially for the days before labor legislation allowed unions to organize a factory merely by winning a representation election. See also Georges Sorel, *Reflections on Violence,* trans. T. E. Hulme (New York: B. W. Huebsch, n.d.), esp. pp. 43 and 289.

violence, but since the more radical *political* movements did not usually occasion similar amounts of violence, this must not have been the ultimate cause. The conservative or "business unionism" philosophy typical of American labor unions was no doubt less offensive to conservative ideologues than communism, socialism, or anarchism; yet it seems to have led to much more violence. The correct explanation surely centers around the need for coercion implicit in attempts to provide collective goods to large groups. If some workers in a particular firm go out on strike, the supply function for labor tends to shift to the left; so for those who continue working, or for outside strikebreakers, wages will if anything be higher than they were before. By contrast, for the duration of the conflict the strikers get nothing. Thus all the economic incentives affecting *individuals* are on the side of those workers who do not respect the picket lines. Should it be surprising, then, that coercion should be applied to keep individual workers from succumbing to the temptation to work during the strike? And that antiunion employers should also use violence?

Violence is apparently the greatest when unions first try to organize a firm.[14] If the employer's forces win the early tests of strength, the union is apt to disappear and peace will be re-established. If the union wins, the hazards of "scabbing" will likewise be evident and workers will soon make it a habit not to cross picket lines, thereby bringing a period of peaceful collective bargaining.

Compulsory membership and picket lines are therefore of the essence of unionism. As Henry George put it: "Labor associations can do nothing to raise wages but by force; it may be force applied passively, or force applied actively, or force held in reserve, but it must be force; they *must* coerce or hold the power to coerce employers; they *must* coerce those among their members disposed to straggle; they *must* do their best to get into their hands the whole field of labor they seek to occupy and to force other workingmen either to join them or to starve. Those who tell you of trades unions bent on raising wages by moral suasion alone are like those who would tell you of tigers who live on oranges."[15] The argument that collective bargaining implies coercion need not be used to attack unions. It can equally well be used to contend, as some students of

14. Bell, pp. 195–197.

15. Henry George, *The Condition of Labor: An Open Letter to Pope Leo XIII* (New York: United States Book Co., 1891), p. 86.

the labor movement have contended, that when the majority of the workers in a particular bargaining unit vote to go out on strike, all of the workers in that unit should be barred by *law* from flouting the majority decision by attempting to continue working.[16] This would leave compulsion to the police and prevent mob violence.

In addition to compulsory membership, picket lines, and violence, some unions have also had selective incentives of a positive kind: they have offered noncollective benefits to those who join the union, and denied these benefits to any who do not. In certain special cases these noncollective goods have been important. Some large labor unions have offered various forms of insurance to those who join the union. Significantly, the first large, national union to prove viable in Great Britain was the Amalgamated Society of Engineers, established in 1851, which offered a wide range of noncollective benefits. As G. D. H. Cole explained:

> The Amalgamated Society of Engineers is commonly acclaimed as a "New Model" in Trade Union organization . . . It became the model for a whole series of "Amalgamated" Societies formed during the next twenty years.
>
> The essential basis of the "New Model" was a close combination of trade and friendly activities. The A.S.E. provided for all its members a wide range of benefits, ranging from dispute and unemployment benefit to sickness and superannuation benefit . . . In short, it was a Trade Union and a Friendly Society almost in equal measure.[17]

The railroad brotherhoods in the United States have at times also attracted members by providing insurance benefits to those who joined the union. In the early days of the railroad unions accident rates were high and many insurance companies did not sell insurance to railroad workers. Thus the fraternal insurance benefits of the railroad brotherhoods offered potential members a considerable incentive for joining. In its early years the conductors' union went so far as to emphasize its insurance program to the virtual exclusion of all else.[18]

---

16. See Neil W. Chamberlain, "The Problem of Union Security," *Proceedings of the Academy of Political Science*, XXVI (May 1954), 1–7, which was also published by the Academy of Political Science as a booklet edited by Dumas Malone and entitled *The Right to Work*.

17. Cole, *Working Class Movement*, p. 173.

18. Toner, pp. 93–114. See also J. Douglas Brown, "The History and Problems of Collective Bargaining by Railway Maintenance of Way Employees," unpub. diss., Princeton University, 1927, pp. 36–38, 69–70, 222.

There were periods, however, when the insurance programs of some of the railroad unions lost money. Then they had to rely mainly on the seniority rule to hold membership. Union members were guaranteed seniority rights in the unions' contracts with the railroad companies, but nonunion workers had to depend on the good will of the railroad companies for any rights of seniority. It is significant that the railroad unions were for certain periods the only major national unions without some form of compulsory membership. The newspaper of the Brotherhood of Locomotive Engineers put it this way: "The closed shop in the industries bears the same relation to the shop craft unions as the senior rule does to the train service brotherhoods. They are the backbone of both and if either are broken down they are no longer effective for collective bargaining. In fact, it would be impossible to maintain an organization today without them." [19]

It seems difficult to find more than a few examples of large unions that have supported themselves primarily by providing noncollective benefits, such as insurance or seniority privileges. On the other hand, most unions do provide something in the way of noncollective benefits, such as insurance, welfare benefits, and seniority rights.[20] A few unions help their members find employment. More important, almost every union handles members' grievances against the employer; that is, it attempts to protect each member against too much (or too little) overtime, against a disproportionate share of the most unpleasant work, against arbitrary foremen, and the like. While unions may process grievances for nonunion members as well, partly to impress them with the usefulness of the union, the nonmember is no doubt aware that his grievance against management may some day be the last to be acted upon if he persists indefinitely in staying out of the union.[21]

19. T. P. Whelan, "The Open Shop Crusade," *Locomotive Engineers' Journal,* LVI (1922), p. 44.

20. *The House of Labor,* ed. J. B. S. Hardman and Maurice F. Neufeld (New York: Prentice-Hall, 1951), pp. 276–319.

21. Leonard R. Sayles and George Strauss, *The Local Union* (New York: Harper, 1953), pp. 27–80; George Rose, "The Processing of Grievances," *Virginia Labor Review,* XXXVIII (April 1952), 285–314; Labor and Industrial Relations Center, Michigan State University, *The Grievance Process* (1956). For quotations from conversations with union members who felt that nonmembers' "gripes" or grievances "won't have any backing," see Joel Seidman, Jack London, and Bernard Karsh, "Why Workers Join Unions," *Annals of the American Academy of Political and Social Science,* CCLXXIV (March 1951), 83, and also McCarthy (note 6 above), p. 93.

Finally, many national unions draw some strength from federation, that is from the fact that their members belong to small union locals, and thus at one stage have the advantages of the small group. The small groups, in turn, can be held in the national union through noncollective benefits provided to the locals by the national union. The national may provide a staff of experts upon which the local unions may draw, and may offer the locals what might perhaps be called "strike insurance" in the form of a centrally administered strike fund. The national may also provide a noncollective benefit to some members directly by arranging for members of a local union who migrate to another community to get access to employment and membership in the local branch of the union in the new community.

With the growth of large-scale industry and the penetration of unions into large manufacturing enterprises in recent times, the small local that was once a major source of strength is becoming less important. Now many union members belong to locals with over a thousand members—to locals so large they are no longer small groups. Moreover the national unions are taking over the functions that union locals once performed.[22] Ordinarily no union local with thousands, or perhaps even hundreds, of members can be an effective social unit. A detailed empirical study of some modern union locals had this finding:

A few unions try to provide a full recreational program for their members as well as protection at work. However, the locals we observed found it impractical to compete with the established social activities in the community. To be sure, a picnic for the entire family in the summer and a dance in the winter will be successful, particularly if the local itself foots a large part of the bill. In fact it was not unusual to observe a union appropriating 10 percent of its treasury for a social affair "so that the members will feel they're getting something for their dues." Parties for the children at Christmas are also popular, but this was the extent of such social activities.[23]

Thus it appears that in many unions (though certainly not all) in the present day, not much strength can be gained from constituent small groups, since even the local units are sometimes large, and with the growth of the average local a union may also not be able to support itself any longer by providing social benefits.

22. Albert Rees, *The Economics of Trade Unions* (Chicago: University of Chicago Press, 1962), pp. 4–7; Reynolds (note 4, above), pp. 40–43.
23. Sayles and Strauss, p. 11.

Probably also the growth of social security and unemployment insurance, sponsored by government, and the proliferation of private insurance companies have made union insurance schemes much less useful for attracting members than they once were. This sort of selective incentive could in any case be provided only in unions with very good business judgment, and it seems that only a few American unions have survived by this means. The noncollective benefits provided through union action on individual members' grievances have also been limited in recent decades by the legal requirement that a union must fairly represent all workers in a given group whether or not they belong to the union. In return for the right to "exclusive jurisdiction" a union is legally required to represent every worker within its jurisdiction.[24] Though it is presumably impossible to ensure that the nonmember's grievances get represented with as much vigor as the member's grievances, this legal requirement must nonetheless reduce the incentive to join a union in order to get action on grievances.

In short, most unions can no longer draw a great deal of strength from small groups, and a union's noncollective benefits cannot usually be sufficient to bring in very many members. Smallness and noncollective benefits can probably now explain only the exceptional union. In most cases it is compulsory membership and coercive picket lines that are the source of the union's membership. Compulsory membership is now the general rule. In recent years roughly 95 per cent of the unionized workers have been covered by various types of "union security" (or sometimes dues check-off) schemes that normally make it impossible, or at least in practice exceedingly difficult, for a worker to avoid being a member of the union under whose jurisdiction he falls.[25] There are admittedly "right-to-work"

24. For an interesting explanation of this requirement see N. W. Chamberlain, "Problem of Union Security," and also Sumner H. Slichter, *The Challenge of Industrial Relations* (Ithaca, N.Y.: Cornell University Press, 1947), pp. 8–14.

25. Orme W. Phelps, *Union Security* (Los Angeles: Institute of Industrial Relations, University of California, 1953), p. 50; Toner, p. 91; Philip D. Bradley in *Public Stake in Union Power*, pp. 143 ff., and the same author's *Involuntary Participation in Unionism* (Washington, D.C.: American Enterprise Association, Inc., 1956); Reynolds, p. 202; E. Wight Bakke, Clark Kerr, and Charles W. Anrod, *Unions, Management, and the Public*, 2nd ed. (New York: Harcourt, Brace, & World, 1960), pp. 96–111. On the great degree of compulsion existing even when there is no closed or union shop, see Seidman, London, and Karsh, "Why Workers Join Unions," pp. 75–84, especially the sections entitled "Joining Despite Opposition," "Dues Inspection Line," and "Forcing Nonmembers to Join."

laws in a number of states (almost all of them nonindustrial states), but these laws are seldom enforced.[26]

This general reliance on compulsory membership should be expected, for labor unions are typically large organizations that strive for benefits for large or latent groups. A labor union works primarily to get higher wages, better working conditions, legislation favorable to workers, and the like; these things by their very nature ordinarily cannot be withheld from any particular worker in the group represented by the union. Unions are for "*collective* bargaining," not individual bargaining. It follows that most of the achievements of a union, even if they were more impressive than the staunchest unionist claims, could offer the rational worker no incentive to join; his individual efforts would not have a noticeable effect on the outcome, and whether he supported the union or not he would still get the benefits of its achievements. The following parts of this chapter will therefore neglect the occasional union that is a small group, and neglect the cases where unions can support themselves by providing very attractive noncollective goods, and will discuss some theories and controversies about labor unions on the oversimplified, but surely basically correct, assumption that unions are, and since they became national organizations have been, institutions working mainly for the *common* interests of *large* groups of workers.

B. LABOR-UNION GROWTH IN THEORY AND PRACTICE

That labor unions are concerned about the "free rider" is well known. But this fact has not been given its due in the principal theories of the labor movement, and has been completely ignored in Selig Perlman's well-known theory of the labor movement,[27] one of the most impressive and outstanding theories of American labor unions. Perlman attempted to explain the growth of American labor unions, and their emphasis on collective bargaining rather than political reform, mainly through what he called "job consciousness." This "job consciousness" is essentially a belief among workers that there is a scarcity of job opportunities, and this belief Perlman thought was due to a pervasive pessimism among manual workers.[28]

---

26. Richard A. Lester, *As Unions Mature* (Princeton, N.J.: Princeton University Press, 1958), p. 145.
27. Selig Perlman, *Theory of the Labor Movement* (New York: Macmillan, 1928).
28. *Ibid., passim,* but esp. p. 6.

Perlman inferred this pessimism among manual workers from the rules and procedures they had developed in their unions. He noted that successful unions strive above all for "job control"—for devices to ensure that their own members will be the first hired and the last fired. The closed shop is viewed not so much as a device for strengthening the union as a technique designed to "conserve" scarce jobs for the workers in a given union.[29] Restrictions on the employer's freedom of dismissal are sought by the union, not so much for the protection of the organization as for apportioning the presumably scarce jobs among all of the members according to a "communism of opportunity."[30] In sum, the unions' efforts to prevent the employers from hiring nonunion men, or from discriminating against unionists in promotion, lay-offs, work assignments, shop discipline, and so on, are according to Perlman designed to facilitate the sharing of scarce jobs among all of those in a certain manual group. By contrast, in the present study the presumption, because of the concept of latent groups, is that such union policies are vital to any large union's strength and existence, and reflect organizational imperatives rather than any endemic pessimism among manual workers.

The view that the unions' desire for control over employers' hiring and firing policies is due to their need for membership, and does not depend upon any pessimistic "job consciousness," is supported by some historical evidence.

American unionism made its first major and lasting advance on a national scale between 1897 and 1904. In that period the number of unionized workers increased from 447,000 to 2,072,000, after which union membership fell off only slightly.[31] This was a time of considerable prosperity; employment was high, and workers presumably should have had less "pessimism" than usual about employment

---

29. *Ibid.*, pp. 237–545 and esp. p. 269.

30. "The scarcity consciousness of the manual worker is the product of two main causes . . . The typical manualist is aware of his lack of capacity for availing himself of economic opportunities [and] knows himself neither the born taker of risks nor the possessor of a sufficiently agile mind ever to feel at home in the midst of the uncertain game of competitive business. Added to this is the conviction that for him the world has been rendered one of scarcity by an institutional order of things, which purposely reserved the best opportunities for landlords, capitalists and other privileged groups." (*Ibid.*, pp. 239–240.)

31. Irving Bernstein, "The Growth of American Unions," *American Economic Review*, XLIV (June 1954), 303; Leo Wolman, *Ebb and Flow in Trade Unionism* (New York: National Bureau of Economic Research, 1936), p. 15–20.

opportunities. The notable gains in union membership in this period were, moreover, closely correlated with the advance of compulsory membership. The influx of new members started with a number of victories in strikes for the union shop in 1897 and 1898. The number of strikes for "union recognition" increased; there were reported to be 140 in 1897 and 748 in 1904. The number of workers on strike for union recognition reportedly increased by almost ten times over the seven-year period.[32] This period marked the climax of an increasing agitation for the closed shop that had begun to gather speed in the 1860's. For the first time unions began to demand that customs and understandings about the closed shop be put in writing.[33] This provoked a bitter reaction among employers. Across the nation employers began the first major open-shop campaign. The National Association of Manufacturers, which had not before concerned itself with labor problems, attacked the closed shop in 1903, and its president spearheaded a national open-shop campaign. Moreover the Theodore Roosevelt administration helped fan the flames of public opposition to compulsory unionism.[34] The increased employer resistance took its toll. Whereas in 1901, 1902, and 1903 the unions had won in one half to two thirds of the establishments in which they called recognition strikes, in 1904 they won in only 37 per cent. The number of lockouts because of controversies over union recognition and union rules also increased with the open-shop campaign, and a great number of these lockouts were successful.[35] Not surprisingly, union membership decreased in 1904 and 1905, but only very slightly. Membership remained rather stable until shortly before World War I.[36]

32. U.S., *Twenty First Annual Report of the Commisisoner of Labor*, 1906 (Washington: Government Printing Office, 1907), table X, pp. 580–613. The figures on strikes and lockouts taken from this government report may well be inaccurate or misleading; so not too much reliance should be placed upon them.

33. Stockton, pp. 37–57, esp. p. 43.

34. *Ibid.*, pp. 44–57; Selig Perlman and Philip Taft, *Labor Movements* (New York: Macmillan, 1935), chap. viii, "The Employers' Mass Offensive," pp. 129–138; David B. Truman, *The Governmental Process* (New York: Alfred A. Knopf, 1958), pp. 80–82.

35. U.S., *Twenty First Annual Report of the Commissioner of Labor*, table X, pp. 580–613, and table XIX, pp. 763–771. See caution in note 32 above.

36. Bernstein, "Growth of American Unions," p. 303; Leo Wolman, *The Growth of American Trade Unions, 1880–1923* (New York: National Bureau of Economic Research, 1924), pp. 29–67.

Labor made its most notable gains between 1935 and 1945.[37] These gains were not due to any unusual pessimism about the availability of jobs. It was at first a period of growing employment, and later a wartime period of labor shortage, or overfull employment. This period of growth begins with the passage of the Wagner Act in July 1935, or perhaps with the acceptance by employers of the bill's constitutionality when the Supreme Court approved it in April 1937. The Wagner Act made collective bargaining a goal of public policy, and stipulated that whenever the majority of the employees in a bargaining unit voted for a particular union in a representation election, the employer *must* bargain collectively with that union about *all* of the employees in that bargaining unit. In order to obtain recognition from an employer after the passage of the Wagner Act, a union had only to persuade a majority of the employees to vote for it; before the passage of this act the union would generally have had to command such support that it could support a strike that would force the employer to submit. The union's task was also made easier by the Wagner Act's prohibition of company unions, and its rules forbidding discrimination against union men. Finally, the Wagner Act specifically allowed the closed shop.[38]

This act, and the wartime period of overfull employment that was soon to follow, apparently helped to bring about what was undoubtedly the most phenomenal increase in membership in the history of modern American unionism. In 1937 alone labor-union membership increased by 55 per cent.[39] There were apparently many strikes for union security.[40] For the first time the big mass-

37. Bernstein, "Growth of American Unions," p. 303; Milton Derber, "Growth and Expansion," in *Labor and the New Deal,* ed. Milton Derber and Edwin Young (Madison, Wis.: University of Wisconsin Press, 1957), pp. 1–45.

38. R. W. Fleming, "The Significance of the Wagner Act," *Labor and the New Deal,* ed. Derber and Young, pp. 121–157; Joseph G. Rayback, *A History of American Labor* (New York: Macmillan, 1959), pp. 341–346; Arthur M. Schlesinger, Jr., *The Coming of the New Deal* (Boston: Houghton Mifflin, 1959), pp. 397–421.

39. Bernstein, "Growth of American Unions," p. 303.

40. See U.S., Bureau of Labor Statistics, *Strikes in the United States, 1880–1936,* Bull. no. 651 (Washington: Government Printing Office, 1938), tables 28–30, pp. 58–77, and *Handbook of Labor Statistics, 1947 ed.,* table E–5, p. 138; and also Irving Bernstein, *The New Deal Collective Bargaining Policy* (Berkeley: University of California Press, 1950), pp. 143–145.

At least the number of strikes involving what the Bureau of Labor Statistics lumps toegther as "union organization" or "union recognition" increased *pari passu* with

production industries were unionized. The vigor of the newly formed CIO added to the momentum of the drive, but the AFL also expanded greatly, soon achieving a larger membership than it had had before the secession of the CIO unions.[41] The biggest years, next to 1937, were the years of the greatest wartime labor shortage, 1942, 1943, and 1944.[42]

Yet there were relatively few strikes in the war years.[43] Probably one important reason for the wartime growth of union membership —in addition to the reason of overfull employment—was the "maintenance of membership" provision forced upon employers by the government whenever there were disputes over the union demands for union security. As other writers have pointed out, the "maintenance of membership" rule added an important element of compulsion,[44] for it required that anyone who joined the union (whether

---

the growth of membership. However, many of the strikes for union recognition did not have to do with compulsory membership, at least directly. In any event the percentage of strikes having to do with union recognition increased from 19 per cent of the total number in 1933 to 47 per cent in 1935 and 57.8 per cent in 1937. And the total number of workers involved in strikes for union recognition increased from 73,000 in 1932 to 288,000 in 1935 and 1,160,000 in 1937.

For the years from 1927 to 1936 the Bureau of Labor Statistics separates out the strikes having to do with the "closed shop." From these separate statistics it appears that the number of strikes for the closed shop alone is much less than the total number of strikes for "union recognition" (though no doubt many of the "union recognition" strikes that were not openly for the closed shop involved devices designed to encourage employees to join the union). But even the number of regular closed-shop disputes is correlated with the gains in union membership.

Admittedly the connection between the number of strikes having to do with union-security matters and the increase in union membership does not prove that these strikes were the cause of the gains in membership. Some might contend the reverse: that the number of strikes over union security increased because the union membership increased. Nonetheless, the obvious fact that a successful strike for a union shop would increase union membership, and the other evidence marshaled in this work, make it seem quite likely that union-security strikes boosted union membership.

41. Rayback, *History of American Labor*, pp. 351–355; see also Walter Galenson, *The CIO Challenge to the AFL* (Cambridge, Mass.: Harvard University Press, 1960), *passim*; Harry A. Millis and Emily Clark Brown, *From the Wagner Act to Taft-Hartley* (Chicago: University of Chicago Press, 1950), pc. 30–271.

42. Bernstein, "Growth of American Unions," p. 303.

43. Rayback, pp. 373–374, 379; Millis and Brown, *Wagner Act to Taft-Hartley*, pp. 274, 298–300.

44. Bradley in *Public Stake in Union Power* (note 10, above), p. 159; Millis and Brown, *Wagner Act to Taft-Hartley*, pp. 296–298.

For a view different from that taken in this study see Joseph Rosenfarb, *Freedom and the Administrative State* (New York: Harper, 1948), p. 144. Rosenfarb there

voluntarily or because of a "dues inspection line," or other forms of intimidation of social pressure, or because of some temporary personal grievance that required union help) had to remain a member of the union at least until the next contract was signed. This also left unions free to concentrate all of their resources on obtaining new members. The "maintenance of membership" arrangement was enforced by the government in order to keep industrial conflict from obstructing the war effort. The War Labor Board had been given power to compel compliance in disputes affecting the defense effort, and it ruled that, when no other form of union security was in effect and the union desired compulsory membership, the "maintenance of membership" arrangement should be imposed. This type of union-security agreement spread quickly during the war.[45]

In World War I the situation had been less clear-cut. But again it appears that there was overfull employment, and thus no special pessimism about a lack of employment opportunities of the kind described by Perlman. And again the crucial position and bargaining power of the unions enabled them to make important advances. Membership increased considerably, though not quite as much as in World War II.[46] In World War I also there was a "War Labor Board." It made awards affecting about 700,000 workers and promoted shop representation committees in previously unorganized industries in the hope that these committees would evolve into full-fledged unions. The relatively favorable attitude of the government was illustrated by the fact that the railway unions won recognition for the nonoperating crafts when the railroads were nationalized during the war, and promptly lost this recognition when the Esch-

---

says: "Those who hug to their breasts the comforting delusion that the growth of unions is due to 'coercion' should have been forewarned by the experience of the National War Labor Board with the 'escape period' during which union security became operative. Only an insignificant fraction of 1 per cent availed themselves of this opportunity." This argument is reminiscent of the claims that certain totalitarian governments are kept in power by the people, because they have received over 99 per cent of the votes cast in an election.

Union leaders have also used these and similar statistics to argue that workers are so enthusiastic about unions that all but an infinitesimal minority of the workers would join unions even if there were no closed shop. But the force of this argument is weakened by their contentions, at other times, that unions will not endure if the union shop is forbidden. (Bradley in *Public Stake in Union Power*, p. 166.)

45. U.S., Bureau of Labor Statistics, *Handbook of Labor Statistics, 1947 Edition*, Bulletin no. 916 (Washington: Government Printing Office), table E–2, p. 133.

46. Bernstein, "Growth of American Unions," p. 303.

Cummins Act returned the railroads to private hands after the war. The shipbuilding industry, moreover, was organized with assistance of the Navy Department.[47] The Reverend Jerome Toner sums it up this way: "Unionism had been protected, if not fostered, by the National War Labor Board during the first world war. The American Federation of Labor, although agreeing not to organize non-union shops during the war, succeeded in enlarging its membership and extending closed shop conditions during and after the war. From 1915 to 1920, there was an increase of 2,503,100 members, and closed shop conditions expanded."[48]

In short, the periods when the unions obtained job control, and restricted jobs to union members, were not periods when workers had the most reason to be pessimistic about shortages of employment opportunities. Nor do the figures on union membership growth suggest that unions necessarily had the most appeal to members during periods of pessimism about job availability. The growth of closed-shop and union-shop provisions, and the growth of union membership, were both most striking in periods of growing employment, and even during periods of wartime labor shortage. It appears that whenever tight labor (and product) markets, or favorable legislation, increased labor's bargaining power, unions demanded and obtained union recognition and generally also some form of compulsory membership. Union membership has then accordingly also increased. This tends to suggest that unions have sought "job control," not so much to protect a stagnant or dwindling supply of job opportunities, as to strengthen, expand, and stabilize unions as organizations.

The foregoing argument, based on historical time patterns, can of course be only suggestive, not definitive. A more compelling argument against Selig Perlman's thesis emerges as soon as the demand function for labor is considered. When unions raise wages the quantity of labor demanded tends to fall. It follows that a union that attempts to raise wages cannot be dominated by any pessimistic

47. *Ibid.*, p. 315; Rayback, pp. 773–777; Perlman and Taft, *History of Labor* (note 34, above), pp. 403–411. Perlman and Taft say, "There was a tangible gain in membership due in large part to the removal by the government of the barriers to unionism created by industry during the previous decade and a half . . . The growth was phenomenal in industries directly active in War Production" (p. 410).

48. Toner, pp. 79–80.

consciousness of job scarcity or any passion to conserve employment opportunities.[49] Attempts to raise wages, moreover, are inconsistent with the "communism of opportunity" Perlman attributed to labor. It is of course possible that on occasion the demand for labor can be extremely inelastic, in which case an increase in wages would tend to bring only a very minor reduction in employment. But then the workers could hardly be pessimistic, for they could enjoy great gains without any significant sacrifice.

Moreover, as Lloyd Ulman has pointed out, unions have used their closed-shop policies and other instruments of job control mainly to bring in *new* members.[50] But if these new workers were kept out of the union, the jobs of the old members would presumably be more secure. This use of union power is accordingly inconsistent with the idea that unions obtain and employ their instruments of compulsion mainly to preserve job opportunities.

Perlman's theory is, however, given some plausibility by the fact that lasting growth in labor-union membership and strength came only when "business unionism" with its emphasis on "job control" was adopted as the philosophy of the American labor movement. Before the formation of the American Federation of Labor in 1886 under Samuel Gompers, there was no stable, lasting labor organization on a national scale;[51] so there is every reason to emphasize the respects in which it differed from most of its predecessors. And the most notable difference between the American Federation of Labor under Gompers and most of the preceding general labor organizations was that the Federation emphasized collective bargaining whereas most of its forerunners had emphasized politics and utopian reform.[52] The reason for the success of the American Federation of Labor, according to Perlman, was that it abjured political activity and concentrated on "job control." This brought it success because

---

49. I have borrowed the argument in this paragraph from Ulman, *Rise of National Trade Union* (note 2, above), pp. 580–581. See also John T. Dunlop, *Wage Determination under Trade Unions* (New York: Augustus M. Kelley, Inc., 1950), pp. 28–44, esp. p. 40. For a different view see Ozanne's previously cited article (note 2, above).

50. Ulman, p. 580.

51. Ware (note 2, above), *passim;* Rayback, *passim;* Phillip S. Foner, *History of the Labor Movement in the United States* (2 vols., New York: International Publishers, 1947–1955).

52. Perlman, *Theory of Labor Movement,* pp. 182–200.

by this time the frontier land had been exhausted and the temporary optimism it had occasioned turned into pessimism about supposedly scarce job opportunities.[53]

John R. Commons, the author of another well-known, important, and stimulating theory about the American labor movement, also thought the emergence of Gompers' collective-bargaining unionism very important. He ascribed the failure of the previous general labor organizations in large part to their emphasis on politics. The timing of the switch to collective bargaining or "business unionism," in Commons' system as in Perlman's, had to do with the passing of the frontier. With the loss of the frontier "safety valve," the pressure for improvement of *wages,* as opposed to concern about free land, currency, and the like, increased. More important, the "widening of the market," the emergence of nationwide competition, somehow drove workers to organize for higher wages.[54]

The success of business unionism, with its attendant union shop or "job control," in contrast with the failure of nineteenth-century political or utopian unionism, can also be explained in terms of the concept of latent groups offered in this study. When a union is engaged in collective bargaining with a particular employer, it can often force the employer to make membership in the union a condition of employment for all of his employees; union members merely need to refuse to work with nonunionists. Once a union achieves adequate recognition from the employer its future can be secure. But the union designed only to work through the political system has no such resource. It cannot make membership in it compulsory; it is not even dealing with the employer, the one who could most easily force workers to join the union. If it did somehow obtain a captive membership it would be in trouble, for as a *purely* political organization it would have no excuse for compulsory membership; compulsion solely for political purposes would seem altogether anomalous in a democratic political system.

The view that the control over jobs that unions demand arises

53. *Ibid.*, pp. 8, 200–207.

54. Commons and Associates, *History of Labour in the United States* (New York: Macmillan, 1953), I, 1–234, esp. 9. For a summary of these theories of American unionism, as well as some original comments about this problem, see John T. Dunlop, "The Development of Labor Organization: A Theoretical Framework," in *Insights into Labor Issues,* ed. Richard A. Lester and Joseph Shister (New York: Macmillan, 1948), pp. 163–193.

primarily from their desire for strength and survival, rather than from any pessimistic job consciousness, is supported by the low level of participation in most labor unions. Sometimes unions fine absent members to obtian attendance at meetings.[55] Students of unions express some surprise at the usual lack of participation:

> If the potential benefits are high, one might expect that most groups would exhibit high participation. Yet over-all activities in the locals studied was low. Frequently less than five percent of the total membership attended meetings, and it was difficult to draft men to accept minor union positions or committee memberships. Most union leaders admitted frankly that apathy was one of their major problems.[56]

Those opposed to unions could argue that this proves that the union shop forces men who do not agree with the policies of the union to remain in the organization, and is evidence that the workers do not really favor unions, much less compulsory membership. But this argument stumbles over the fact that impartially conducted elections have shown again and again that unionized workers support union-shop provisions. The Taft-Hartley law's sponsors apparently thought that workers would often throw off union-shop provisions in free elections; so they required unions, in order to qualify for a union shop, to petition the National Labor Relations Board for a secret-ballot election and then obtain a majority of those eligible to vote— not just a majority of those voting. These hopes were frustrated. In the first four months under the act the unions won all but four out of the 664 union-shop elections held, with more than 90 per cent of the employees voting for compulsory union membership. In the first four years, 44,795 union shops were authorized in such elections; 97 per cent of the elections were won by the unions. Accordingly in 1951 the act was amended so that the elections are no longer required.[57]

55. Lester, *As Unions Mature, passim,* but esp. pp. 17 and 31; Hjalmer Rosen and R. A. Hudson Rosen, *The Union Member Speaks* (New York: Prentice-Hall, 1955), pp. 80–85; Rose (note 21, above), pp. 88–90; Arnold L. Tannenbaum and Robert L. Kahn, *Participation in Union Locals* (Evanston, Ill.: Row, Peterson, 1958), *passim;* Clark Kerr, *Unions and Union Leaders of Their Own Choosing* (New York: Fund for the Republic, 1957), p. 15.

56. Sayles and Strauss, *Local Union,* p. 190. See also David Riesman, Nathan Glazer, and Reuel Denney, *The Lonely Crowd* (Garden City, N.Y.: Doubleday, 1956), p. 203.

57. Phelps, *Union Security,* pp. 40–41.

Thus there is a paradoxical contrast between the extremely low participation in labor unions and the overwhelming support that workers give to measures that will force them to support a union. *Over 90 per cent will not attend meetings or participate in union affairs; yet over 90 per cent will vote to force themselves to belong to the union and make considerable dues payments to it.* An interesting study by Hjalmer Rosen and R. A. Hudson Rosen illustrates this paradox well.[58] The Rosens conducted an opinion survey of District 9 of the International Association of Machinists and found many workers who told them that, since fines for absences from union meetings had been discontinued, attendance had dropped, as one member put it, "something awful." There was more dissatisfaction among the members over the poor attendance than on any other point covered in the extensive survey; only 29 per cent were satisfied with the attendance at meetings. The Rosens inferred from this that the members were probably inconsistent. "If the rank and file feel that members should attend meetings and are dissatisfied when they don't, why don't they correct the situation by all going to the meetings? The condition they are dissatisfied with is certainly in their power to change."[59]

In fact the workers were not inconsistent: *their actions and attitudes were a model of rationality when they wished that everyone would attend meetings and failed to attend themselves.* For if a strong union is in the members' interest, they will presumably be better off if the attendance is high, but (when the fines for failure to attend meetings are not in effect) an individual worker has no economic incentive to attend a meeting. He will get the benefits of the union's achievements whether he attends meetings or not and will probably not by himself be able to add noticeably to those achievements.[60]

58. Rosen and Rosen, *Union Member Speaks*.

59. *Ibid.,* pp. 82–83.

60. Max Weber, when he theorizes about "closed" and "open" groups, seems to assume that when a group restricts participation in certain activities to its own members, it usually does so in order to keep from sharing monopolies or other special privileges with others, or for the sake of being exclusive. But an organized group might insist that only its own members be allowed to participate in a certain activity or privilege, not with the idea of restricting advantages to those already in the group, but for the purpose of increasing the membership and power of the group organization. Weber may have realized this, of course, but he does not mention this motive for the "closed shop" in his discussion of "Closed and Open Relationships," even

This sort of situation, in which workers do not participate actively in their union, yet wish that members in general would, and support compulsory membership by overwhelming majorities, is of course analogous to the characteristic attitude of citizens toward their government. Voters are often willing to vote for higher taxes to finance additional government services, but as individuals they usually strive to contribute as little as the tax laws allow (and on occasion even less). Similarly, farmers often increase their output, even when the demand is inelastic and this is contrary to their common interests, and then vote for government controls that *force* them to reduce output.

The conclusion of this analysis is that the union shop cannot be explained by any pessimism among workers about any lack of job opportunities, and that the union shop, or other forms of compulsion, are highly important to the strength and stability of labor unions. It is the union as an organization, not the worker directly, that needs the "job control" that Perlman thought was the essence of American unionism. Small, local unions may exist without compulsion in industries where the workplaces are very small. Occasionally, too, some large unions may be able to survive if they can manage very attractive insurance schemes, or offer other adequate non-collective benefits. It is even possible that for brief periods unions could survive even for reasons completely different from those described in this study; that is, because of emotions so strong that they would lead individuals to behave irrationally, in the sense that they would contribute to a union even though a single individual's contribution would have no perceptible effect on a union's fortunes, and even though they would get the benefits of the union's achievements whether they supported it or not. But it does not seem to be the case that large, national labor unions with the strength and durability of those that now exist in this country could exist without some type of compulsory membership. No doubt ideological motives could provoke occasional outbursts of organization, but it is unlikely that many large unions could last longer or accomplish more than the Locofocos or the Knights of Labor, without at least some measure of coercion.

though he there mentions the closed shop. See his *Theory of Social and Economic Organization,* trans. Talcott Parsons and A. M. Henderson (New York: Oxford University Press, 1947), pp. 139–143.

C. THE CLOSED SHOP AND ECONOMIC FREEDOM IN THE LATENT GROUP

If the conclusion that compulsory membership is usually essential for an enduring, stable labor movement is correct, then it follows that some of the usual arguments against the union shop are fallacious. One of the most common arguments against compulsory unionism, one used even by some professional economists,[61] depends on an analogy with ordinary private business. In essence the argument is that, since a firm must please its customers if it is to retain their patronage, a union should also be forced to stand the test of an open shop, in which case it would still succeed if its performance pleased the potential members. This "right-to-work" argument often comes from those who are most ardent in support of a free-enterprise system based on the "profit motive." But if the same profit motive that is assumed to activate consumers and businessmen also stimulates workers, the enforcement of "right-to-work" laws would bring about the death of trade unions.[62] A rational worker will not voluntarily contribute to a (large) union providing a collective benefit since he alone would not perceptibly strengthen the union, and since he would get the benefits of any union achievements whether or not he supported the union.

Arguments about compulsory union membership in terms of "rights" are therefore misleading and unhelpful. There are of course many intelligent arguments against unions and the union shop. But none of them can rest alone on the premise that the union shop and other forms of compulsory unionism restrict individual freedom, unless the argument is extended to cover all coercion used to support the provision of collective services. There is no less infringement of "rights" through taxation for the support of a police force or a

---

61. For example, Bradley in *Public Stake in Union Power,* esp. pp. 151–152.

62. Edward H. Chamberlin, in arguing the case for legislation to restrict the power of labor unions, does not make any explicit references to the collective nature of the service that unions provide, and thus he lessens the clarity of his argument. He refers to the union's privilege to ignore the "right to work," along with other legal immunities enjoyed by labor unions but not by private business. Then he says: "Certainly the appeal of equal treatment for all is a strong one in a democracy. Why should it not apply in this area?" Later, still referring apparently to the legal advantages that trade unions enjoy and companies do not, he says: "I have seen a statement by an important labor leader . . . to the effect that even to raise the question of whether unions have too much power is to question their very right to exist . . . Yet what could be more absurd? Has anyone ever held that to reduce and regulate monopoly power in the business area was to question the right of business to exist?" Chamberlin, "Can Union Power Be Curbed?" *Atlantic Monthly* (June 1959), p. 49.

judicial system than there is in a union shop. Of course, law and order are requisites of all organized economic activity; the police force and the judicial system are therefore presumably more vital to a country than labor unions. But this only puts the argument on the proper grounds: do the results of the unions' activities justify the power that society has given them? The debate on the "right-to-work" laws should center, not around the "rights" involved, but on whether or not a country would be better off if its unions were stronger or weaker.

To be consistent, those who base their case against the union shop solely on "right-to-work" grounds must also advocate the "unanimous consent" approach to taxation put forth by Knut Wicksell in the 1890's.[63] Wicksell was often an advocate of laissez faire policies (though by no means in any basic sense a conservative),[64] who argued that "coercion is always an evil in itself" and that therefore the state should never exact taxes from a citizen without his consent. He recognized, however, that the state could not support the essential public services through a market system, since the citizen could get the benefits from these services whether he purchased any or not. Accordingly the only just method of financing the state services was to require that virtually every appropriation of government funds obtain a unanimous vote. If a proposed expenditure could not, under *any* distribution of the tax burden, command unanimous support in parliament it should be rejected. Otherwise some citizens would be forced to pay taxes for a government service that they did not want at all or did not want enough to help pay for it. Thus in the sphere of government, as in the free market economy, no one would be forced to spend money for things he did not want.[65] (More recently, James Buchanan and Gordon Tullock have in a

63. Knut Wicksell, "A New Principle of Just Taxation," *Classics in the Theory of Public Finance*, ed. Richard A. Musgrave and Alan T. Peacock (London: Macmillan, 1958), pp. 72–119.

64. Wicksell went to jail for a lecture that lampooned the chastity of the Virgin Mary, refused to take an oath of allegiance to the Swedish King, refused to legalize his marriage, and devoted much of his life to the advocacy of birth control at a time when that was quite unpopular. He wanted government policies more favorable to the working class, and was considered an ally by many socialists. See Torsten Gardlund, *The Life of Knut Wicksell*, trans. Nancy Adler (Stockholm: Almquist & Wiksell, 1958).

65. Obviously this approach is not consistent with the use of taxes for the redistribution of income, and it also neglects the likelihood that people would hide their true preferences for services in the bargaining over the distribution of the tax burden.

similar spirit suggested that something approaching a unanimous vote be required before some types of expenditure should be allowed.)[66]

Wicksell's old-fashioned liberalism is reminiscent of John Maynard Keynes' attitude toward conscription during World War I. Keynes opposed conscription, but he was not a pacifist. He opposed conscription because it deprived the citizen of the right to decide for himself whether or not to join in the fight. Keynes was exempt as a civil servant from conscription; so there is no need to question his sincerity.[67] Apparently his belief in the rights of the individual against a majority of his compatriots was very strong indeed.

Most of the present generation would think Wicksell's unanimous-consent theory of taxation and Keynes' total opposition to conscription carried the laissez-faire philosophy to an altogether impractical, and perhaps even fantastic, extreme. But Wicksell's and Keynes' views are nothing more than consistent applications of the liberal premise embodied in the arguments of those who oppose the union shop on the ground that it denies the "right to work." For if, under all circumstances, the individual has a "right to work" (the right to work without paying union dues), surely he must have the "right not to fight" (the right to avoid military service), and the "right to spend" (the right to avoid paying taxes for government services he does not want). Collective bargaining, war, and the basic governmental services are alike in that the "benefits" of all three go to everyone in the relevant group, whether or not he has supported the union, served in the military, or paid the taxes. Compulsion is involved in all three, and has to be. Accordingly the consistent critic of the closed shop will either go all the way down the liberal road with Wicksell and Keynes, or else argue simply that unions are so harmful, or ineffective, or unimportant,[68] that the country should

66. James Buchanan and Gordon Tullock, *The Calculus of Consent* (Ann Arbor: University of Michigan Press, 1962), pp. 263–306.

67. Sir Roy Harrod doubts that Keynes went so far as to *apply* for exemption from conscription as a conscientious objector, emphasizing that Keynes was in any event exempt from military service as an important civil servant. But there can be little doubt that Keynes at least at some time held the view described above, for there is among his records a handwritten note stating this view fully and precisely. See Harrod's "Clive Bell on Keynes," *Economic Journal*, LXVII (December 1957), 692–699, and Elizabeth Johnson's correction of Harrod, with Harrod's concession and comment, in the *Economic Journal*, LXX (March 1960), 160–167.

68. An intelligent attack on the closed shop might well center around the argument

not be concerned about their viability nor tolerant of their privileges.[69]

It may seem strange to draw an analogy between the union and the state. Some have supposed, with Hegel, that the state must be different in all of the more important respects from every other type of organization.[70] But normally both the union and the state provide mostly common or collective benefits to large groups. Accordingly, the individual union member, like the individual taxpayer, will not be able to see by himself that the collective good is provided, but will, whether he has tried to have this good provided or not, nonetheless get it if it is provided by others. The union member, like the individual taxpayer, has no incentive to sacrifice any more than he is forced to sacrifice.

D. GOVERNMENT INTERVENTION AND ECONOMIC FREEDOM IN THE LATENT GROUP

This approach to the unions and the rights or freedoms of their members can also clarify some of the popular arguments about the role of the government and the economic freedom of the citizen. There are many who argue that socialism and the growing activities

---

that labor unions do not increase the wage earners' share of the national income, yet may tend to promote inflation.

69. Of course, when unions use the closed shop, not to bring members into the union, but to keep certain workers out of a particular kind of employment (because of race, personal bias, or whatever), then the power of compulsion is not at all necessary to the survival of the union, and the foregoing arguments no longer apply. On the manifold legal complications posed in many countries by the naive assumption that unions are voluntary associations, see R. W. Rideout, *The Right to Membership of a Trade Union* (University of London: Athlone Press, 1963).

70. See particularly Georg W. F. Hegel, *Philosophy of Right*, trans. T. M. Knox (Oxford: Clarendon Press, 1949); see also George H. Sabine, *A History of Political Theory* (New York: Henry Holt, 1937), who summarizes this aspect of Hegel's thought simply and briefly: "The state must be governed by principles quite different from those which govern its subordinate members" (p. 643). Aristotle, on the other hand, argued that the state has something in common with other types of organizations: "Observation shows us, first, that every polis (or state) is a species of association, and, secondly, that all associations are instituted for the purpose of attaining some good . . . We may therefore hold . . . that all associations aim at some good." (Politics i.1.1.1252a, as translated by Ernest Barker.) The following books also find some parallel between the state and other associations: A. D. Lindsay, *The Modern Democratic State* (London: Oxford University Press, 1943), *passim*, but esp. I, 240–243; Earl Latham, *The Group Basis of Politics* (Ithaca, N.Y.: Cornell University Press, 1952), p. 12; and Arthur Bentley, *The Process of Government* (Evanston, Ill.: Principia Press, 1949), pp. 258–271.

of government will usually or inevitably restrict economic freedom, and perhaps threaten political rights as well.[71] Others deny that the *economic* activities of the state in any way restrict "freedom," holding that freedom is essentially a political concept involving democracy and civil rights rather than economic policy.[72]

This controversy is often complicated by purely semantic misunderstandings and by confusions about what the exact areas of disagreement are. Thus it is necessary here to distinguish three aspects of the controversy.

One aspect has to do with the relationships between economic institutions and political liberties. Many conservative thinkers claim that a free, democratic political system can exist only as long as the role of the state in economic life is reasonably small; that socialism, government planning, and the welfare state will in the long run inevitably bring dictatorship on the Stalinist or Hitlerian models.[73] Many others argue the reverse—that only bold government planning and liberal welfare measures will prevent the depression, distress,

71. Friederich A. Hayek, *The Road to Serfdom* (Chicago: University of Chicago Press, 1944), and *The Constitution of Liberty* (Chicago: University of Chicago Press, 1960); John M. Clark, "Forms of Economic Liberty and What Makes Them Important," in *Freedom, Its Meaning,* ed. Ruth Nanda Anshen (New York: Harcourt, Brace, 1940), pp. 305–329.

72. See Karl Mannheim, *Freedom, Power, and Democratic Planning* (New York: Oxford University Press, 1950), esp. pp. 41–77; Thomas Mann, "Freedom and Equality," in *Freedom, Its Meaning,* ed. Anshen, pp. 68–84; Joseph Rosenfarb, *Freedom and the Administrative State* (New York: Harper, 1948), pp. 74–84; John R. Commons, *Legal Foundations of Capitalism* (Madison: University of Wisconsin Press, 1957), pp. 10–130.

Some other critics of the view that socialism and "big government" restrict freedom rely instead on a definition of freedom in terms of range of choice, or wealth, rather than in terms of freedom from coercion, thus enabling themselves to hold that any government activities that increase income for some class of people also could increase freedom, however coercive these government activities might be. See for example: John Dewey, "Liberty and Social Control," *The Social Frontier,* II (November 1935), 41–42; Denis Gabor and Andre Gabor, "An Essay on the Mathematical Theory of Freedom," *Journal of the Royal Statistical Society,* CXVII (1954), 31–60, and discussion on this paper, 60–72; Harold J. Laski, *Liberty in the Modern State,* 3rd ed. (London: George Allen & Unwin, 1948), esp. pp. 48–65; Bertrand Russell, "Freedom and Government," in *Freedom, Its Meaning,* ed. Anshen, pp. 249–265, esp. p. 251.

For a perceptive and detached analysis of various concepts of freedom see Martin Bronfenbrenner, "Two Concepts of Economic Freedom," *Ethics,* LXV (April 1955), 157–170.

73. Hayek, *Road to Serfdom.* For a much more moderate argument expressing concern about this danger, see Clark's essay in *Freedom, Its Meaning,* ed. Anshen, p. 306. See also Thomas Wilson, *Modern Capitalism and Economic Progress* (London: Macmillan, 1950), pp. 3–19.

and disaffection that bring dictatorial governments in their wake.[74] This aspect of the controversy is not relevant to this study.

Another aspect of the controversy over economic freedom has to do with the question of by whom and for what economic liberties are restrained. Many, perhaps most, thinkers would be very concerned about whether or not controls or limitations on individual freedom were imposed through a democratic election in the interests of the group involved, or whether they were imposed by a dictator or oligarchy that was not concerned about the interests of the group it controlled. Some would say that in the former case the "compulsion" is not really compulsion, whereas in the latter case it is.[75] This distinction would emerge most clearly in the peculiar case of a group that voted unanimously to impose such a compulsory rule upon itself because if everyone followed the rule everyone would be better off. In this special case there would be no more infringement upon the freedoms of those involved than when two people freely sign a contract, which obviously restricts their freedom by legally compelling or forcing them to do some thing in the future. This case of absolutely unanimous support for compulsion would admittedly be altogether unusual. Nonetheless, in the more general situation where there is a majority vote, but not unanimous support, for some coercive measure in the group interest, most people would find this compulsion much less objectionable than the compulsion imposed by a dictator unmindful of the interests of his subjects. On the other hand, many others, especially laissez-faire enthusiasts, would argue that the economic tyranny of the majority in a democracy, or the benevolent paternalism of a political leader, is as much of an outrage against human freedom as any other form of compulsion.[76] This aspect of the disagreement about economic freedom is very important, but it is not the aspect that is central to this study.

The third and most fundamental aspect of the controversy about economic freedom involves economic liberty itself—freedom from any coercive control of an individual's economic life, no matter what the political implications or political arrangements of such control

74. Albert Lauterbach, *Economic Security and Individual Freedom* (Ithaca, N.Y.: Cornell University Press, 1948), esp. pp. 5, 11, 12; Thomas Mann in *Freedom, Its Meaning,* ed. Anshen, pp. 80–81.

75. I am thankful to Professor Thomas C. Schelling for explaining the importance of this distinction and persuading me to discuss it in this study.

76. Hayek, *Constitution of Liberty.*

might be.[77] This aspect of the controversy over economic liberty is directly relevant to this study. There can be varying views about the importance of economic liberty in this strict sense—that is largely a matter of personal values—but not about its existence or reality.[78] There is meaning to the idea of freedom to spend one's money as one likes, of "freedom of choice in the disposal of one's income," [79] though a great many think small changes in the amount of this freedom are not important.[80]

If it is granted that economic freedom in this third and most proper sense is a meaningful concept, and that it is to some people at least an important concept, the next step is to analyze its relation to different degrees of government intervention in economic life. What types of government activity infringe upon economic freedom? Does the government's economic activity always rest on coercion? Or is it sometimes no more dependent on the use of force than private enterprise?

Here the concept of latent groups can be helpful. Some goods and services, it was shown, are of such a nature that all of the members of the relevant group must get them if anyone in the group is to get them. These sorts of services are inherently unsuited to the market mechanism, and will be produced only if everyone is forced to pay his assigned share. Clearly many governmental services are of this kind. Therefore they restrict freedom. They replace individual decisions made freely with collective decisions backed by force.[81]

---

77. *Ibid.*, pp. 11–21. Here Hayek trenchantly and fairly shows the need to distinguish this concept of liberty from others that have lately been put forward. See also Isaiah Berlin, *Two Concepts of Liberty* (Oxford: Clarendon Press, 1958).

78. See Bronfenbrenner, "Two Concepts of Economic Freedom," pp. 157–170. Even ardent advocates of governmental economic planning concede the importance of this type of freedom, e.g. Barbara Wooton, in *Freedom under Planning* (Chapel Hill: University of North Carolina Press, 1945). For a lengthy discussion of the need to distinguish the various meanings of the word "liberty" see Maurice Cranston, *Freedom, A New Analysis* (London: Longmans, Green, 1953). Frank Knight surely goes too far in contending that no objective meaning can be given to the idea of freedom; see his "Freedom as Fact and Criterion," *International Journal of Ethics*, XXXIX (1929), 129–147.

79. Richard S. Thorn, "The Preservation of Individual Economic Freedom," in *Problems of U.S. Economic Development*, published by the Committee for Economic Development (New York, 1958).

80. See J. K. Galbraith, *The Affluent Society* (Boston: Houghton Mifflin, 1958).

81. On this subject see Anthony Downs, *An Economic Theory of Democracy* (New York: Harper, 1957), pp. 195–196. There would of course be no coercion if all decisions were unanimous.

Improvements in the defense forces, the police forces, and the judicial system at least cannot be financed without in some sense reducing the economic freedoms of the citizenry, without increasing taxes and thereby reducing the individual's freedom to spend.

But if the government decides to form a public corporation to manufacture some product it is not clear that there *necessarily* has to be any reduction in anyone's economic freedom. The consumers are not necessarily any less free if they buy from a public rather than a private corporation; nor are the workers necessarily less free because they work for one rather than the other. The institutional arrangements have been changed to be sure, and the magnitude of the public sector is greater, but no one necessarily must have lost his economic freedom.

The conclusion is that when the government provides collective goods and services it restricts economic freedom; when it produces the noncollective goods usually produced by private enterprise it need not restrict economic freedom. But how paradoxical. For it is the financing of the traditional services of government—notably the army and the police, the defenders of the established order—that most restricts economic freedom; and it is the socialistic incursions into the private economy that need not do so. It is conservatives, who historically have advocated the most military spending, and who have more property in need of police protection, that restrict economic freedom, as well as the socialists.[82] Of course, since governments normally have a monopoly on the major means of violence, they characteristically have the power to restrict the freedom of citizens whenever they want to, even when producing or distributing noncollective goods, or when undertaking any activity whatever. If, for example, a government distributes noncollective goods for free, it is reducing economic freedom.[83] The point, however, is that the pro-

82. If some modern advocates of laissez faire can be accused of imprecision when they discuss economic freedom, the same cannot be said of Wicksell. His plan for "unanimous consent" for government expenditures attacked the real problem, the collective services, rather than the size of the governmental sector. In his day government spending was concentrated almost exclusively on the military forces, and on the maintenance of domestic order and tranquility. The adoption of his plan would perhaps not have limited the *sphere* of the government's activities; it would merely have enforced more economical and perhaps more pacific national policies (Wicksell opposed Sweden's heavy expenditure on armaments and her bellicose attitude toward Russia). See Gardlund's *Life of Wicksell*.

83. Liberal or left-wing proposals to restrict the production of certain products also

vision of the public goods traditionally provided by government inevitably entails a limitation of economic freedom, while the government-owned socialistic enterprise producing noncollective good does not necessarily entail any such loss of freedom. It is therefore possible that the widespread belief that the growth of the governmental sector is equivalent to a decline in economic freedom owes something to the association of *all* governmental activity wtih the traditional governmental services, and particularly with the higher taxes and conscription required for a larger military establishment.[84]

The foregoing argument is not meant to label any government activity good or bad; it is intended instead to show that it is the provision of collective goods and services, not the public or private nature or other characteristics of the institutions that provide these services, that largely determines whether economic freedom must be curtailed. The growth of cartels capable of disciplining firms that undercut established prices restricts economic freedom, even though the cartels are private associations. Similarly, if the main argument of this chapter is correct, the development of collective bargaining for large groups must normally restrict economic freedom in that it implies that those who do not join the union must be deprived of the right to work in the unionized enterprise. In other words, the large labor union, though not a part of the government, must be coercive, if it attempts to fulfill its basic function and still survive. This is largely because its basic function is to provide a collective good—collective bargaining—to a large group, just as the basic function of government is to provide traditional collective goods like law, order, and defense. On the other hand, a government (or a labor union or any other organization) can provide noncollective goods without restricting economic freedom. There are of course many

---

limit economic freedom, but so do effective private cartels. And the nationalization of an industry, though it need not affect the freedom of the workers and managers in that industry, or the consumers of the industry's product, could, if the government prohibited private competition, restrict the freedom to become an entrepreneur in that particular industry. But this freedom would not affect many people, and then only if the government prohibited competition.

On the effects of nationalization on economic freedom see Wooton, *passim*.

84. For psychological, anthropological, and sociological approaches to the problem of liberty, see Erich Fromm, *Escape from Freedom* (New York: Holt, Rinehart & Winston, 1941); and George C. Homans, *The Human Group* (New York: Harcourt, Brace, 1950), pp. 332–333.

other important factors that have not been considered here that also help to determine how much economic freedom there will be in any given situation; the subject is much more complex than the present discussion would indicate. It would take this study far from its central theme to do justice to this profound problem. Yet it is already evident that the conventional creed which says that unions should not have the power of coercion because they are private associations, and that the expansion of the public sector inevitably entails the loss of economic freedom, is based on an inadequate understanding. No analysis of the limits of economic freedom or the uses of coercion by government, labor unions, or organizations of any kind can do justice to the complexity of the subject without taking account of the distinction between collective and noncollective goods.

IV

Orthodox Theories of State and Class

A. THE ECONOMISTS' THEORY OF THE STATE

Most economists accept a theory which implies that the basic services of government can be provided, as the last chapter argued, only through compulsion. This is the theory of "public goods." Most economists have accordingly also accepted the basic premise of this study—that organizations work for a common good or benefit—in the case of one special type of organization, the state. The idea that the state provides a common benefit, or works for the general welfare, goes back more than a century.

But simple and basic as this idea appears to be, more than a generation of discussion and disagreement passed before it was clearly understood, even for the special case of the state. The discussion of this question had begun in the early part of the nineteenth century if not before. Heinrich von Storch, in a work written for the instruction of the Czar's family, appeared to have some vague conception of the distinction between a collective good and an individual benefit, for he argued that individual enterprise could not secure life and property from attack, though it could best supply all other needs.[1] J.-B. Say later endorsed and elaborated Storch's argument.[2] Later Friederich von Wieser asked why there was an

---

1. Henri (Heinrich Friedrich von) Storch, *Cours d'économie politique* (St. Petersburg: A. Pluchart, 1815), I, 3–7. I learned of Storch's writing on this subject from William J. Baumol's *Welfare Economics and the Theory of the State* (Cambridge, Mass.: Harvard University Press, 1952), chap. xii, pp. 140–157. In that chapter Professor Baumol has a fuller discussion of the history of the theory of public goods than will be found here. His discussion has, however, a different focus. More recent elaborations of the theory of public goods, as they relate to welfare economics, are discussed in the second edition of Baumol's book, which is now in press.

2. "Indépendamment des besoins que ressentent les individus et les familles, et qui donnent lieu aux consommations privées, les hommes en société ont des besoins qui leur sont communs, et qui ne peuvent être satisfaits qu'au moyen d'un concours d'individus et même quelquefois de tous les individus qui la composent. Or, ce concours ne peut être obtenu que d'une institution qui dispose de l'obéissance de tous, dans

equality in the consumption of those goods and services provided by the state while there was such a remarkable inequality in the distribution of the products of the private sector. Wieser also noticed a similarity between the state and private associations in this respect. But Wieser also showed that he did not fully understand the question by saying that "the public economy does not in itself create productive income." [3]

Emil Sax distinguished publicly owned enterprises from state activities that benefit the whole citizenry. He also remarked parenthetically that there was a similarity between the state and private associations. But the fact that the theory of public goods was not yet properly understood is evident, for Sax wrongly ascribed the support of the state and other associations to "a kind of altruism created by the need for joint action towards a common end, and designed for mutual assistance to the exclusion of self interest if necessary." [4] If this were true, governments would not need to make taxes compulsory. [5]

The Italian economist Ugo Mazzola came nearer to analyzing the state's collective services correctly. He rightly emphasized the "indivisibility" of what he called "public goods," and realized that the basic state services benefited everyone. His error came in contending there was a "complementarity" between public and private goods which implied that the amount of public goods consumed depended on the amount of private goods consumed. Somehow Mazzola concluded from this that each citizen got at the margin exactly as much utility from the public goods as from private goods, and was ac-

---

les limites qu'admet la forme du gouvernement." Jean-Baptiste Say, *Cours complet d'économie politique pratique* (Paris: Guillaumin Libraire, 1840), II, 261. This reference was discovered in Baumol, just cited, pp. 146–149.

3. Friederich von Wieser, "The Theory of Public Economy," in *Classics in the Theory of Public Finance,* ed. Richard A. Musgrave and Alan T. Peacock (London: Macmillan, 1958), pp. 190–201. Most of the following references will be to this anthology of classics. The following account is not an original, much less a thorough, history of economic thought on this question. A full account would be an unnecessary digression here.

4. Emil Sax, "The Valuation Theory of Taxation," in *Classics,* p. 181 and pp. 177–179.

5. Adolph Wagner's approach was better than Sax's in that it recognized that the state must be coercive. Wagner seemed, however, to give more emphasis to the historical circumstances affecting the size of the government than to any abstract conceptions of public goods. See his "Three Extracts on Public Finance," *Classics,* pp. 1–16.

cordingly in an equilibrium position,[6] that is, one that he would not voluntarily change unless the basic situation changed.

But, as Wicksell later pointed out, the individual taxpayer could hardly be in an equilibrium position, for, "if the individual is to spend his money for private and public uses so that his satisfaction is maximized, he will obviously pay nothing whatsoever for public purposes." Whether the taxpayer pays much or little to the treasury he "will affect the scope of public services so slightly that for all practical purposes he himself will not notice at all."[7] Taxes therefore are compulsory exactions which keep the taxpayer in what might better be called a disequilibrium position.

Thus these continental writers on public finance had learned from each other's errors and progressively improved the analysis, which after many decades culminated in Wicksell's conception of the problem in the essay in which he propounded his "unanimous consent" theory of taxation. Wicksell had a correct conception of the problem of financing the collective services provided by government, whatever may be thought of his practical proposal for taxation. Wicksell confined his discussion to the special case of the government, however, and did not consider the general problem faced by all economic organizations. Nor did he consider how small a "public" must be before the theory no longer applies.

Generally speaking, economists writing after Wicksell have accepted his analysis of the basic problem of the theory of public expenditure.[8] Hans Ritschl has been perhaps the most forceful among those few economists[9] who have not accepted the "individualistic" or Wicksellian approach. Ritschl argued that:

The fatherland and mother tongue make us all brethren together. Anyone is welcome to the exchange society who obeys its regulations.

6. Ugo Mazzola, "The Formation of the Prices of Public Goods," *Classics*, pp. 159–193. See also Maffeo Pantaleoni, "Contributions to the Theory of the Distribution of Public Expenditure," *Classics*, pp. 16–27.

7. Knut Wicksell, "A New Principle of Just Taxation," *Classics*, pp. 81–82.

8. For example, see Richard Musgrave, *The Theory of Public Finance* (New York: McGraw-Hill, 1959), esp. chaps. iv and vi; Paul A. Samuelson, "The Pure Theory of Public Expenditure," *Review of Eonomics and Statistics*, XXXVI (November 1954), 387–390; Erik Lindahl, "Just Taxation—A Positive Solution," *Classics*, pp. 168–177 and 214–233.

9. Others are Gerhard Colm, "Theory of Public Expenditures," *Annals of the American Academy of Political and Social Science*, CLXXXIII (January 1936), 1–11; and Julius Margolis, "A Comment on the Pure Theory of Public Expenditure," *Review of Economics and Statistics*, XXXVII (November 1955), 347–349.

But to the national community belong only the men and women of the same speech, of the same ilk, the same mind . . . Through the veins of society streams the one, same money; through those of the community the same blood . . .

Any individualistic conception of "the State" is a gross aberration . . . [and] nothing but a blind ideology of shopkeepers and hawkers.

The State economy serves the satisfaction of communal needs . . . If the State satisfies needs which are purely individual, or groups of individual needs which can technically not be met otherwise than jointly, it does so for the sake of revenue only.

In the free market economy the economic self-interest of the individual reigns supreme and the almost sole factor governing relations is the profit motive, in which the classical theory of the free market economy was appropriately and securely anchored. This is not changed by the fact that more economic units, such as those of associations, cooperatives or charities, may have inner structures where we find motivations other than self-interest. *Internally, love or sacrifice, solidarity or generosity may be determining: but irrespective of their inner structures and the motives embodied therein, the market relations of economic units with each other are always governed by self-interest* [italics mine].

In the exchange society, then, self-interest alone regulates the relations of the members; by contrast, the state economy is characterized by communal spirit within the community. Egotism is replaced by the spirit of sacrifice, loyalty and communal spirit . . . This understanding of the fundamental power of the communal spirit leads to a meaningful explanation of coercion in the state economy. Coercion is a means of assuring the full effectiveness of the communal spirit, which is not equally developed in all members of the community.

The objective collective needs tend to prevail. Even the party stalwart who moves into responsible government office undergoes factual compulsion and spiritual change which makes a statesman out of a party leader . . . There is not a single German statesman of the last twelve years . . . who escaped compliance with this law.[10]

Ritschl's argument is exactly the opposite of the approach in this book. He assumes a curious dichotomy in the human psyche such that self-interest rules supreme in all transactions among individuals, whereas self-sacrifice knows no bounds in the individual's relationship to the state and to the many types of private associations. The organizations supported by this self-sacrifice are nonetheless selfish in all dealings with other organizations. The state and the race (and

10. Hans Ritschl, "Communal Economy and Market Economy," *Classics*, pp. 233–241.

with Marxian writers, the class) become metaphysical entities, with "objective" needs and purposes beyond those of the individuals who compose them.

The most notable tradition in nineteenth-century economics—the British laissez-faire tradition—largely ignored the theory of public goods. Admittedly, many of the best-known British economists enumerated the functions they thought the state should perform. The lists were generally very brief, though they included at least provision for national defense, for police forces, and for law and order generally. But these economists did not point out what the various activities appropriate to the state had in common.[11] They had a comprehensive theory which explained why most economic needs should be met by private enterprise; so it is natural to ask for a systematic explanation of the exceptional class of functions they thought should be fulfilled by the state. Except for a few imprecise comments by John Stuart Mill and Henry Sidgwick,[12] it appears that the leading British economists largely ignored the problem of collective goods. Even in this century, Pigou, in his classic treatise on public finance, gave collective goods for the most part only implicit treatment.[13]

B. THE MARXIAN THEORY OF STATE AND CLASS

Although the British classical economists can be accused of failing to develop an explicit theory of the state, no such charge can be leveled at Karl Marx. For Marx developed an interesting and provocative *economic* theory of the state at a time when most other economists had not even begun to consider the question. In Marx's theory the state is the instrument through which the ruling class dominates the other, oppressed classes. In the capitalistic period of history the state is the "executive committee of the bourgeoisie"; it protects the property of the capitalist classes and adopts whatever policies are in the interest of the bourgeoisie. The Communist Manifesto says that "political power, properly so called, is merely the organized power of one class for oppressing another."[14]

11. Baumol, p. 11.
12. *Ibid.*, pp. 140–156, for long quotations from Mill's *Principles* and Sidgwick's *Principles,* on this problem, and for a discussion of the casual comments found on this matter in Frédéric Bastiat, J. R. McCulloch, and Friedrich List. See *Classics* for relevant comments by Enrico Barone and Giovanni Montemartini.
13. A. C. Pigou, *A Study in Public Finance,* 3rd rev. ed. (London: Macmillan, 1949). However, see his p. 33 for an explicit mention of this matter.
14. Karl Marx and Friederich Engels, *The Communist Manifesto* (New York:

This theory of the state springs naturally from Marx's theory of social classes. Marx believed that "the history of all hitherto existing society is a history of class struggles."[15] Classes were "organized human interest groups."[16] Social classes were also uniformly selfish: they put the class interest above the national interest and had no concern whatever for the interests of the classes that opposed them. For Marx, a social class was not any particular group of people sharing a certain social status or included in a particular income bracket. Classes were defined in terms of property relationships. It was the owners of productive capital, i.e., the "expropriators" of surplus value, who made up the exploiting class, and the exploited propertyless wage earners that made up the proletariat.[17]

This point of definition is important. If Marx had defined classes in terms of the social position or prestige of their members, he would *not* have been justified in speaking of their common interests, for people with different sources of income (i.e., income from labor or income from capital) might nonetheless have similar amounts of prestige. Instead Marx defined a class in terms of the ownership of productive property. Thus all of those in the capitalist class have common interests, and all of those in the proletariat have common interests, as these are groups whose members gain or lose together as prices and wages change. The one group expropriates the surplus value that the other produces; eventually the exploited class understands that it is in its interest, and within its capability, to revolt, thus ending this type of exploitation. In short, the classes are defined in terms of their economic interests, which they will use all methods, including violence, to further.

Just as the class is selfish, so too is the individual. Marx had nothing but contempt for the utopian socialists and others who assumed a benevolent human nature. Much of the self-interest Marx saw around him he attributed to the capitalistic system and bourgeois

---

League for Industrial Democracy, 1933), p. 82; see also Ralf Dahrendorf, *Class and Class Conflict in Industrial Society* (Stanford, Calif.: Stanford University Press, 1959), p. 13.

15. Marx and Engels, *Communist Manifesto*, p. 59.

16. Dahrendorf, p. 35.

17. Dahrendorf, pp. 30–31; see also Mandell M. Bober, *Karl Marx's Interpretation of History*, rev. ed. (Cambridge, Mass.: Harvard University Press, 1948), esp. pp. 95–96. In this respect Marx was not far different from James Madison, who wrote in the Federalist papers (Number Ten) that "the most common and durable source of factions has been the various and unequal distribution of property. Those who hold and those who are without property have ever formed distinct interests in society."

ideology. "The bourgeoisie...has left remaining no other nexus between man and man than naked self-interest, than callous 'cash payment.' It has drowned the most heavenly ecstasies of religious fervor, of chivalrous enthusiasm, of philistine sentimentalism, in the icy water of egotistical calculation."[18] But if self-interest was most blatant in bourgeois society, it was typical of all of the history of civilized man. "Bare-faced covetousness was the moving spirit of civilization from its first dawn to the present day; wealth, and again wealth, and for the third time wealth; wealth, not of society, but of the puny individual was its only and final aim."[19] Marx attacked as hypocritical almost everything for which people said they were willing to make sacrifices; ideologies were cloaks to hide vested interests; the bourgeois spent great sums on the "evangelization of the lower orders," knowing that this would render the workers "submissive to the habits of the masters it had pleased God to put above them."[20] He wrote that "the English Established Church, for example, will more readily pardon an attack on 38 of its 39 articles than on 1/39th of its income."[21] Only in communism, the primitive communism of the tribe or post-revolutionary communism, would the selfish propensities not control human behavior.

Marx's emphasis on self-interest, and his assumption that classes will be conscious of their interests, has naturally led most critics to think of Marx as a utilitarian and a rationalist. Some think that this is his main failing and that he emphasizes self-interest and rationality far too much. One example of this view deserves quotation at length. The late C. Wright Mills argued that before class action can come about, there must be:

1) a rational awareness and identification with one's own class interests;
2) an awareness of and a rejection of other class interests as illegitimate; and 3) an awareness of and a readiness to use collective political means to the collective political end of realizing one's interests...Underlying the general Marxian model there is always...the political psychology

18. Marx and Engels, *Communist Manifesto*, p. 62.

19. Friedrich Engels, quoted in Bober, *Karl Marx's Interpretation*, p. 72. Bober writes: "If the older English economists assumed the economic man in pecuniary dealings, if Machiavelli constructed the political man in the domain of politics, Marx went farther" (pp. 74–75).

20. Friedrich Engels, *Socialism, Utopian and Scientific*, trans. Edward Aveling (New York: 1892), pp. xxv, xxxi, xxxvi.

21. Karl Marx, *Capital*, Everyman ed. (London: J. M. Dent, 1951), II, 864–865. See also Bober, chaps. vi and vii, pp. 115–156.

of "becoming conscious of inherent possibilities." *This idea is just as rationalist as liberalism in its psychological assumptions.* For the struggle that occurs proceeds on the rational recognition by competing classes of incompatible material interests; reflection links material fact and interested consciousness *by a calculus of advantage.* As Veblen correctly pointed out, the idea is utilitarian, and more closely related to Bentham than Hegel.

Both Marxism and liberalism make the same rationalist assumptions that men, given the opportunity, will naturally come to political *consciousness of interests, of self or of class* [italics mine].

The error of the Marxian view that people will be utilitarian and rationalistic enough to see the wisdom of engaging in class action is proven, in Mills' view, by the widespread political apathy. "Indifference," says Mills, "is the major sign of the . . . collapse of socialist hopes."

But the most decisive comment that can be made about the state of U.S. politics concerns the fact of widespread public indifference . . . [Most of the people] are strangers to politics. They are not radical, not liberal, not conservative, not reactionary; they are inactionary; they are out of it.[22]

Briefly, Marx sees self-interested individuals and self-interested classes acting to achieve their interests. Many critics attack Marx for emphasizing self-interest and individual rationality too much. They feel that most people must not *know or care* what their class interests are, since class conflict is not the overwhelming force Marx thought it would be.

C. THE LOGIC OF THE MARXIAN THEORY

It is *not* in fact true that the absence of the kind of class conflict Marx expected shows that Marx overestimated the strength of rational behavior. On the contrary, the absence of the sort of class action Marx predicted is due in part to the predominance of rational utilitarian behavior. *For class-oriented action will not occur if the individuals that make up a class act rationally.* If a person is in the bourgeois class, he may well want a government that represents his

---

22. All of these quotations are from C. Wright Mills, *White Collar* (New York: Oxford University Press, 1951), pp. 325–328. Talcott Parsons also argues that Marx was basically a utilitarian; see "Social Classes and Class Conflict in the Light of Recent Sociological Theory," in his *Essays in Sociological Theory,* rev. ed. (Glencoe, Ill.: Free Press, 1954), p. 323.

class. But it does not follow that it will be in his interest to work to see that such a government comes to power. If there is such a government he will benefit from its policies, whether or not he has supported it, for by Marx's own hypothesis it will work for his class interests. Moreover, in any event one individual bourgeois presumably will not be able to exercise a decisive influence on the choice of a government. So the *rational* thing for a member of the bourgeoisie to do is to ignore his *class* interests and to spend his energies on his *personal* interests. Similarly, a worker who thought he would benefit from a "proletarian" government would not find it rational to risk his life and resources to start a revolution against the bourgeois government. It would be just as reasonable to suppose that all of the workers in a country would voluntarily restrict their hours of work in order to raise the wages of labor in relation to the rewards for capital. For in both cases the individual would find that he would get the benefits of the class action whether he participated or not.[23] (It is natural then that the "Marxian" revolutions that have taken place have been brought about by small conspiratorial elites that took advantage of weak governments during periods of social disorganization. It was not Marx, but Lenin and Trotsky, who provided the theory for this sort of revolution. See Lenin's *What Is to Be Done*[24] for an account of the communist's need to rely on a committed, self-sacrificing, and disciplined minority, rather than on the common interests of the mass of the proletariat.)

Marxian class action then takes on the character of any endeavor to achieve the collective goals of a large, latent group. A class in Marxist terms consists of a large group of individuals who have a common interest arising from the fact that they do or do not own productive property or capital. As in any large, latent group, each individual in the class will find it to his advantage if all of the costs or sacrifices necessary to achieve the common goal are borne by others. "Class legislation" by definition favors the class as a whole

---

23. John R. Commons has also made this mistake; see "Economists and Class Partnership," in his collection of essays entitled *Labor and Administration* (New York: Macmillan, 1913), p. 60.

24. V. I. Lenin, *What Is to Be Done* (New York: International Publishers, 1929); see also Edmund Wilson, *To the Finland Station* (New York: Harcourt, Brace, 1940), pp. 384–404. Crane Brinton has shown that the major revolutions, communist or otherwise, were carried out by strikingly small numbers of people; see *The Anatomy of Revolution* (New York: Random House, n.d.), pp. 157–163.

rather than particular individuals within the class and thus offers no incentive for individuals to take "class-conscious" action. The worker has the same relation to the mass of the proletariat, and the businessman has the same relation to the mass of the bourgeois, as the taxpayer has to the state, and the competitive firm to the industry. The comparison of the Marxian class to the ordinary large economic group or organization is not at all far-fetched. Marx at times restricted the term "class" to organized groupings: "In so far as the identity of their interests does not produce a community, national association, and political organizations—they do not constitute a class." [25] Marx also emphasized the importance of the trade union and the strike to the class action of the proletariat. Marx and Engels describe the process of proletarian action this way in the Communist Manifesto:

> The collisions between individual workmen and individual bourgeois take more the character of collisions between the two classes. Thereupon the workers begin to form combinations (Trades' Unions) against the bourgeois; they club together in order to keep up the rate of wages; they found permanent associations in order to make provision beforehand for these occasional revolts. Here and there the contest breaks into riots.
>
> Now and then the workers are victorious, but only for a time. The real fruit of their battles lies, not in the immediate result, but in the ever expanding union of the workers.[26]

But the workers who would start the opening round of the class struggle by forming a union to raise wages must face the fact that it is not in the interest of the individual worker to join a union for such a purpose.[27] The crux of the matter, then, is that Marx's theory

25. Quoted in Dahrendorf, p. 13.
26. *Communist Manifesto*, pp. 68–69. Many students think the growth of unions lessens the chances of a communist revolution, since this growth institutionalizes strife and tends to keep it within bounds. Communist revolutions have been most successful in countries where there were not strong unions. See Seymour Martin Lipset, *Political Man* (Garden City, N.Y.: Doubleday, 1960), pp. 21–22.
27. Marx on occasion appeared to recognize this problem, but his answer to it is hardly very clear, as the following quotation suggests: "Large-scale industry concentrates in one place a crowd of people unknown to each other. Competition divides their interests. But the maintenance of wages, this common interest which they have against their boss, unites them in a common thought of resistance—*combination* . . . combinations, at first isolated, constitute themselves into groups . . . and, faced with always united capital, the maintenance of the association becomes more necessary to them than that of wages . . . In this struggle—a veritable civil war—are united and

of social classes is inconsistent insofar as it assumes the rational, selfish pursuit of individual interests. When the class-oriented action Marx predicted does not materialize, it does *not* indicate that the economic motivation is not predominant, as some of his critics imply, but rather than there are *no* individual economic *incentives* for class action. Many of those who criticize Marx as though he were logically consistent but psychologically unrealistic are not only giving Marx's theory credit for a consistency it may not have, but are also wrong in assuming that apathy and the absence of the degree of class action that Marx expected are due to the lack of rational economic behavior: they could logically be due to its strength.

This is not to deny that a theory of *irrational* behavior leading to class action might in certain cases be of some interest. Class differences resulting from sociological factors might lead individuals irrationally and emotionally to act in a class-oriented way.[28] A theory of class action that emphasized emotion and irrationality, rather than the cold and egotistical calculation Marx often emphasized, would be at least consistent. Marx was unfortunately not a precise writer, and there is uncertainty about what he actually meant, and so it is conceivable that he could have had such an irrational, emotional, and psychological theory of class action in mind, rather than the rational, economic, and utilitarian theory of class action that is normally ascribed to him. This is conceivable, but perhaps unlikely, for if Marx had wanted to develop such a theory he would have been logically obliged to emphasize the sincere, selfless sublimation of individual interests in favor of class-oriented action. He would have had to argue that the individual bourgeois were so unselfish and

---

developed all the elements necessary for a coming battle. Once it has reached this point, association takes on a political character." This passage, from *The Poverty of Philosophy,* was also quoted and emphasized by Lenin; see his essay on "Karl Marx," in Karl Marx, *Selected Works in Two Volumes,* prepared by the Marx-Engels-Lenin Institute, Moscow, under the editorship of V. Adoratsky (New York: International Publishers, n.d.), I, 48–50.

28. Such a sociologically determined, irrational class attitude might nonetheless be influenced by the economic position of the class; economic conditions can affect social attitudes. But this fact does not destroy the distinction between such a sociologically oriented class theory and one that assumes that class action is due to (imagined) individual incentives for class-conscious action. On the influence of class on American political behavior see Samuel Lubell, *The Future of American Politics* (New York: Harper, 1952), *passim,* but especially *circa* p. 59, and his *Revolt of the Moderates* (New York: Harper, 1956), pp. 103–120; V. O. Key, *Politics, Parties and Pressure Groups,* 4th ed. (New York: T. Y. Crowell, 1958), pp. 269–279.

dedicated that they would neglect their individual interests to further the goals of their class. But, as explained above, this was hardly Marx's position. He emphasized individual selfishness and bourgeois calculation at every opportunity. He even defined classes in terms of property relationships, and therefore economic interests.[29] And he gave little or no attention to the sociological and psychological processes by which an irrational, emotional class consciousness might develop. For these reasons Marx probably did not have only a theory of irrational and uneconomic class action in mind.[30]

Much of the evidence suggests instead that Marx was offering a theory based on rational, utilitarian individual behavior. And if so his

29. On the other hand, Marx in some places seems to sense the fact that individual interests do not provide a basis for the organized class action that he proclaimed as the decisive force in history. See his comments about competition among the workers and among the bourgeois breaking down the unity of each class in the *Communist Manifesto,* especially p. 69, as well as in his other writings. See also the quotation from Marx's "Ideology—'Saint Max' " quoted in Lipset, *Political Man,* pp. 24–25.

Marx also gives great emphasis to the derivation of moral ideas from the class position. See Friederich Engels, *Herr Eugen Duhring's Revolution in Science (Anti-Duhring),* trans. Emile Burns (New York, 1939), pp. 104–105. In this connection the apparent tendency for revolutionary movements to draw their adherents from those with the *weakest* class ties should be noticed; some scholars contend that those who are déclassé, or "alienated" from the major groups of their society, are the most apt to turn to radical religious or political movements like communism, the John Birch Society, and the like. See Eric Hoffer, *The True Believer* (New York: New American Library, 1958), and William Kornhauser, *The Politics of Mass Society* (Glencoe, Ill.: Free Press, 1959), pp. 14–15. See also Erich Fromm, *Escape from Freedom* (New York: Holt, Rinehart & Winston, 1960), and David Riesman, *The Lonely Crowd* (New York: Doubleday Anchor, 1956).

30. There is some possibility that Marx had neither a theory of rational nor a theory of irrational behavior in mind, but was merely putting forward an unempirical, metaphysical assertion derived from Hegel's dialectical philosophy. Marx again and again referred to the importance of dialectical reasoning for an understanding of social phenomena, and said that he had found Hegel's dialectic standing on its head and had turned it right side up. The essence of history is an inexorable movement by which one ruling class replaces another, just as each thesis has its antithesis. To the extent that Marx's theory of class conflict has such a metaphysical basis, it frustrates any criticism of the sort above; for if replacement of one ruling class by another inevitably is brought about by some immanent force in history, it matters not whether the rational pursuit of self-interest of the persons in the different classes can bring this about; the dialectical movement of historical change will ensure the change in class rule in any event. But however small or large the part of the dialectic in Marx's work, it is clear that such a metaphysical concept has no part whatever to play in an empirical discipline like economics. For an argument that there is an "element of mysticism in the dialectic," see Bober, p. 44. For a different view see Joseph Schumpeter, *Capitalism, Socialism, and Democracy,* 4th ed. (London: George Allen & Unwin, 1954), p. 10.

theory is inconsistent. But even if Marx really had irrational emotional behavior in mind, his theory still suffers, for it is hard to believe that irrational behavior could provide the motive power for *all* social change throughout human history. Therefore Marx's theory of social classes is, as Joseph Schumpeter described it, only a "crippled sister" of his more comprehensive Economic Interpretation of History.

V

Orthodox Theories of Pressure Groups

A. THE PHILOSOPHICAL VIEW OF PRESSURE GROUPS

Just as Marxians glorify and magnify class action, many non-Marxian scholars glorify and magnify the pressure group. Many well-known scholars, especially in the United States, enthusiastically endorse or contentedly accept the results of pressure-group activity, and scoff at the journalists and casual observers[1] who worry about the power of pressure groups. The scholars who praise the pressure groups differ considerably among themselves. Still there is perhaps a common element in the views of most of them; they tend to write approvingly of the functions that the pressure groups fulfill and of the beneficial effects of their activities. Many of them contend that the pressure groups generally counterbalance one another, thus ensuring that there will not be a result unduly favorable to one of them and unjustly harmful to the rest of the society.

It would be difficult to trace exactly the development of the view that pressure groups are generally beneficial, or at least benign. But one type of thinking that has probably helped create an intellectual climate favorable to the growth of this view is that known as "pluralism." Pluralism, to be sure, deals with much more than pressure groups: indeed it deals with them only tangentially. It is the political philosophy which argues that private associations of all kinds, and especially labor unions, churches, and cooperatives, should have a larger constitutional role in society, and that the state should not have an unlimited control over the plurality of these private associations. It opposes the Hegelian veneration of the nation state, on the one hand, but fears the anarchistic and laissez-faire individual-

---

1. See Robert Luce, *Legislative Assemblies* (Boston: Houghton Mifflin, 1924); Stuart Chase, *Democracy Under Pressure: Special Interests vs. the Public Welfare* (New York: Twentieth Century Fund, 1945); Robert Brady, *Business as a System of Power* (New York: Columbia University Press, 1943); Kenneth G. Crawford, *The Pressure Boys* (New York: Julian Messner, 1939).

istic extremes, on the other, and ends up seeking safety in a society in which a number of important private associations provide a cushion between the individual and the state.[2]

Pluralism tends to create a mood favorable to pressure groups (even though that is not its principal purpose) primarily because it emphasizes the spontaneity, the liberty, and the voluntary quality of the private association in contrast with the compulsory, coercive character of the state.[3] The pluralist political theorist, A. D. Lindsay, put it this way:

> The common life of society is lived by individuals in all manner of social relationships—churches, trade unions, institutions of all kinds. The religious, the scientific, the economic life of the community develop through these. Each has its own development. *There is in them a sphere of initiative, spontaneity, and liberty.*
>
> *That sphere can not be occupied by the state with its instruments of compulsion* [italics mine].[4]

The pluralists inherited this view in part from two famous legal scholars, Otto von Gierke of Germany and F. W. Maitland of England.[5] These two scholars were primarily concerned with the legal

2. Francis W. Coker, "Pluralism," *Encyclopaedia of the Social Sciences,* XII (New York: Macmillan, 1934), 170–173; M. P. Follett, *The New State—Group Organization the Solution of Popular Government* (New York: Longmans, Green, 1918); Harold Laski, *A Grammar of Politics,* 4th ed. (London: George Allen & Unwin, 1939), pp. 15–286; Sir Ernest Barker, *Political Thought in England, 1848–1914* (London: Oxford University Press, 1947), pp. 153–160 and 221–224, and *Principles of Social and Political Theory* (Oxford: Clarendon Press, 1951), pp. 47–88. More recently a new, sociological type of pluralist theory has contended that a multitude of political groups besides the state are necessary if a society is to avoid susceptibility to "mass movements" like Nazism and Communism. See William Kornhauser, *The Politics of Mass Society* (Glencoe, Ill.: Free Press, 1959), and Harry Eckstein, *A Theory of Stable Democracy* (Princeton, N.J.: Center of International Studies, Princeton University, 1961). I am indebted to a conversation with Professor Talcott Parsons for the suggestion that this variety of sociological thinking should be regarded as a new type of pluralism.

3. "The pluralist regards these [voluntary associations] . . . as implying respect for the independence and initiative of 'spontaneous' economic, professional, and local groups which correspond to 'natural' unities of interest and function." Coker in *Encyclopaedia of the Social Sciences,* XII, 172. See also Francis Coker, *Recent Political Thought* (New York: Appleton-Century-Crofts, 1934), pp. 497–520.

4. A. D. Lindsay, *The Modern Democratic State* (London: Oxford University Press, 1943), I, 245.

5. Otto von Gierke, *Political Theories of the Middle Age,* translated with an introduction by F. W. Maitland (Cambridge, Eng.: Cambridge University Press, 1900), and *Natural Law and the Theory of Society, 1500–1800,* translated with an introduc-

difficulties that resulted when private associations were not given "legal personality"—the status of units bearing legal rights and duties—and they found in medieval thought and practice a view of organized groups or associations which emphasized their spontaneous origin and organic unity and which they thought a proper basis for modern legal thinking. The view that the private organization was an independent, voluntary, spontaneous outgrowth was further strengthened by several scholars who, though not always pluralists, nonetheless shared the enthusiasm for the voluntary association. John Dewey, the American social critic, was one of these.[6] And in French corporate thought there was a somewhat pluralistic emphasis on the private association. Joseph Paul-Boncour, later a French prime minister, argued that the history of professional or occupational associations showed that in all ages and countries such groups had arisen spontaneously and had in time become a decisive force in their industry or occupation.[7] Emile Durkheim, the great French sociologist, was, like Paul-Boncour, something of a "corporatist" in that he believed in the sociologically natural causes and psychologically desirable effects of a network of occupationally organized associations, and wanted a system of government in which such groups played a much larger role.[8]

The idea of the "corporate state"—a government organized around representation and administration through industrial-occupational groups rather than through territorial divisions—has perhaps some similarity to the view that pressure groups should, because of their beneficial effects, play a larger role. The corporate state theory has

tion by Ernest Barker (Cambridge, Eng.: Cambridge University Press, 1950); F. W. Maitland, "Moral Personality and Legal Personality," in *Maitland—Selected Essays,* ed. H. D. Hazeltine, G. Lapsley, and P. H. Winfield (Cambridge, Eng.: Cambridge University Press, 1936), pp. 223–239.

6. John Dewey, *The Public and Its Problems,* 3rd ed. (Denver: Allan Swallow, 1954), pp. 22–23, 26–27, 28–33, 72–73, and 188.

7. Joseph Paul-Boncour, *Le Fédéralisme économique; étude sur les rapports de l'individu et des groupements professionnels* (Paris: Felix Alcan, 1900), and *Reflections of the French Republic,* trans. George Marion, Jr. (New York: Robert Speller & Sons, 1957), I, 40 and 138–147.

8. Emile Durkheim, *Le Suicide* (Paris: Felix Alcan, 1897), and *The Division of Labor in Society,* trans. George Simpson (Glencoe, Ill.: Free Press, 1947), esp. pp. 1–31. See also Mathew H. Elbow, *French Corporative Theory, 1789–1948* (New York: Columbia University Press, 1953), pp. 100–118. For an English politician's view of the need for an occupational or "social" parliament, see L. S. Amery, *Thoughts on the Constitution* (London: Oxford University Press, 1953), pp. 64–69.

been popular for a long while on the continent, and especially in France, where one version of it has been supported by many Roman Catholic groups—it has been encouraged officially by the Vatican[9]— as well as by President Charles de Gaulle.[10] The emphasis on political organization on a functional or occupational-industrial basis rather than on a geographic basis was of course also characteristic of some varieties of syndicalist and fascist thought, and was to a degree put into practice in fascist Italy and Vichy France.[11]

B. INSTITUTIONAL ECONOMICS AND THE PRESSURE GROUP— JOHN R. COMMONS

Probably the most thoughtful advocacy of occupational as opposed to geographic representation in America came from the institutional economist John R. Commons.[12] And in his case the concern for occupational-industrial representation was directly tied up with his strong support for the pressure group. At one point Commons advocated direct election of representatives for each interest group, which representatives would be the effective legislature of the country.[13]

9. Pius XI, *Quadragesimo Anno.*

10. Elbow, *passim,* esp. pp. 81–96, 100–118, 197–204.

11. Coker, *Recent Political Thought,* pp. 229–290, 460–496; Elbow, *passim;* Richard Humphrey, *Georges Sorel* (Cambridge, Mass.: Harvard University Press, 1951), *passim,* esp. pp. 193–194. In some respects Adolph Berle's ideas on the political role that corporations might play is also similar to pluralism; see *The Twentieth Century Capitalist Revolution* (New York: Harcourt, Brace, 1954), and *Power without Property* (New York: Harcourt, Brace, 1959).

12. John R. Commons, *Representative Democracy* (New York: Bureau of Economic Research, n.d.); *Institutional Economics* (Madison: University of Wisconsin Press, 1959), II, 877–903; *The Economics of Collective Action* (New York: Macmillan, 1950).

13. See chap. ii, entitled "Representation of Interests," in Commons' *Representative Democracy.* "To get back to first principles of representative government (historically as well as logically), each of these diverse interests should be permitted to assemble by itself and elect its spokesman. The negroes would then elect Booker T. Washington; the bankers would elect Lyman J. Gage and J. Pierpont Morgan; . . . the Trade Unions would elect Samuel Gompers and P. M. Arthur; the clergy would elect Archbishop Corrigan and Dr. Parkhurst; the Universities would elect Seth Low and President Eliot . . . But scarcely one of these men could today be elected by popular suffrage in the limited wards or districts where they happen to sleep . . . But at the same time this original principle is unconsciously forcing its way forward. There is no social movement of the past twenty years more quiet nor more potent than the organization of private interests" (pp. 23–24). See also Harvey Fergusson, *People and Power* (New York: William Morrow, 1947), esp. pp. 110–111. One shortcoming of such a pressure-group parliament is that no one legislator can feasibly trade off one interest in favor of another, and therefore the degree of compromise necessary to a continuing democracy may be unattainable.

(G. D. H. Cole and other Guild Socialists advocated a somewhat similar political system in England.)[14] But most of the time Commons argued only that pressure groups were the most representative and beneficial forces affecting American economic policy.

The basis for Commons' thinking was the view that the market mechanisms did not of themselves bring about fair results to the different groups in the economy, and the conviction that this unfairness was due to disparities in the bargaining power of these different groups. These disparities would not be removed by collective action promoted by the government unless pressure groups forced through the necessary reforms, since machine politicians and men of wealth controlled the legislatures. Thus pressure groups were to Commons virtually an indispensable means for the achievement of a just and rational economic order.[15] The conflicts among different interest groups were the vehicles of reform and progress. The economist, Commons believed, should not look for economic legislation that would be in the interest of the whole of society; he should rather attach himself to some pressure group or class and counsel it on the measures that were in its long-run interest. It was after all through their identification with the rising commercial and industrial classes of nineteenth-century England that the classical economists came to have a decisive influence on British economic policy.[16]

But the most important part of Commons' thought for the present

14. "It is nonsense to talk of one man representing another, or a number of others; . . . there is no such thing as representation of one person by another, because in his very nature a man is such a being that he cannot be represented . . . We say that the only way in which there can be real representation is when the representative represents not another person but some group of purposes which men have in common; that you never ought to try to represent Smith and Jones and Brown by means of Robinson, but that, if Smith, Jones, and Brown have a common interest in some particular thing whether as producers or as football players or in any other capacity, it is quite legitimate for them to choose Robinson to execute for them and on their behalf their common purpose. That is to say, all true representation, if we are right, is not representation of persons, but only representation of common purposes; or, to put it in other words, any real representation is necessarily functional representation." This is from G. D. H. Cole, "Guild Socialism," as excerpted in *Introduction to Contemporary Civilization in the West,* published and prepared by Columbia University, II, 889. See also Cole's *Self-Government in Industry* (London: G. Bell & Sons, 1917).

15. Commons, *Economics of Collective Action, passim,* esp. pp. 33, 59, 262–291; *Institutional Economics, passim;* and *The Legal Foundations of Capitalism* (Madison: University of Wisconsin Press, 1957), *passim.*

16. "Economists and Class Partnership," in *Labor and Administration* (New York: Macmillan, 1913), a collection of articles by Commons, pp. 51–71 and esp. pp. 54 and 67.

purpose was his belief that the economic pressure groups were more representative of the people than the legislatures based on territorial representation. In his last book, in which he summed up his thought with the help of Kenneth Parsons, he wrote: "A notable fact about the pressure groups is the recent concentration of their headquarters in Washington, D.C., the political capital of the country. *The economic pressure groups really become an occupational parliament of the American people, more truly representative than the Congress elected by territorial divisions* [italics mine]. They are the informal counterpart of Mussolini's 'corporate state,' the Italian occupational state." [17] Commons' encouragement of the economic pressure group went so far as to suggest that the pressure groups, and especially the labor unions, farm organizations, and cooperatives, were the most vital institutions in society and the lifeblood of democracy. The freedom to form pressure groups mattered more than any of the other democratic freedoms. The traditional legislature, he felt, was worth preserving against the assaults of Communism and Fascism mainly because it in turn would allow the freedom to associate in interest groups or pressure groups to be maintained.

But far more important than other reasons for improving the legislatures is *the protection they may give to voluntary associations* . . . The rights of man are now his rights of free association . . . the civil liberties that make possible the voluntary associations of labor unions, farmers' unions, business cooperatives, and political parties. *It is these associations rather than the older individualism of free individual action, that are the refuge of modern Liberalism and Democracy* from Communism, Fascism, or Banker Capitalism [italics mine].[18]

This aspect of Commons' thought has more recently been developed by Kenneth Parsons, Commons' most thoughtful disciple and interpreter.[19] And some aspects of John Kenneth Galbraith's theory of countervailing power, which may come through political action by pressure groups, have a slight similarity to Commons' theories.[20]

17. Commons, *Economics of Collective Action*, p. 33; see also pp. 59, 262–277, and 291. Yet sometimes Commons argued, inconsistently it would seem, that some important groups were not at all well organized. This was especially true of the farmers. *Ibid.*, p. 213, and *Institutional Economics*, II, 901–902.

18. Commons, *Institutional Economics*, II, 901–903.

19. Kenneth Parsons, "Social Conflicts and Agricultural Programs," *Journal of Farm Economics*, XXIII (November 1941), 743–764.

20. John Kenneth Galbraith, *American Capitalism: The Concept of Countervailing*

C. MODERN THEORIES OF PRESSURE GROUPS—BENTLEY, TRUMAN, LATHAM

It is not among economists, but rather among political scientists, that the opinion of pressure groups which Commons held is the most common. For political scientists have evolved a theory of group behavior strikingly similar to that which Commons advocated. The idea that group interests are absolutely fundamental determinants of economic and political behavior is accepted by many, perhaps most, political scientists. As Earl Latham pointed out in his book *The Group Basis of Politics,* "American writers on politics have increasingly accepted the view that the group is the basic political form." [21] Professor Latham himself holds to this view: "It has been pointed out, and repeated, that the structure of society is associational. Groups are basic . . . What is true of society is true of the . . . economic community." [22]

The parallelism between Commons' thinking on group behavior in economics and politics and the trend of thought in political science can easily be illustrated. Professor Latham illustrates this parallelism most clearly:

The concept of the group . . . has been helpful in bringing to economics a knowledge of the human institutions through which men dig coal, make soap and battleships, create credit, and allocate the resources of production. Commons, Veblen, Clark, Andrews, and other pioneers in the empirical study of such economic group forms as banks, corporations, granges, unions, cooperatives, railroads, brokerage houses, and exchanges did much to rectify the notion that some objective law, heedless of men, somehow filled each purse to the exact limit justified by the contribution of its owner to the total of the goods and services of society. The economic theory of a century ago fixed the nature of the economic universe by definition and tended to derive its characteristics by deduction, an economic world inhabited by a multiplicity of individuals in isolation, where combination was a pathological deviation. Such a *defined* (not observed) universe could not fail to work—in the realm of discourse. So far have we come from this view that a whole new vocabulary has been invented to explain the operations of an economic community formed of aggregations, clusters, blocs, and combinations of

---

Power (London: Hamish Hamilton, 1952), esp. chap. x, "Countervailing Power and the State," pp. 141–157.

21. Earl Latham, *The Group Basis of Politics* (Ithaca, N.Y.: Cornell University Press, 1952), p. 10; see also David B. Truman, *The Governmental Process* (New York: Alfred A. Knopf, 1958), pp. 46–47.

22. Latham, p. 17.

people and things—not individuals in isolation. Few modern writers on economics would be able to discuss their subject matter without reference to "oligopoly," "imperfect competition," "monopolistic competition," and other group phenomena in the economic community.[23]

What is significant in this quotation is not the neglect of the fact that monopolistic and imperfect competition alike are in fact based on assumptions fully as individualistic as perfect competition, but rather the belief that group interests and group behavior are the primary forces in economic as well as in political behavior. The essence of this tradition in political science seems to be that one looks to group interests rather than to individual interests to see the basic forces at work in both the economy and the polity. For Commons and Latham alike, group interests are dominant, individual interests secondary.

Latham quite plausibly emphasizes the close connection between the "group theory" of modern American political science and the tradition of pluralism. The original pluralist thinkers, the "philosophical pluralists," are credited with understanding "the group basis of society, both in its political and economic communities." [24] While the original pluralists are praised for seeing the fundamental and inevitable character of economic and political action on behalf of group interests, they are chided for failing to examine the group's "forms, mutations, and permutations in a scientific spirit." [25] The modern political scientists, since they deal with the plurality of group forms, should also be called pluralists, but because of their "scientific" and theoretical rigor the adjective "analytical" should be added to distinguish them from the original or "philosophical" pluralists.[26] All of the modern "group theorists," then, are "analytical pluralists," and it is by this name that they shall be known in this study.

The most important of the "modern" or "analytical" pluralists was Arthur F. Bentley, for it is his book, *The Process of Government*,[27] that has inspired most of the political scientists who have

23. *Ibid.*, pp. 4–5.
24. *Ibid.*, p. 8.
25. *Ibid.*, p. 9.
26. *Ibid.*, p. 9.
27. Arthur F. Bentley, *The Process of Government* (Evanston, Ill.: Principia Press, 1949). Although this book was first published in 1908, and thus is contemporaneous with many of the original or "philosophical" pluralist writings, its approach is completely in harmony with modern political science.

followed the "group approach."[28] His book, probably one of the most influential in American social science, is partly an attack on certain methodological errors that had troubled the study of politics, but mostly a discussion of the dominant role that pressure groups play in economic and political life.

The economic aspect was very important to Bentley. He had previously written about economic history, and considered himself for much of his life an economist.[29] Wealth, he thought, was the main source of group division in society.[30] Apparently he turned to the study of pressure groups primarily because of his interest in economic affairs. "I will say," he wrote in *The Process of Government,* "that my interest in politics is not primary, but derived from my interest in economic life; and that I hope from this point of approach ultimately to gain a better understanding of economic life than I have succeeded in gaining hitherto."[31]

His idea that group pressure was the basic force was not, however, confined to the economic sphere, though that was apparently the most important. "The great task in the study of any form of social life is the analysis of these groups," he contended; "when the groups are adequately stated, everything is stated. When I say everything, I mean everything."[32] It was group *interests,* moreover, that were basic. "*There is no group without its interest.* An interest, as the term will be used here, is the equivalent of a group."[33] These group interests were to be found by empirical study. Bentley thought that no "interest" could be considered to exist unless it manifested itself in group action.

Whereas group interests were everything, individual interests were nothing. What mattered were the common interests of groups of people, not the losses and gains to single individuals. "The individual stated for himself, and invested with an extra-social unity of his own, is a fiction. But every bit of the activity, which is all we

28. Truman, p. ix; Latham, p. 10; Robert T. Golembiewski, " 'The Group Basis of Politics': Notes on Analysis and Development," *American Political Science Review,* LIV (December 1960), 962; William J. Block, *The Separation of the Farm Bureau and the Extension Service* (Urbana: University of Illinois Press, 1960), p. 2.

29. Myron Q. Hale, "The Cosmology of Arthur F. Bentley," *American Political Science Review,* LIV (December 1960), 955.

30. Bentley, p. 462.

31. *Ibid.,* p. 210.

32. *Ibid.,* pp. 208–209.

33. *Ibid.,* p. 211; italics mine.

know of him, can be stated either on the one side as individual, or on the other side as social group activity. The former statement is in the main of trifling importance in interpreting society; the latter statement is essential, first, last, and all the time." [34] Just as the idea of the individual interest was a fiction, so was the idea of the national interest. All group interests pertained to groups comprising only a part of a nation or society.[35] "Usually we shall find," wrote Bentley, "on testing the 'social whole,' that it is merely the group or tendency represented by the man who talks of it, erected into the pretense of a universal demand of the society." [36] This situation was logically necessary in Bentley's model, since he defined groups in terms of their conflict with one another, and thought that "no interest group has meaning except with reference to other interest groups." [37]

By defining group interests in terms of their conflict with one another, thereby excluding the idea of an interest of society as a whole, Bentley was then able to say that the resultant of the group pressures was the one and only determinant of the course of government policy. "Pressure, as we shall use it, is always a group phenomenon. It indicates the push and resistance between groups. The balance of group pressures *is* the existing state of society." [38] Government, in Bentley's theory, was "considered as the adjustment or balance of interests." [39] Now the outline of the model is evident. By assuming that there are no effective individual interests, that every group has its interests, that these interests always result in group action, and that there is no one group interest that includes everyone in society, Bentley was able to claim that all things involving government, all things great and small, are determined by the conflicting group pressures.[40] This was the key to understanding government in general and economic policy in particular.

34. *Ibid.,* p. 215; see also pp. 166–170 and 246–247.

35. "The 'state' itself is, to the best of my knowledge and belief, no factor in our investigation. It is like the 'social whole': we are not interested in it as such, but exclusively in the processes within it." *Ibid.,* p. 263; see also pp. 217–222, 271, 422, 443–444, and R. E. Dowling, "Pressure Group Theory: Its Methodological Range," *American Political Science Review,* LIV (December 1960), 944–954, and esp. 944–948.

36. Bentley, p. 220; for a similar view see Truman, p. 51.

37. Bentley, p. 271; he also says that the "activity that reflects one group, however large it may be, always reflects the activity of that group against the activity of some other group" (p. 240).

38. *Ibid.,* pp. 258–259.

39. *Ibid.,* p. 264.

40. Bentley went all the way with his model. Everything that mattered in the control of social and economic policy could fit into the model of conflicting group

Not only was the resultant of all the group pressures always the determinant of social policy, but it was also, in Bentley's mind, for the most part a reasonably just determinant. Groups had a degree of power or pressure more or less in proportion to their numbers. The larger, more nearly general, interest would usually tend to defeat the smaller, narrower, special interest. He considers a situation in which a relatively small group of team owners with heavy wagons are tending to damage the public roads in a town to the detriment of the majority of the taxpayers and citizens in the town. Bentley asserts that eventually the interest of the larger number will win out over the special interests of the minority: the mass of taxpayers is "bound to win" eventually and require wider tires for the teamsters' wagons, despite the fact that many in the majority may not even be aware of the controversy.[41] This result was typical. "The greater proportion of the detail of government work . . . is composed of habitual actions which are adjustments forced by large, united weak interests upon less numerous, but relatively to the number of adherents, more intense interests. If there is anything that could probably be meant by the phrase 'control by the people' just as it stands, it is this." [42] Legislatures, he concedes, were at times working quite imperfectly, but when special interests got too large a hand, a hue and cry arose against them.[43] The logrolling of special interests was not to be feared: it was an excellent, efficient device for adjusting group interests.[44]

---

pressures. Differences in the quality of political leadership? This was mainly the result of different group patterns. If a group leader was weak, it meant that there were quarreling subgroups within the group he was attempting to lead. The type of government? Group pressures would triumph, whether there was dictatorship, constitutional monarchy, oligarchy, or democracy. Even the most powerful dictator was a mediator among groups, the army, the church, the landowners, or whatever; even the slaves' interests had their effect on the outcome. The separation of powers? Group pressures would determine the outcome however the government was organized, though each different agency or part of the government was itself a group with an interest of its own which would in turn affect the balance of pressures. Even the judicial decisions could be understood in terms of group pressures. The extent of the franchise? A group would have power whether or not it had the vote. Whether women were enfranchised mattered little, for if they were not they would still affect the resultant of group pressures through the family, an important subgroup.

41. Bentley, pp. 226–227.
42. *Ibid.*, p. 454.
43. *Ibid.*, pp. 454–455.
44. "Log-rollling is, however, in fact, the most characteristic legislative process. When one condemns it 'in principle,' it is only by contrasting it with some assumed pure public spirit which is supposed to guide legislators, or which ought to guide

For all his emphasis on the importance and beneficence of group pressures, Bentley said very little about *why* the needs of the different groups in society would tend to be reflected in politically or economically effective pressure. Nor did he consider carefully what it is that causes groups to organize and act effectively. Or why some groups are important in some societies and other groups important in other societies and periods.[45] Bentley's disciples, however, have attempted to fill this gap in his thinking.

David Truman, in his well-known book *The Governmental Process,* has given particularly careful attention to this lacuna in Bentley's book. Essentially Professor Truman tried to develop a variant of the sociological theory of voluntary associations to show that organized and effective group pressures will emerge when necessary.[46] As a society becomes more complex, Truman argued, and its group needs become more numerous and varied, it will naturally tend to form additional associations to stabilize the relationships of the various groups in the society. With more specialization and social complexity, more associations are needed, and more will arise, because it is a basic characteristic of social life that associations emerge to satisfy the needs of society.

With an increase in specialization and with the continual frustration of established expectations consequent upon rapid changes in the related techniques, *the proliferation of associations is inescapable* [italics mine]. So closely do these developments follow, in fact, that the rate of association formation may serve as an index of the stability of a society, and their number may be used as an index of its complexity. Simple societies have no associations (in the technical sense of the term); as they grow more complex, i.e., as highly differentiated institutionalized groups increase in number, societies evolve greater numbers of associations.[47]

This "inescapable" increase in the number of associations will inevitably have its impact on government. The associations will acquire

them, and which enables them to pass judgment in Jovian calm on that which is best 'for the whole people.' Since there is nothing which is literally best for the whole people, group arrays being what they are, the test is useless, even if one could actually find legislative judgments which are not reducible to interest-group activities. And when we have reduced the legislative process to the play of group interests, then log-rolling, or give and take, appears as the very nature of the process. It is compromise . . . It is trading. It is the adjustment of interests." (*Ibid.,* pp. 370–371.)

45. See however his pp. 460–464.
46. Truman, pp. 23–33, 39–43, and 52–56.
47. *Ibid.,* p. 57.

connections with the institutions of government whenever government is important to the groups in question.[48] This tendency for associations to arise to fill the needs of the groups in society is especially evident in the economic sphere.

There are, undoubtedly, a number of reasons for the prevalence of associations growing out of economic institutions . . . There has been a series of disturbances and dislocations consequent upon the utopian attempt, as Polanyi calls it, to set up a completely self-regulating market system. This attempt involved a policy of treating the fictitious factors of land, labor, and capital as if they were real, ignoring the fact that they stood for human beings or influences closely affecting the welfare of humans. Application of this policy inevitably meant suffering and dislocation—unemployment, wide fluctuation in prices, waste, and so forth. *These disturbances inevitably produced associations—of owners, of workers, of farmers—operating upon government to mitigate and control the ravages of the system* through tariffs, subsidies, wage guarantees, social insurance and the like.[49] [Italics mine.]

Truman then appears to contend that "suffering," "dislocation," and "disturbance" will almost inevitably result in *organized* political pressure. Those disadvantaged groups that need an organization will in fact come to have an organization. But the facts of recent political life do not necessarily substantiate this view. By Truman's standard, more associations should have been formed during the industrial revolution (when there was a great deal of "suffering" and "dislocation"). But, as he points out, the rate at which associations have been formed has been highest in recent years[50] (which have been mainly prosperous and stable).

Apart from this attempt to amend Bentley's theory (by adding an

48. *Ibid.*, pp. 52, 55.

49. *Ibid.*, p. 61. Truman also gives the rapid rate of technical change in modern industry part of the credit for the preponderance of economic associations.

50. *Ibid.*, pp. 55, 60. By Truman's theory, the major national British labor unions should have begun during the Industrial Revolution, not in the placid period after 1850, and American unions should have grown most during the tumultuous years of industrial change after the Civil War, or from 1929 to 1933, not before and during the two world wars. Admittedly, the legal environment was possibly also a factor; British unions, for example, were outlawed during part of the Industrial Revolution. Admittedly also Truman is persuasive in finding that discontent and disaffection are greatest during periods of economic dislocation; I have committed myself to a similar argument in "Rapid Growth as a Destabilizing Force," *Journal of Economic History*, XXIII (December 1963), 529–552. The trouble with Truman's theory here is that it assumes *organized* groups arise because there is a dislocation or "need" for them, and this is neither factually nor theoretically substantiated.

explanation of why group needs and interests would result in organized political pressure), Truman tended to follow every twist and turn in Bentley's account. Truman, like Bentley, neglected individual interests; group interests, group attitudes, and group pressures were the only things that mattered.[51]

Truman not only shared Bentley's belief that group pressures alone determined the final equilibrium position of the social system, but was, if anything, even less qualified in his belief that this group equilibrium tended to be just and desirable.[52] There were two main reasons for Professor Truman's benign view of the results of pressure-group politics. He thought, in the first place, that most pressure groups would be weak and divided in those circumstances in which they asked for too much from society, since their members also had "overlapping" memberships in other groups with different interests and would thus tend to oppose excessive demands. Tariff-seeking manufacturers were also consumers, churchmen, and so on, so that if the manufacturers' association went too far it would alienate some of its own members.[53] Moreover, in the second place, there were "potential groups" that would arise and organize to do battle with the special interests if the special interests got far out of line.[54] If the tariff proposed was excessive, presumably the consumers would organize a lobby that would oppose it. And the very existence

51. Truman also resembled his master in his neglect of the all-inclusive social or national interest. "In developing a group interpretation of politics," he commented on p. 51, "we do not need to account for a totally inclusive interest, because one does not exist."

52. It does not follow that the results of pressure-group activity would be harmless, much less desirable, even if the balance of power equilibrium resulting from the multiplicity of pressure groups kept any one pressure group from getting out of line. Even if such a pressure group system worked with perfect *fairness* to every group, it would still tend to work *inefficiently*. If every industry is favored, to a fair or equal degree, by favorable government policies obtained through lobbying, the economy as a whole will tend to function less efficiently, and every group will be worse off than if none, or only some, of the special-interest demands had been granted. Coherent, rational policies cannot be expected from a series of separate *ad hoc* concessions to diverse interest groups. For a related argument, see Peter H. Odegard, "A Group Basis of Politics: A New Name for an Ancient Myth," *Western Political Quarterly,* XI (September 1958), 700.

53. Truman, pp. 506–516.

54. This idea is now apparently so widely accepted that it is passed on to the young in the textbooks almost without qualification. See James MacGregor Burns and James Walter Peltason, *Government by the People,* 4th ed. (Englewood Cliffs, N.J.: Prentice-Hall, 1960), pp. 310–311.

of these potential groups, and the fear that they would organize, keeps the organized interests from making excessive demands.

Thus it is only as the effects of overlapping memberships and the functions of unorganized interests and potential groups are included in the equation that it is accurate to speak of governmental activity as the product or resultant of group activity ... To assert that the organization and activity of powerful interest groups constitutes a threat to representative government without measuring their relation to and the effects upon the widespread potential groups is to generalize from insufficient data and upon an incomplete conception of the political process.[55]

So confident was Professor Truman of the generally salutory effects of group pressures that he belittled almost all attempts to improve the system of legislation and lobbying.[56]

D. THE LOGIC OF GROUP THEORY

There is an inconsistency in the thinking of Commons, Bentley, Truman, Latham, and some of the pluralist and corporatist writers who have emphasized the pressures of the different economic groups. Many of these stimulating and important writers, especially Bentley, Truman, and Latham, have taken for granted that large economic groups working for their economic interests are absolutely fundamental in the political process. They have at times affirmed the existence of groups with something other than self-interested economic purposes, but still self-interested economic groups always play

---

55. Truman, pp. 515–516.

56. In a section on "Nostrums and Palliatives," Truman ridiculed the idea of the direct representation of the different economic interests in a "social parliament." In this he distinguished himself from J. R. Commons (who for all his faith in the results of pressure-group activity had once advocated election of representatives from the different occupational groups) as well as from many of the guild socialist and corporatist writers in Europe. Of the recommendations for an occupationally rather than a territorially based parliament, Professor Truman said that "these proposals are worth noting . . . because their recurrence shows how easily the political process may be misunderstood." There are many disadvantages to any system of functional representation and Professor Truman is right to bring these to mind. But the question remains whether or not he is right in assuming that, whatever the institutional arrangements, the needs of all groups in society will nonetheless tend to be reflected in effective political pressure and appropriate government policies. This same contentment about the wisdom and justice of the policies resulting from the equilibrium of group pressures also led Truman to be rather negative about proposals for the regulation of lobbying, for constitutional reforms, and for responsible political parties. (See Truman, pp. 524–535.)

the largest role in their writings.[57] Professor Latham has been the most explicit on this point; for him self-interest is important, if not dominant, even in spiritual and philanthropic groups:

> Groups organize for the self-expression and security of the members that comprise them. Even where a group is a benevolent, philanthropic association devoted to the improvement of material and spiritual fortunes of people outside its membership—a temperance or missionary organization, for example—the work toward this goal, the activity of the organization, is a means through which the members express themselves . . . The philanthropic organization devoted to good works often regards other agencies in the same field with a venomous eye. Councils of social agencies in large cities are often notorious for the rancor with which the struggle for prestige and recognition (that is self-expression and security) is conducted one with the other.[58]

If the groups, or at least the economic groups, are often interested primarily in their own welfare, it could only be so because the *individuals* in these groups were primarily interested in their own welfare. So the "group theorists" under consideration here have committed themselves, usually implicitly and sometimes also explicitly, to the idea that, at least in economic groups, self-interested behavior is quite common. It can scarcely be emphasized too strongly that the analytical pluralists see the results of pressure-group activity as benign, not from any assumption that individuals always deal altruistically with one another, but rather because they think that the different groups will tend to keep each other in check because of the balance of power among them.

Here then is the logical failing in the analytical pluralists' treatment of economic groups. They generally take for granted that such groups will act to defend or advance their group interests, and take it for granted that the individuals in these groups must also be concerned about their individual economic interests. But if the individuals in any large group are interested in their own welfare, they will *not* voluntarily make any sacrifices to help their group attain its political (public or collective) objectives. Often the groups that the analytical pluralists expect will organize whenever they have any reason or incentive to do so are latent groups. Although in relatively small groups ("privileged" or "intermediate" groups) indi-

57. Truman, pp. 58–61; Bentley, pp. 210, 226–227, 462; Latham, p. 17.
58. Latham, pp. 28–29.

viduals may voluntarily organize to achieve their common objectives, this is not true in large or latent groups. It follows that the analytical pluralists, the "group theorists," have built their theory around an inconsistency. They have assumed that, if a group had some reason or incentive to organize to further its interest, the rational individuals in that group would also have a reason or an incentive to support an organization working in their mutual interest. But this is logically fallacious, at least for large, latent groups with economic interests.

Professor Truman developed a variant of the sociological theory of voluntary associations (which was explained in Chapter I of this study) to buttress his assumption that groups of individuals will organize to protect their interests. But his variant of the sociological theory of voluntary organizations, like that theory itself, is insufficient. It is, like that theory, based on the mistaken belief that large groups could attract membership and support as easily as the small, primary groups that dominated primitive society. Previous chapters of this book argued that this assumption was logically untenable and moreover inconsistent with the available evidence. Because of the differences between small (privileged and intermediate) groups and large (latent) groups, there is no reason to suppose, as Truman does, that as problems that small primary groups cannot handle begin to emerge, large voluntary associations will arise to deal with those problems.

The distinction between the privileged and intermediate groups, on the one hand, and the latent group, on the other, also damages the pluralistic view that any outrageous demands of one pressure group will be counterbalanced by the demands of other groups, so that the outcome will be reasonably just and satisfactory. Since relatively small groups will frequently be able voluntarily to organize and act in support of their common interests, and since large groups normally will not be able to do so, the outcome of the political struggle among the various groups in society will not be symmetrical. Practical politicians and journalists have long understood that small "special interest" groups, the "vested interests," have disproportionate power. The somewhat too colorful and tendentious language with which the men of affairs make this point should not blind the scholar to the important element of truth that it contains. The small oligopolistic industry seeking a tariff or a tax loophole will sometimes attain its objective even if the vast majority of the population loses as a result. The smaller groups—the privileged and intermediate groups—can often defeat the large groups—the latent groups—which are normally supposed to prevail in a democracy. The privileged and intermediate groups often triumph over the numerically superior forces in the latent or large groups because the former are generally organized and active while the latter are normally unorganized and inactive. The greater degree of organization and activity of small groups is not difficult to illustrate; the late V. O. Key argued in his standard textbook that "the lobbyists for electrical utilities, for example, are eternally on the job; the lobbyists for the consumers of this monopolistic service are ordinarily conspicuous by their absence."[59]

The conflict between the theory of analytical pluralism and the facts of political life is, however, somewhat obscured by the emphasis the analytical pluralists give to the "potential" (that is unorganized and inactive) group. The analytical pluralists generally, and Professor Truman particularly, emphasize the influence of the group that, even though unorganized and inactive, could and allegedly would organize and act if its interests were seriously threatened. The argument is that politicians know that a group, if its interest is seriously damaged or threatened, will organize and then wreak vengeance on its enemies. Therefore politicians will be almost as solicitous of the unorganized and inactive group as they are of the organized and active interest group. This contention is rather difficult to test empirically, because, if a group does not organize and act, the analytical pluralist can say that the damage to its interests was not serious or that there was in fact no group interest.

Accordingly the analytical pluralists tend to belittle the importance of formal organization and other observable evidences of group action. "Organization," according to Professor Truman, "indicates merely a stage or degree of interaction."[60] Bentley did not think formal organization amounted even to that,[61] and compared formal organization with the singing with which armies of old went into battle: it is merely a "technique" designed to improve the spirit and efficiency of the group that has little effect on the results.[62] But would

---

59. V. O. Key, Jr., *Politics, Parties, and Pressure Groups*, 4th ed. (New York: Crowell, 1958), p. 166.

60. Truman, p. 36.

61. Bentley, pp. 434–446 and 463–464.

62. *Ibid.*, p. 442.

not the comparison between a disciplined, coordinated army and an undisciplined, leaderless mob provide a better analogy to the difference between the organized and unorganized group? Practical politicians often emphasize the importance of "organization" and the power of the "machine." They would not often think of "lobbying" without a "lobby." The textbook writers in political science, moreover, discuss the achievements of organized pressure groups at great length, but they list few if any specific examples of the influence of unorganized groups.[63]

But even if the analytical pluralists should be correct in emphasizing the "potential" group and belittling the existing organization, their theory is still inadequate unless they can show *how* damage to a large group's interests—how an incentive for group organization and action—would necessarily provide an incentive or stimulus for the members of that large group to sacrifice their individual interests on behalf of the group goal. They must show *why* the individual member of the large, latent group will voluntarily support the group goal when his support will not in any case be decisive in seeing that the group goal is achieved, and when he would be as likely to get the benefits from the attainment of that goal whether he had worked for its attainment or not. The group theorists are on this point logically inconsistent. Their references to "potential" groups and their lack of concern for organization may blur the contrast between their theoretical conclusions and the facts of everyday observation, but they cannot negate the fact that their theories, insofar as they relate to large economic groups at least, are logically inconsistent.

The foregoing argument against the analytical pluralists also applies to John R. Commons' interesting view that the pressure groups' lobbies actually assembled in Washington are more "representative" than the territorially elected Congress is.[64] The foregoing argument also damages, though it does not destroy, a few of the

63. See for example Key, pp. 21–177.

64. The theory presented here does not, however, weaken, and might even strengthen, the idea, expressed by Commons and some corporatist thinkers, that the parliament ought to be elected by each economic group. To the extent that the theory shows how different groups would be unequally represented in a territorially elected legislature, it could be used to support a social or occupational parliament. But this theory destroys the corporatist idea that occupational groups naturally tend to form corporate organizations because of some spontaneous unity within them.

arguments of some of the older or "philosophical" pluralists and the advocates of a corporate organization of society. The various philosophical pluralists and the diverse advocates of corporatism mentioned at the beginning of this chapter differ a great deal among themselves and no one criticism can apply equally to them all. Their different theories are, moreover, almost all so broad the theory developed in this study can apply only to parts of them. Still, to the extent that the philosophical pluralists and the corporatists argue that any *private* organizations representing different occupational and industrial groups would have a firm foundation in the "natural unities of interest and function" of those groups, and that those groups could or would create "spontaneous and voluntary" organizations without the unnatural, coercive characteristics of the state, they are weakened by the theory developed in this study. Certainly the pluralist idea that the private group, even if it is rather large (and provides a collective service), can be natural, harmonious, and voluntary, and thus stand in contrast to the coercive state, is mistaken, however valuable other aspects of pluralist thought may be.

The pluralistic view that private organizations spring up voluntarily and spontaneously in response to the needs, beliefs, and interests of the various groups has much in common with one aspect of the theory of anarchism. Many anarchists believed that once the existing, repressive, exploitive state was overthrown, a new, voluntary, natural unity would somehow emerge to take its place. As Bakunin saw it, "the political unity of the State is a fiction . . . it artificially produces discord where, without this intervention by the State, a living unity would not fail to spring up." [65] He continued, "When the states have disappeared, a living, fertile, beneficent unity of regions as well as of nations . . . by way of free federation from below upward—will unfold itself in all its majesty, not divine but human." [66] According to Prince Kropotkin, once the leading anarchist intellectual, a natural feeling that man should cooperate with his fellows for their "mutual aid" would ensure that after the anarchistic overthrow of the state a spontaneous and natural order would

65. Mikhail A. Bakunin, *Bakunin: Scientific Anarchism*, ed. G. P. Maximoff (Glencoe, Ill.: Free Press, 1953), p. 272.

66. *Ibid.*, p. 273, also pp. 259, 293–300, 309. See also Paul Eltzbacher, *Anarchism*, trans. Steven T. Byington (New York: Libertarian Book Club, 1960).

develop. "The sophisms of the brain," said Kropotkin, "can not resist the mutual-aid feeling." [67]

The anarchistic assumption that in the absence of the oppressive state a natural, spontaneous unity would spring up to take its place is now regarded as evidence of hopeless eccentricity. The consistent critic of anarchism must, however, attack with equal force all of those who suppose that large groups will whenever the need arises voluntarily organize a pressure group to deal with the state, or a labor union to deal with an employer. Bentley, Truman, Commons, Latham, and many of the pluralist and corporatist thinkers are fully as guilty of the "anarchistic fallacy" as the anarchists themselves. The anarchists supposed that the need or incentive for organized or coordinated cooperation after the state was overthrown would ensure that the necessary organization and group action would be forthcoming. Is the view that workers will voluntarily support a trade union, and that any large group will organize a pressure-group lobby to ensure that its interests are protected by the government, any more plausible?

Because of the inconsistency, the anarchistic fallacy, in the prevailing (pluralistic) theory of pressure groups, this theory is not sufficient. The "group theory" that dominates the discussions of pressure groups is inadequate for large economic groups, at least, and there is accordingly a need for a new theory. It is to the development of such a theory that the next chapter will be devoted.

67. P. Kropotkin, *Mutual Aid, A Factor of Evolution,* rev. ed. (London: William Heinemann, 1904), p. 277.

VI

The "By-Product" and "Special Interest" Theories

A. THE "BY-PRODUCT" THEORY OF LARGE PRESSURE GROUPS

If the individuals in a large group have no incentive to organize a lobby to obtain a collective benefit, how can the fact that some large groups are organized be explained? Though many groups with common interests, like the consumers, the white-collar workers, and the migrant agricultural workers, are not organized,[1] other large groups, like the union laborers, the farmers, and the doctors have at least some degree of organization. The fact that there are many groups which, despite their needs, are not organized would seem to contradict the "group theory" of the analytical pluralists; but on the other hand the fact that other large groups have been organized would seem to contradict the theory of "latent groups" offered in this study.

But the large economic groups that are organized do have one common characteristic which distinguishes them from those large economic groups that are not, and which at the same time tends to support the theory of latent groups offered in this work. This common characteristic will, however, require an elaboration or addition to the theory of groups developed in this study.

The common characteristic which distinguishes all of the large economic groups with significant lobbying organizations is that these groups are also organized for some *other* purpose. The large and powerful economic lobbies are in fact the by-products of organizations that obtain their strength and support because they perform some function in addition to lobbying for collective goods.

1. "When lists of these organizations are examined, the fact that strikes the student most forcibly is that *the system is very small*. The range of organized, identifiable, known groups is amazingly narrow; there is nothing remotely universal about it." E. E. Schattschneider, *The Semi-Sovereign People* (New York: Holt, Rinehart & Winston, 1960), p. 30.

The lobbies of the large economic groups are the by-products of organizations that have the capacity to "mobilize" a latent group with "selective incentives." The only organizations that have the "selective incentives" available are those that (1) have the authority and capacity to be coercive, or (2) have a source of positive inducements that they can offer the individuals in a latent group.

A purely political organization—an organization that has no function apart from its lobbying function—obviously cannot legally coerce individuals into becoming members. A political party, or any purely political organization, with a captive or compulsory membership would be quite unusual in a democratic political system. But if for some nonpolitical reason, if because of some other function it performs, an organization has a justification for having a compulsory membership, or if through this other function it has obtained the power needed to make membership in it compulsory, that organization may then be able to get the resources needed to support a lobby. The lobby is then a by-product of whatever function this organization performs that enables it to have a captive membership.

An organization that did nothing except lobby to obtain a collective good for some large group would not have a source of rewards or positive selective incentives it could offer potential members. Only an organization that also sold private or noncollective products, or provided social or recreational benefits to individual members, would have a source of these positive inducements.[2] Only such an organiza-

2. An economic organization in a perfectly competitive market in equilibrium, which had no special competitive advantage that could bring it a large amount of "rent," would have no "profits" or other spare resources it could use as selective incentives for a lobby. Nonetheless there are many organizations that do have spare returns they can use for selective incentives. First, markets with some degree of monopoly power are far more common than perfectly competitive markets. Second, there are sometimes important complementaries between the economic and political activities of an organization. The political branch of the organization can win lower taxes or other favorable government policies for the economic branch, and the good name won by the political branch may also help the economic branch. For somewhat similar reasons, a social organization may also be a source of a surplus that can be used for selective incentives.

An organization that is not only political, but economic or social as well, and has a surplus that provides selective incentives, may be able to retain its membership and political power, in certain cases, even if its leadership manages to use some of the political or economic power of the organization for objectives other than those desired by the membership, since the members of the organization will have an incentive to continue belonging even if they disagree with the organization's policy. This may help explain why many lobbying organizations take positions that must be uncongenial to

tion could make a joint offering or "tied sale" of a collective and a noncollective good that could stimulate a rational individual in a large group to bear part of the cost of obtaining a collective good.[3] There are for this reason many organizations that have both lobbying functions and economic functions, or lobbying functions and social functions, or even all three of these types of functions at once.[4] Therefore, in addition to the large group lobbies that depend on coercion, there are those that are associated with organizations that provide noncollective or private benefits which can be offered to any potential supporter who will bear his share of the cost of the lobbying for the collective good.

The by-product theory of pressure groups need apply only to the large or latent group. It *need not* apply to the privileged or intermediate groups, because these smaller groups can often provide a lobby, or any other collective benefit, without any *selective* incentives, as Chapter I showed. It applies to latent groups because the individual in a latent group has no incentive voluntarily to sacrifice his time or money to help an organization obtain a collective good; he alone cannot be decisive in determining whether or not this collective good will be obtained, but if it is obtained because of the efforts of others he will inevitably be able to enjoy it in any case. Thus he would support the organization with a lobby working for collective goods only if (1) he is coerced into paying dues to the lobbying organization, or (2) he has to support this group in order to obtain some other noncollective benefit. Only if one or both of these conditions hold will the potential political power of a latent group be mobilized.

---

their membership, and why organizations with leaders who corruptly advance their own interests at the expense of the organization continue to survive.

3. The worth of the noncollective or private benefit would have to exceed its cost by an amount greater than the dues to the lobbying branch of the organization, or the joint offering would not be sufficient to attract members to the organization. Note that on page 51, note 72, selective incentives were defined to be values larger in absolute magnitude than an individual's share of the costs of the collective good.

4. An organization that lobbied to provide a collective good for a large group might even obtain its selective incentives by lobbying also for noncollective "political" goods, like individual exceptions to (or advantageous interpretations of) a general rule or law, or for patronage for particular individuals, etc. The point is not that the organization must necessarily also be economic or social as well as political (though that is usually the case); it is rather that, if the organization does not have the capacity to coerce potential members, it must offer some noncollective, i.e., selective, benefit to potential members.

This chapter will attempt to show how the largest economic pressure groups in the United States are in fact explained by the by-product theory. It will argue that the main types of large economic lobbies—the labor unions, the farm organizations, and the professional organizations—obtain their support mainly because they perform some function besides lobbying. It will argue that labor unions are a dominant political force because they also deal with employers, who can be forced to employ only union members; that farm organizations obtain their members mainly through farm cooperatives and government agencies; and that professional associations rely in part on subtle forms of coercion and in part on the provision of noncollective services to get their membership. Finally, it will argue that the many organizations representing industries with small numbers of firms are explained by a theory of "special interests," which rests on the special capacity for organized action in small groups.

B. LABOR LOBBIES

The labor union is probably the most important single tpye of pressure-group organization and accordingly deserves first place in any discussion of large lobbying organizations. Though the opponents of the labor unions are exaggerating when they claim that the Democratic candidates in industrial states are merely puppets of labor leaders, it is quite clear that the Democrats in these states are normally very friendly to labor, and that the Republicans usually treat the labor unions as the major source of enemy strength. The membership of the AFL–CIO is *several times larger* than the membership of any other lobbying organization. The labor unions have, moreover, an impressive organizational network to match their numbers: there are about 60,000 to 70,000 union locals in this country.[5] Labor leaders have claimed that they could influence about 25 million voters.[6] Their purely political expenditures are measured in the millions.[7] In 1958 some candidates may have been elected as a result of the large labor vote brought out by "right-to-work" proposals on the ballot in some industrial states. In Michigan the Demo-

5. V. O. Key, *Politics, Parties, and Pressure Groups,* 4th ed. (New York: Crowell, 1958), p. 62.

6. Dayton David McKean, *Party and Pressure Politics* (Boston: Houghton Mifflin, 1949), p. 464.

7. For example, *ibid.,* pp. 475–476.

cratic party came out of the doldrums as labor organization grew.[8] There were about 200 unionists who were either delegates or alternate delegates to the 1952 Democratic national convention.[9] The late Sumner Slichter argued that "the American economy is a laboristic economy, or at least is rapidly becoming one." By this he meant "that employees are the most influential group in the community and that the economy is run in their interest more than in the interest of any other economic group." [10] Professor Slichter may have been mistaken, but if so only because many business, professional, and agricultural organizations unite in intense opposition to what they regard as the excessive claims of labor.

Just as there can be little doubt that labor unions are a significant political force, neither can there be much question that this political force is a by-product of the purely industrial activities that unions regard as their major function. As Chapter III pointed out, it was only when labor unions began to concentrate on collective bargaining with employers and abandoned the mainly political orientation of the earlier American unions, that they came to have any stability or power. It was only when the labor unions started to deal with the employers, who alone had the power to *force* the workers to join the union, that they began to prosper. It is, moreover, hard to see how the labor unions could have obtained and maintained the "union shop" in a democratic country like the United States if they had been solely political organizations. Labor unions came to play an important part in the political struggle only long after they had forsaken political action as a major goal. It is worth noting that the Wagner Act, which made organizing a union with compulsory membership much easier, and which led to the greatest increase in union membership, was passed *before* labor unions came to play a really important role in politics. The experience of Great Britain also shows that a democratic nation is often happy to overlook compulsory membership in organizations that engage in collective bargaining, but hesitant to make membership in a political organization in any degree automatic. Although, as Chapter III explained, it has long been taken for granted in Britain that unionists will often not work with nonunion men, there has been a great deal of bitter con-

---

8. Key, p. 73.   9. *Ibid.*
10. Sumner H. Slichter, *The American Economy* (New York: Alfred A. Knopf, 1950), p. 7.

troversy over whether union men should "contract in" or "contract out" of a contribution to the Labour party. (The vast majority of the members of that party, incidentally, are a by-product of the trade unions' activities; all except a small minority belong through the trade unions.)[11] If, then, it is true that a democratic nation would not normally want to make membership in a purely political union compulsory, and that compulsion is essential to a stable labor movement of any size, then it follows that the political power of unions is a by-product of their nonpolitical activities.

C. PROFESSIONAL LOBBIES

Many of those who criticize organized labor because of the coercion entailed in labor unions are themselves members of professional organizations that depend upon compulsion as much as unions do. Many organizations representing prosperous and prestigious professions like the law and medicine have also reached for the forbidden fruits of compulsory membership. There is in fact a pervasive tendency towards compulsion in professional associations generally. "The trend," writes Frances Delancey, "is toward the professional guild."[12] This is what many other scholars have also observed. "A characteristic of the politics of the professional association," according to V. O. Key, "is their tendency to seek the reality, if not invariably the form, of a guild system."[13] J. A. C. Grant argues that the guild "has returned. Its purposes are the same as in the Middle Ages."[14] The guild form of organization is often adopted not only by the ancient and learned professions, but also by undertakers, barbers, "beauticians," "cosmeticians," plumbers, opticians, and other groups interested in professional status.[15] This adoption of the guild form of

11. B. C. Roberts, *Trade Union Government and Administration in Great Britain* (Cambridge, Mass.: Harvard University Press, 1956), pp. 369–380 and 551–553; G. D. H. Cole, *A Short History of the British Working Class Movement, 1789–1947*, new ed. (London: George Allen & Unwin, 1948), pp. 296–299, 310–315, 423–424; Charles Mowat, *Britain Between the Wars* (Chicago: University of Chicago Press, 1955), pp. 336–337; and Martin Harrison, *Trade Unions and the Labour Party Since 1945* (London: Ruskin House, George Allen & Unwin, 1960), *passim*.

12. Frances Priscilla DeLancey, *The Licensing of Professions in West Virginia* (Chicago: Foundation Press, 1938), p. 140.

13. Key, p. 136.

14. J. A. C. Grant, "The Gild Returns to America," *Journal of Politics*, IV (August 1942), 316.

15. Grant, "The Gild Returns to America, II," *ibid.*, IV (November 1942), 463–476.

organization is evidence for the by-product theory of large pressure groups, for compulsory membership has always been, Grant points out, "the first rule" of the guild system.[16]

The self-regulating guild with compulsory membership has reached its furthest degree of development in many state bar associations. Many state legislatures have been induced to require *by law* that *every* practicing lawyer must be a member of the state bar association.[17] These bar associations have closed shops enforced by government, and thus should be the envy of every labor union.

The modern professional associations or guilds are moreover coming to resemble "miniature governments."[18] They have "all the types of power normally exercised by government."[19] State governments often give the professional groups authority to govern themselves (and to a degree their clients) and to discipline any members of the profession that do not maintain the "ethical" standards the profession finds it expedient or appropriate to maintain. It follows that, even when membership in these associations is not a legal requirement, the individual in professional practice knows that he has an interest in maintaining membership in good standing with the professional association.

The advantages of maintaining membership and good relationships with a professional association may be illustrated by the fact that it was not found expedient to release the name of a doctor who had written to a congressional committee to argue that "the central organization of the AMA in Chicago has no idea what the average physician wants his patients to have."[20] Oliver Garceau, author of the classic work on the American Medical Association, has argued that the recalcitrant doctor in trouble with organized medicine may face "a genuine economic threat."[21] When the American Medical Association blocked the Denver city council's program for Denver General Hospital in 1945, a Denver councilman, according to *Time* magazine, was driven to exclaim: "Nobody can touch the American

16. Grant's first installment (August 1942), 304.

17. M. Louise Rutherford, *The Influence of the American Bar Association on Public Opinion and Legislation* (Philadelphia, 1937), pp. 32–34; McKean, p. 568.

18. Grant (August 1942), 324.

19. *Ibid.*

20. U.S. Congress, House Committee on Interstate and Foreign Commerce, 83d Cong., 2d Sess., *Health Inquiry,* Part 7 (1954), p. 2230, quoted in Key, p. 139.

21. Oliver Garceau, *The Political Life of the American Medical Association* (Cambridge, Mass.: Harvard University Press, 1941), pp. 95, 103.

Medical Association . . . Talk about the closed shop of the AFL and the CIO—they are a bunch of pikers." [22]

The role of coercion, even in its subtler forms, in the American Medical Association is, however, probably less important as a source of membership than the noncollective benefits the organization provides its membership. According to Garceau, there is "one formal service of the society with which the doctor can scarcely dispense. Malpractice defense has become a prime requisite to private practice." [23] One doctor who had founded a cooperative hospital, and lost his membership in his medical society, discovered that not only had he lost his chance to have other doctors testify in his behalf during malpractice suits, but that he had lost his insurance as well.[24] The many technical publications of the American Medical Association, and the state and local medical societies, also give the doctor a con-

22. *Time* (Feb. 19, 1945), p. 53, quoted in McKean, p. 564.

23. Garceau, p. 103.

24. *Ibid.*, p. 104. Those who are not members of thier local medical societies can, now at least, usually get malpractice insurance, though they must apparently pay higher rates. One student of the economics of medicine, Reuben Kessel, describes the situation in this way:

"County medical societies play a crucial role in protecting their members against malpractice suits. Physicians charged with malpractice are tried by their associates in the private judicial system of organized medicine. If found innocent, then local society members are available for duty as expert witnesses in the defense of those charged with malpractice. Needless to say, comparable services by society members for plaintiffs in such actions are not equally available. By virtue of this monopoly over the services of expert witnesses and the tacit coalition of the members of a society in the defense of those charged with malpractice, the successful prosecution of malpractice suits against society members is extremely difficult.

"On the other hand, for doctors who are *persona-non-grata* with respect to organized medicine, the shoe is on the other foot. Expert witnesses from the ranks of organized medicine are abundantly available for plaintiffs but not for defendants. Therefore the position of the plaintiff in a suit against a non-society member is of an order of magnitude stronger than it is for a suit against a society member. Consequently it should come as no surprise that the costs of malpractice insurance for non-society members is substantially higher than it is for society members. Apparently some non-society members have experienced difficulty in obtaining malpractice insurance at any price."

Kessell also argues that the nonmember of the county medical society may have difficulty getting on a hospital staff. "This control over hospitals by the AMA has been used to induce hospitals to abide by the Mundt Resolution. This resolution advises hospitals that are certified for intern training that their staff ought to be composed solely of members of local medical societies. As a result of this AMA control over hospitals, membership in local medical societies is a matter of enormous importance to practicing physicians. Lack of membership implies inability to become a member of a hospital staff." Reuben Kessell, "Price Discrimination in Medicine," *Journal of Law and Economics,* I (October 1958), 2–53, esp. 30–31 and 44–45.

siderable incentive to affiliate with organized medicine. The American Medical Association publishes not only its celebrated *Journal,* but also many other technical periodicals on various medical specialties. Since the nineteenth century the *Journal* alone has provided a "tangible attraction for doctors." [25] The importance of this attraction is perhaps indicated by a survey conducted in Michigan, which showed that 89 per cent of the doctors received the *Journal of the American Medical Association,* and 70 per cent read a state society journal, but *less than 30 per cent* read any *other* type of medical literature.[26] The *Journal* has been, moreover, the "prime money maker of the organization." [27] Much of the organization's revenue, according to Garceau, comes from drug companies' advertisements—advertisements which Garceau believes helped companies obtain the AMA seal of approval for their products.[28] The conventions of the American Medical Association and many of its constituent organizations also provide technical information needed by doctors, and thus give the member a "direct return in education" [29] for the investment in dues, just as the medical journals do.

In short, by providing a helpful defense against malpractice suits, by publishing medical journals needed by its membership, and by making its conventions educational as well as political, the American Medical Association has offered its members and potential members a number of selective or noncollective benefits. It has offered its members benefits which, in contrast with the political achievements of the organization, can be withheld from nonmembers, and which accordingly provide an incentive for joining the organization.

The American Medical Association, then, obtains its membership partly because of subtle forms of coercion, and partly because it provides noncollective benefits. It would have neither the coercive power to exercise, nor the noncollective benefits to sell, if it were solely a lobbying organization. It follows that the impressive political power of the American Medical Association and the local groups that compose it is a by-product of the nonpolitical activities of organized medicine.

It is interesting to ask why no organization of college professors has acquired anything like the political power of the American Medi-

25. Garceau, p. 15.   26. *Ibid.*, p. 99.
27. *Ibid.*, p. 16.   28. *Ibid.*, p. 89.
29. *Ibid.*, p. 66.

cal Association. Probably the most important factor is that, in the academic profession, the learned societies are independent of the political association.[30] If the American Association of University Professors could usurp the functions of the learned societies, it could rival the AMA. If subscriptions to the scholarly journals, and attendance at the conventions of the learned societies, were restricted to members of the AAUP, professors would probably be as well organized and as powerful as doctors. If the AAUP published as many technical journals as the American Medical Association, almost every faculty member would have an incentive to join, and the AAUP membership would presumably rise above its present level,[31] and dues and participation could perhaps also increase.

D. THE "SPECIAL INTEREST" THEORY AND BUSINESS LOBBIES

The segment of society that has the largest number of lobbies working on its behalf is the business community. The *Lobby Index*,[32] an index of organizations and individuals filing reports under the Lobbying Act of 1946 and 1949, reveals that (when Indian tribes are excluded), 825 out of a total of 1,247 organizations represented business.[33] Similarly, a glance at the table of contents of the *Encyclopedia of Associations* shows that the "Trade, Business, and Commercial Organizations" and the "Chambers of Commerce" together take up more than ten times as many pages as the "Social Welfare Organizations," for example.[34] Most of the books on the subject

30. "One important structural difference exists between the AAUP and the AMA. The AMA performs two kinds of functions for its members. In addition to serving physicians in the capacity of a craft union, i.e., protecting and advancing their economic interest, it provides the services of an outstanding scientific organization. For example, it publishes scientific journals, standardizes drugs, protects the public from harmful medicines, and provides a forum for scientific papers. The AAUP, on the other hand, has but one dimension: it is a craft union for college teachers. For scientific services its members look to the professional organizations serving their subject fields." Melvin Lurie, "Professors, Physicians, and Unionism," *AAUP Bulletin*, XLVIII (September 1962), 274.

31. As of January 1, 1965, the AAUP had 66,645 members. *AAUP Bulletin*, LI (March 1965), 54.

32. U.S. Congress, House, Select Committee on Lobbying Activities, *Lobby Index, 1946–49*, Report No. 3197, 81st Cong., 2d Sess., 1950, H.R. 298.

33. Schattschneider, *Semi-Sovereign People* (note 1, above), p. 30.

34. *Encyclopedia of Associations*, 3rd ed. (Detroit: Gale Research Co.), I, 3. See also U.S. Department of Commerce, *Directory of Trade Associations* (Washington, 1956), p. iii; in addition see W. J. Donald, *Trade Associations* (New York: McGraw-Hill, 1933); Benjamin S. Kirsh, *Trade Associations in Law and Business* (New York:

agree on this point. "The business character of the pressure system," according to Schattschneider, "is shown by almost every list available."[35] This high degree of organization among businessmen, Schattschneider thinks, is particularly important in view of the fact that most other groups are so poorly organized: "only a chemical trace" of the nation's Negroes are members of the National Association for the Advancement of Colored People; "only one sixteen hundredths of 1 per cent of the consumers" have joined the National Consumers' League; "only 6 per cent of American automobile drivers" are members of the American Automobile Association, and only "about 15 per cent of the veterans" belong to the American Legion.[36] Another scholarly observer believes that "of the many organized groups maintaining offices in the capital, there are no interests more fully, more comprehensively, and more efficiently represented than those of American industry."[37] Burns and Peltason say in their text that "businessmen's 'unions' are the most varied and numerous of all."[38] V. O. Key points out that "almost every line of industrial and commerical activity has its association."[39] Key also expresses surprise at the extent of the power of organized business in American democracy: "The power wielded by business in American politics may puzzle the person of democratic predilections: a comparatively small minority exercises enormous power."[40]

The number and power of the lobbying organizations representing American business is indeed surprising in a democracy operating according to the majority rule. The power that the various segments of the business community wield in this democratic system, despite the smallness of their numbers, has not been adequately explained. There have been many rather vague, and even mystical, generalizations about the power of the business and propertied interests, but

Central Book Co., 1938); Clarence E. Bonnett, *Employers' Associations in the United States* (New York: Macmillan, 1922) and *History of Employers' Associations in the United States* (New York: Vantage Press, 1956); and Trade Association Division, Chamber of Commerce of the United States, "Association Activities" (Washington, 1955), mimeo.

35. Schattschneider, *Semi-Sovereign People,* p. 31.

36. *Ibid.,* pp. 35–36.

37. E. Pendleton Herring's comment in *Group Representation before Congress* (Washington: Brookings Institution, 1929), p. 78, which is quoted approvingly by McKean, pp. 485–486.

38. James MacGregor Burns and Jack Walter Peltason, *Government by the People,* 4th ed. (Englewood Cliffs, N.J.: Prentice-Hall, 1960), p. 293.

39. Key, p. 96.

40. *Ibid.,* p. 83.

these generalizations normally do not *explain why* business groups have the influence that they have in democracies; they merely assert that they always have such an influence, as though it were self-evident that this should be so. "In the absence of military force," said Charles A. Beard, paraphrasing Daniel Webster, "political power naturally and necessarily goes into the hands which hold the property."[41] But why? Why is it "natural" and "necessary," in democracies based on the rule of the majority, that the political power should fall into the hands of those who hold the property? Bold statements of this kind may tell us something about the ideological bias of the writer, but they do not help us understand reality.

The high degree of organization of business interests, and the power of these business interests, must be due in large part to the fact that the business community is divided into a series of (generally oligopolistic) "industries," each of which contains only a fairly small number of firms. Because the number of firms in each industry is often no more than would comprise a "privileged" group, and seldom more than would comprise an "intermediate" group, it follows that these industries will normally be small enough to organize voluntarily to provide themselves with an active lobby— with the political power that "naturally and necessarily" flows to those that control the business and property of the country. Whereas almost every occupational group involves thousands of workers, and whereas almost any subdivision of agriculture also involves thousands of people, the business interests of the country normally are congregated in oligopoly-sized groups or industries. It follows that the laboring, professional, and agricultural interests of the country make up large, latent groups that can organize and act effectively only when their latent power is crystallized by some organization which can provide political power as a by-product; and by contrast the business interests generally can voluntarily and directly organize and act to further their common interersts without any such adventitious assistance. The multitude of workers, consumers, white-collar workers, farmers, and so on are organized only in special circumstances, but business interests are organized as a general rule.[42]

41. Charles A. Beard, *The Economic Basis of Politics* (New York: Alfred A. Knopf, 1945), p. 103; see also McKean, p. 482.
42. The advantage in having a small number of large units in a group can be illustrated very simply by considering the extreme case of the very large firm with a

The political advantages of the small groups of large units—the business interests—may account for some of the concern about "special interests." As Chapter V pointed out, there may be a sense in which the narrow "special interests" of the small group tend to triumph over the (often unorganized and inactive) interests of "the people." Sometimes the contrast drawn between the "special interests" and the "people" is nothing more than a convenient rhetorical device for politicians and journalists. At other times, however, practical observers may be sensing the fact that the organized and active interest of small groups tend to triumph over the unorganized and unprotected interests of larger groups. Often a relatively small group or industry will win a tariff, or a tax loophole, at the expense of millions of consumers or taxpayers in spite of the ostensible rule of the majority. This is what the distinction between privileged and intermediate groups, on the one hand, and large, latent groups, on the other, would lead one to expect.

The main type of organization representing the business interests is the trade association, and it is not difficult to show how small and "special" the interests the trade associations represent are. Professor Schattschneider points out how few members most trade associations have:

> Of 421 trade associations in the metal products industry listed in *National Associations of the United States,* 153 have a membership of less than 20. The median membership was somewhere between 24 and 50. Approximately the same scale of memberships is to be found in the lumber, furniture and paper industries where 37.3 per cent of the associations listed had a membership of less than 20 and the median membership was in the 25 to 50 range.

The statistics in these cases are representative of nearly all other classifications of industry.[43]

---

political interest unique to itself. Such a firm is a "group of one," and analogous to the monopoly or monopsony in the marketplace. When a large firm is interested in legislation or administrative regulations of unique importance to itself, there is little doubt that it will act in its interest. It is in an even more favorable position than the firms in the privileged group. In the case of the single large firm, the ordinary rules of the market tend to apply. Markets evolve. Washington is said to be host to numerous lawyers, former officials, and retired congressmen who are adept at helping individual businesses get what they want from the government. These services are provided for a fee: a market has developed. The language is a shibboleth of the fact that in this sphere of politics collective goods are not involved, and that an informal, sometimes shadowy, price system exists: consider the "influence peddler."

43. Schattschneider, *Semi-Sovereign People,* p. 32.

"Pressure politics," Schattschneider concludes, "is essentially the politics of small groups."[44] V. O. Key points out that the effective or supporting membership of these trade associations is often much smaller than would be expected; "in almost half of them," he says, "nearly 50 per cent of the cost is borne by a handful of members."[45]

The trade associations are therefore normally rather small, and this smallness must be the principal reason that so many of them exist. Many of the trade associations, however, are able to derive still further strength because they provide some noncollective services for their members in addition to lobbying. They provide noncollective or nonpublic benefits the same way that many nonbusiness organizations do, and thus they have not only the advantage of being composed of rather small numbers of rather substantial or well-to-do business members, but in addition all the opportunities that other organizations have to provide a noncollective good to attract members. Many trade associations distribute trade statistics, provide credit references on customers, help collect bills, provide technical research and advisory services, and so on. Merle Fainsod and Lincoln Gordon list seventeen different functions which trade associations perform *in addition* to their political or lobbying duties.[46] By performing these additional functions the trade associations offer a further incentive to membership.

The disproportionate political power of the "special interests" or particular business interests should not, however, lead one to suppose that the whole business community necessarily has disproportionate power in relation to organized labor, the professions, or agriculture. Although particular industries normally have disproportionate power on questions of particular importance to themselves, it does not follow that the business community has disproportionate power when dealing with broad questions of national concern. For the business community as a whole is not well organized in the sense that particular industries are. The business community *as a whole* is not a

44. *Ibid.*, p. 35.
45. Key, p. 96.
46. Merle Fainsod and Lincoln Gordon, *Government and the American Economy*, rev. ed. (New York: W. W. Norton, 1948), pp. 529–530. E. Pendleton Herring, in *Group Representation before Congress*, p. 98, describes the diverse functions of the trade associations thus: "The trade association has succeeded upon its merits. It fulfills a definite need in industry. There are so many matters in which cooperation is necessary and economic that a clearing house such as a trade association is considered desirable."

small privileged or intermediate group—it is definitely a large, latent group. As a result it has the same problems of organization as the other segments of society.

The two major organizations purporting to speak for business as a whole—the National Association of Manufacturers and the Chamber of Commerce of the United States—illustrate this point rather well. Neither of them has disproportionate power in relation to the AFL-CIO, the AMA, or the American Farm Bureau Federation.

The Chamber of Commerce of the United States is only a "federation of federations."[47] Its principal members are the many local chambers of commerce and similar organizations around the country. These local chambers of commerce are normally small groups, and on that ground can normally organize with relative ease. They are made the more attractive to members by the fact that they are good places for businessmen to make "contacts" and exchange information. The Chamber of Commerce of the United States is built up from these local chambers of commerce on the principle of federation; but in the process of federation much of the strength is lost. The national organization provides various informational and organizational services to the local organizations, but nonetheless the individual member and even the individual local chamber of commerce are essentially only individual units in a latent group. They can make no decisive contribution to the success of the national organization, and will get the benefit of any achievements of the national organization whether they have participated or not. A number of very large businesses will gain or lose so much from changes in national policy that they will find it expedient to make significant contributions—and the Chamber has found it necessary to sell special individual memberships to such large businesses.[48] The money derived from big business, and a vague federal connection with the local chambers of commerce, can give the Chamber of Commerce of the United States a certain amount of power, but certainly not disproportionate power.

The National Association of Manufacturers is also based on the small group. It is in fact based on a *single* small group of very large businesses. Though nominally the NAM has a few thousand mem-

47. Burns and Peltason, p. 293.
48. McKean, p. 486.

bers, it is in practice supported and controlled by a handful of really big businesses. As Dayton McKean describes it: "The president of the Association is usually a small manufacturer of very conservative views, who serves for one or two years. The presidents of the giant corporations, which by general agreement dominate the Association because their concerns provide the funds by which it operates, do not serve as its president. About 5 per cent of the membership contribute about half the money." [49] About eight tenths of one per cent of the members of the NAM have held 63 per cent of all directorships.[50] Although these few big businesses have made it possible for the NAM to spend as much as 5.5 million dollars per year for political purposes,[51] they are still a small group, and are by no means more powerful than the major organizations representing labor, the professions, or the farmers. The NAM has not been successful in preventing the passage of measures it opposes, and its support of a cause is sometimes regarded as the "kiss of death." [52]

The business community as a whole, which is certainly a large, latent group, is therefore not fully organized. It has two organizations that attempt to represent it, but these two organizations draw much of their support from a small group of giant businesses: they do not attract the direct support of the whole business community. A small group is powerful in matters relating to a particular industry, because then it is normally the only organized force, but it is less formidable when questions which divide the entire nation are involved, for then it must take on organized labor and other large organized groups. The business community in the aggregate is for this reason not uniquely effective as a pressure group.

The judgment that the "special interests"—the individual industry groups—have disproportionate power, though the business community as a whole does not, is apparently consistent with the general trend of current affairs. For it seems that particular interests do win tax loopholes, favorable tariffs, special tax rulings, generous regula-

---

49. *Ibid.*, p. 489; Robert A. Brady, *Business as a System of Power* (New York: Columbia University Press, 1943), pp. 211–212.

50. Alfred S. Cleveland, "NAM: Spokesman for Industry?" *Harvard Business Review*, XXVI (May 1948), 353–371.

51. Key, p. 100.

52. R. W. Gable, "NAM: Influential Lobby or Kiss of Death?" *Journal of Politics*, XV (1953), 253–273.

tory policies, and the like, but that the business community as a whole has been unsuccessful in its attempts to stop the trend toward social-welfare legislation and progressive taxation.

E. GOVERNMENT PROMOTION OF POLITICAL PRESSURE

The most striking fact about the political organization of farmers in the United States is that there has been so little. Farmers have not on the whole been well organized, except perhaps in recent years. And what organization the farmers have had has tended to be unstable. Many farm organizations have come and gone, but only a few have come and stayed.

There was no lasting, significant farm organization or lobby in this country until after the Civil War,[53] though farmers were the largest group in the population throughout the early history of the country. The first farm organization worth mentioning was the Grange—the Patrons of Husbandry. The Grange was started in 1867, and in the first few years of its life it spread like a prairie fire across the plains of the country.[54] It had very soon acquired an impressive membership and a considerable amount of power. But the Grange soon collapsed as fast as it had grown. By the 1880's it was already insignificant.[55] The Grange has survived with a small membership to the present day, but has never regained the power and glory of its youthful years. Indeed, the precipitous decline it suffered apparently affected the spirit as well as the body of the Grange, for since then it has generally avoided controversial economic or political issues. It has become to a great degree a social organization, and is no longer an aggressive pressure or lobbying organization, though it does some low-keyed lobbying.[56]

The remarkable achievement of the Grange is that it has managed to survive at all, when so many other farm organizations formed since it began have passed away. The Farmers' Alliances, the Greenback movement, the Free Silver movement, the Agricultural

53. Fred A. Shannon, *American Farmers' Movements* (Princeton, N.J.: D. Van Nostrand, 1957), pp. 8–48.

54. *Ibid.*, pp. 54–57; Charles M. Gardner, *The Grange—Friend of the Farmer* (Washington, D.C.: National Grange, 1949), pp. 3–12.

55. Solon J. Buck, *The Agrarian Crusade* (New Haven, Conn.: Yale University Press, 1920), pp. 60–76.

56. Gardner, *passim;* David Lindstrom, *American Farmers' and Rural Organizations* (Champaign, Ill.: Garrard Press, 1948), p. 177.

Wheel, the Gleaners, Populism, the Equity, the Brothers of Freedom, and other such organizations died within a few years of their birth.[57] This indeed has been the general pattern.

The Farmers Union and the Farm Bureau are the two distinct exceptions to that pattern. But these two organizations also have had their difficulties. The Farmers Union, the older of the two, was started in Texas in 1902.[58] During its early years it acquired a significant membership in the South. This membership was lost after the First World War and the organization nearly succumbed to this tragedy.[59] The organization began a new life in the Great Plains states during the interwar years, but its membership in this period was very small. In the late 1930's and in the 1940's the Farmers Union built a firmer base of support in the states of the Missouri Valley, however, and it is from this region that it presently draws most of its strength.[60]

The Farm Bureau, which is now the largest of the farm organizations, and the only one with a nationwide membership, was from the very beginning completely different from other farm organizations. For the Farm Bureau was created by the government. The Smith-Lever Act of 1914 provided that the federal government would share, with the states, the cost of programs for providing what has come to be called "county agents," who furnish farmers information on improved methods of husbandry developed by the agricultural colleges and agricultural experiment stations.[61] Many of the state governments decided that no county could receive any government money for a county agent unless it organized an association of farmers that would be evidence of an interest in getting more information on modern agricultural methods. These county organizations came to be called "Farm Bureaus."[62] They were the beginning of the Farm Bureau movement that exists today. There were, it is true, a

57. Carl C. Taylor, *The Farmers' Movement, 1620–1920* (New York: American Book Co., 1953), *passim*.

58. Theodore Saloutos, *Farmer Movements in the South, 1865–1933* (Berkeley and Los Angeles: University of California Press, 1960), pp. 184–212.

59. Lindstrom, p. 208; Taylor, pp. 335–364.

60. Key, p. 43; Theodore Saloutos and John D. Hicks, *Agricultural Discontent in the Middle West, 1900–39* (Madison: University of Wisconsin Press, 1951), pp. 219–254.

61. Gladys L. Baker, *The County Agent* (Chicago: University of Chicago Press, 1939), pp. 36–40.

62. *Ibid.*, p. 16.

handful of these county Farm Bureaus a year or two before the government started providing money for county agents,[63] but these were so few in number that they were totally insignificant, and they were in any case like the county Farm Bureaus started by the government in that their purpose was simply to obtain better information on agricultural methods.[64]

The expenditure of government funds for "extension work," that is for the county agents, increased greatly during World War I, so the number of county Farm Bureaus naturally increased *pari passu*. These county Farm Bureaus, normally under the guidance of the county agent (who often had to maintain the Farm Bureau in his county or else lose his job), soon combined to form statewide Farm Bureaus. These state organizations in turn formed a national organization, the American Farm Bureau Federation, in 1919.[65]

Up to this time the Farm Bureau was, first, a quasi-official organization, set up in response to financial incentives provided by government, and second, an organization that provided individualized or *noncollective* benefits to its members. The second point is especially important. The farmer who joined his county Farm Bureau got technical assistance and education in return. The farmer who joined was normally put on the mailing list for technical publications: the farmer who did not join was not. The farmer who joined had first call on the county agent's services: the farmer who did not, normally had last call, or no call at all. A farmer thus had a specific incentive to join the Farm Bureau. The dues he had to pay were an investment (and probably a good investment) in agricultural education and improvement.

Under the stimulus furnished by the increasing government expenditures on agricultural extension work, the membership of the county and state Farm Bureaus, and therefore of the American Farm Bureau Federation, increased very rapidly. By 1921, the Federation had a membership of 466,000.[66] In the next year, however, the membership was considerably less, and it continued to fall more or less steadily until 1933, by which time it was only 163,000.[67]

---

63. Orville Merton Kile, *The Farm Bureau Movement* (New York: Macmillan, 1921), pp. 94–112.

64. *Ibid.*, pp. 94–112.

65. *Ibid.*, pp. 113–123; Grant McConnell, *The Decline of Agrarian Democracy* (Berkeley and Los Angeles: University of California Press, 1953), pp. 44–54.

66. McConnell, p. 185.

67. *Ibid.*, p. 185.

At the very time that its membership was falling, there was every reason to suppose that the value of the services the Farm Bureau was providing to farmers was increasing.[68] The Farm Bureau was taking on new functions. It had helped create the powerful "farm bloc" and was bringing the passage of much legislation that was popular among (and helpful to) the farmers. At the same time, with the help of the county agents, it was promoting a number of cooperatives designed to bring savings to farmers. Why then did the membership of the Farm Bureau continue to fall? The answer, almost certainly, is that, as the Farm Bureau took on these new functions, it naturally increased the competition of the political and business organizations already in the field. The result was that the nation began to notice that the Farm Bureau was at once a pressure group, and a (cooperative) business organization, subsidized by public funds. The situation was so anomalous that it naturally stimulated a negative reaction. The criticism led to the "True-Howard" agreement, which restricted the extent to which the county agent could work for the Farm Bureau organization or for Farm Bureau members alone.[69] The county agent was no longer supposed to "organize farm bureaus or similar organizations, conduct membership campaigns, solicit memberships, receive dues, handle farm bureau funds, edit and manage the farm bureau publications," and so on.[70] Though the extent to which the government could subsidize the Farm Bureau was then limited, these subsidies were not stopped altogether. The county agents continued to assist the farm bureaus, but they did so less regularly and less conspicuously as time went on.[71]

It was presumably this limitation on the amount of help that the county agent could give the farm bureaus that accounted for the decline in membership at the very time the organization was expanding its programs. As it became more convenient for farmers who were not members of the Farm Bureau to get the technical help of the county agent, and as it became harder for the farm-bureau organization to obtain the governmentally subsidized labor of the county agent, the incentive to join the Farm Bureau decreased.

This decline in the membership of the Farm Bureau Federation

68. Kile, *Farm Bureau Movement, passim.*

69. Orville Merton Kile, *The Farm Bureau Through Three Decades* (Baltimore: Waverly Press, 1948), pp. 110–111.

70. *Ibid.*, p. 110.

71. William J. Block, *The Separation of the Farm Bureau and the Extension Service* (Urbana. Ill.: University of Illinois Press, 1960).

came to a halt in 1933. In this year the Roosevelt administration began a vast program of aid to agriculture under the Agricultural Adjustment Act. To get the program off to a rapid start, that administration had to rely on the only nationwide administrative system that had any experience with agriculture—the Agricultural Extension Service, with its county agents in every county. The county agents then took over the task of administering the programs that controlled how much farmers could plant, how much they had to plow down, and how large their subsidy checks were. This development naturally favored the Farm Bureau, and increased its membership.[72] Although stories of county agents sending farmers their government checks in the same envelopes in which they sent bills for Farm Bureau dues[73] are no doubt exceptional, there can be no question that, at a time when the county agent was the channel through which the farmer got both his government aid and his agricultural education, it was often expedient to join the county agent's organization: the Farm Bureau. Accordingly, in this period the Farm Bureau enjoyed a moderate increase in its membership, though it failed to reach the level of membership it had enjoyed in 1921.[74]

Later in the 1930's the Farm Bureau lost this particular source of strength. The Farm Bureau had cooperated wholeheartedly with the New Deal agricultural program and Secretary of Agriculture Henry Wallace in the first few years of the Roosevelt administration, but this cooperation became more difficult as time went on. The Roosevelt administration soon set up an administrative system independent of the county agent to administer the Agricultural Adjustment Act. A new federal hierarchy was created, and in each county this federal administrative machine was helped by "farmer-elected committeemen." These commmitteemen were farmers who were elected by their neighbors to help administer the farm program in the county, and who worked part time in the pay of the government. The establishment of this new administrative system not only weakened the county agent, and therefore the Farm Bureau; it also set up what inevitably became, especially during the Truman administration, another farm organization. The farmer-elected committeemen were

72. *Ibid.*, pp. 15–16.
73. Sam B. Hall, *The Truth About the Farm Bureau* (Golden, Colo.: Golden Bell Press, 1954), pp. 10–12.
74. McConnell, p. 185.

in constant touch with the Department of Agriculture, and they soon began to form, along with their friends and neighbors, a subtle but relatively influential farm organization that often opposed the Farm Bureau.[75]

F. FARM COOPERATIVES AND FARM LOBBIES*

There was, meanwhile, one state in which the Farm Bureau was developing important new organizational techniques, and in which it was making its best progress. These organizational techniques, which have since been widely copied, have unfortunately never been explained or analyzed in any single publication, and as a result the problems of the farm organizations in general, and the Farm Bureau in particular, have often been misunderstood. Throughout the thirties and forties the Farm Bureau in Illinois was coming to have more and more membership in relation to the other major agricultural states. The Illinois Farm Bureau (which strictly speaking should be called the "Illinois Agricultural Association") had a tenth fewer members than the Iowa Farm Bureau (the most nearly comparable organization) in 1925, but it had twice as many members by 1933 and an even bigger lead over the Iowa Farm Bureau by 1938.[76]

The progress of the Farm Bureau in Ilinois was due to the extensive system of cooperative business organizations it had set up in that state. But these cooperatives were not the "Rochdale" type of cooperatives normally found in this country, but rather a new type, which is appropriately called the "Kirkpatrick" type of "cooperative," because it was designed primarily by Donald Kirkpatrick, the general

---

* Most of what I shall have to say in this section is based upon many hundreds of interviews with leaders and members of the Farm Bureau and the Farmers Union, and on an extended examination of some of the publications and documents of these two organizations and their cooperatives and other business affiliates. To the best of my knowledge, the relationship of the farm organizations and their affiliates has never been explained, at least in detail. I had planned (and still hope) to write at some length on this subject, and for this reason undertook detailed research into some of the relevant primary sources.

75. On this whole question of the relation between governmental units and agencies and lobbying strength see Charles M. Hardin, *The Politics of Agriculture* (Glencoe, Ill.: Free Press, 1952), *passim;* and also John D. Black, *Federal-State-Local Relations in Agriculture*, National Planning Association, Planning Pamphlet No. 70 (February 1950).

76. From an undated mimeographed set of figures entitled "Memberships Paid to American Farm Bureau Federation," which was prepared by the American Farm Bureau Federation.

counsel for the Illinois Agricultural Association.[77] The "Kirkpatrick" cooperatives differ from other cooperatives, first of all, in that they are controlled, not by their patrons, but by a legally separate organization. All of the voting stock in the cooperative business and mutual insurance companies associated with the Illinois Agricultural Association is held, not by their patrons, but by the Illinois Agricultural Association itself—the political or lobbying organization.[78] The cooperative marketing, supply, and insurance companies associated with the Farm Bureau in Illinois are run, then, by an organization that is legally completely separate, and which has legislative and lobbying objectives rather than the business or economic objectives cooperatives and mutual insurance companies normally have. The system was set up in such a way that the business purposes of the purely economic parts of the system would *always* be completely subordinate to the political part of the system. As an official pamphlet on the history of the Farm Bureau insurance companies in Illinois points out, "men of vision were drafting policies and *systems of control* that placed the insurance companies *forever* under the direction of the parent organization."[79] (Italics mine.)

The proof that the interest of the political arm of the Farm Bureau is important even in the management of the business side of the movement is found in the fact that *some of the business enterprises are not allowed to sell their product to anyone who is not, and will not become a member of the political organization.* This is true primarily of the mutual casualty insurance companies. The marketing and farm-supply cooperatives controlled by the Farm Bureau in Illinois will normally do business with anyone, but *they generally will not pay a "patronage dividend" to anyone who is not a member of the Illinois Agricultural Association.* This means many farmers find that, if they do not join the Farm Bureau, they lose patronage

---

77. Illinois Agricultural Association, *Guardians of Tomorrow,* undated pamphlet published by IAA insurance service, p. 10.

78. "Business Services Developed," *The Illinois Agricultural Association Record* (January 1941), pp. 34–42; Wilfred Shaw, "The Farm Bureau as Parent Organization" (an undated typescript written by Shaw as a staff member of the Illinois Agricultural Association).

79. *Guardians of Tomorrow,* pp. 8–9. For interesting comments on the Illinois Agricultural Association, see Arthur Moore, *The Farmer and the Rest of Us* (Boston: Little, Brown, 1945), pp. 80–98. This section of my book has benefited from criticisms by W. E. Hamilton, director of research for the American Farm Bureau Federation, who feels, however, that certain aspects of this discussion are mistaken or misleading.

dividends or other noncollective business benefits amounting to far more money than the Farm Bureau dues; thus it would cost them money, sometimes a lot of money, to stay out. So the Farm Bureau dues often come indirectly out of the earnings of Farm Bureau business enterprises. Obviously, arrangements of this kind do not exist primarily for business reasons. The requirement that the benefits from patronizing a Farm Bureau business organization should normally go only to Farm Bureau members in maintained in the interests of the political organization. The publications of the organization admit this. For example: "Still another avenue of vision and hope was being explored in the field of commercial services with the thought that offering them through the state association would bring about greater membership participation . . . Thus, in looking into the possibilities of establishing commercial services to be offered by the state association, it was in the hope that such services would be confined to Farm Bureau members only." [80]

The Kirkpatrick type of cooperative, then, is distinguished from other cooperatives, first, in that it is controlled by a lobbying or legislative organization, and second, by the fact that it generally restricts the benefits of trading with it to members of that lobbying or legislative organization. This Kirkpatrick plan has worked very well indeed in Illinois. In recent years the membership of the Illinois Agricultural Association has come to include almost every farmer in the state (as well as a sizable number of nonfarmers who have dealt with its business organizations). It is sometimes said (though this is no doubt an exaggeration) that it is economically almost impossible to operate a farm in Illinois without patronizing some Farm Bureau business and therefore becoming a member of the Farm Bureau. The Farm Bureau businesses in Illinois deal in a vast variety of products.[81] By 1951 the Illinois Farm Supply Company, which is only one of the Farm Bureau business organizations, had paid out (along with its local affiliates) over 41.5 million dollars in patronage dividends.[82] The Country Mutual Casualty Company, another Farm Bureau company in Illinois, had 337,000 insurance policies in force. Since there are

80. *Guardians of Tomorrow*, pp. 5–6.

81. Illinois Agricultural Association, "The Farm Bureau Idea," n.d., mimeo.; Illinois Farm Supply Co., *Men of Illinois Farm Supply Co., 1926–1951* (1951).

82. *Men of Illinois Farm Supply Co., 1926–1951*. See also Illinois Farm Supply Co., *32nd Annual Report*, Chicago: Nov. 18, 1958.

not nearly that many farmers in the state,[83] some farmers must have more than one policy and many nonfarmers must have dealt with the company. These policies obviously have brought a good proportion of the farmers in the state into the Illinois Agricultural Association. The membership in this organization has grown *pari passu* with the expansion of its business affiliates.

The success of the Kirkpatrick type of business organization in Illinois bred imitation by state Farm Bureaus throughout the nation.[84] By now Farm Bureau business organizations of one kind or another are operating in almost every state. These organizations are generally, but not invariably, patterned in the exact image of those in Illinois. They are normally controlled by the state Farm Bureaus and generally restrict their benefits to Farm Bureau members. They have normally been quite profitable. This profitability often owes something to the favorable tax treatment given cooperatives, but that is not the only explanation. The Farm Bureau has created an especially large number of automobile insurance companies, and these may have profited from the fact that their clientele was largely rural, and thus at times probably less apt to drive in congested areas and be involved in traffic accidents. It is interesting that the two largest automobile insurance companies in the nation, State Farm and Nationwide, both started out selling insurance to farmers in affiliation with the Farm Bureau.[85]

As the Kirkpatrick type of business organization has been adopted by state Farm Bureaus all over the nation, the membership in the Farm Bureau has increased manyfold. The membership in the American Farm Bureau Federation was 163,000 in 1933, 444,000 in 1940, 828,000 in 1944, and 1,275,000 in 1947, and since 1953 has been in excess of a million and a half.[86] The growth in membership has

83. *Guardians of Tomorrow*, p. 19.

84. On the extent to which Farm Bureau insurance companies cover the nation, see American Agricultural Mutual Insurance Company, "Directory of State Farm Bureau Insurance Companies," March 25, 1959, mimeo., and "Summary of Insurance in Farm Bureau Companies," Oct. 1, 1948.

85. Murray D. Lincoln, *Vice President in Charge of Revolution* (New York: McGraw-Hill, 1960); Karl Schriftgiesser, *The Farmer from Merna: A Biography of George J. Mecherle and A History of the State Farm Insurance Companies* (New York: Random House, 1955).

86. "Memberships Paid" (note 76, above). There is an interesting contrast here between the farm organizations' successes in using business institutions to provide noncollective benefits and the inability of most labor unions to provide noncollective benefits through business activities that are sufficient to maintain their membership.

followed the expansion of the business organizations that tend to restrict their benefits to Farm Bureau members. The American Farm Bureau Federation now has what no farm organization in America has ever had before: a large, stable, nationwide membership.

The size and relative stability of the American Farm Bureau Federation, then, has been the result of two factors. One is that for a long while it was the natural channel through which farmers could get technical aid and education from the government; the other is that it controls a vast variety of business institutions that normally provide special benefits to Farm Bureau members. The Farm Bureau is of course also a lobbying organization—one of the nation's largest. But there is almost no evidence that the lobbying the Farm Bureau has done accounts for much of its membership. The fluctuations in its membership clearly cannot be explained by any changes in its legislative policies, or in the popularity of its policies. On the contrary, the Farm Bureau seems to have grown very rapidly in periods when, if the results of polls and elections can be believed, its policies were the least popular. The theory of latent groups would suggest that the lobbying activities of an organization as large as the Farm Bureau would not provide an incentive that would lead rational individuals to join the organization, even if they were in complete agreement with its policies. Therefore, large pressure-group organizations must derive their strength as a by-product of some nonpolitical functions. The lobbying strength of the Farm Bureau seems, then, to have been a by-product of the county agents, on the one hand, and the Farm Bureau business organizations, on the other.

The Farm Bureau is not, however, the only farm organization whose political power is a by-product of its nonpolitical functions. The Farmers Union, which had such a troubled and unstable existence until the late thirties, has now found a stable, solid membership in the Great Plains, and it has got this stability through the

---

Presumably the main explanation of the contrast is that farmers—especially the larger ones who are the most likely to belong to farm organizations—have special needs arising out of the farm business that farm cooperatives can satisfy. The farmer needs marketing facilities for his farm production and a vast variety of agricultural supplies, and there is no similar special demand on the part of industrial wage earners. Another factor that may help to explain the contrast is that farmers have experience in running their farm businesses and thus are able to manage cooperatives more efficiently than industrial workers could. It is perhaps significant that such unions as have had successful business ventures have tended to represent relatively skilled workers.

farm cooperatives and insurance companies with which it is associated. The Farmers Union has sponsored some mutual insurance companies which are like the Farm Bureau insurance companies in that they normally do business only with those who are or will become members of the political branch of the movement. In addition, it has arrangements with a number of farm cooperatives which further increase its strength. Those farm cooperatives associated with the Farmers Union normally "check off" membership in the Farmers Union—that is to say they simply subtract the dues to the Farmers Union from the patronage dividends the farmer earns by patronizing the cooperative. In addition, these cooperatives normally pay five per cent of their earnings to an "Educational Fund" which is spent by the Farmers Union for lobbying, organizational work, and the like.[87]

Because of the recreational and social benefits the Grange provides for its members, and because of the limited character of its lobbying activities, the Grange probably has less need for business enterprises than the Farm Bureau or the Farmers Union. Yet it, too, has a considerable variety of business organizations associated with it, and many of these buinesses also provide an incentive for membership in the Grange.[88]

There is one farm organization that has tried not to use business institutions or governmental agencies to obtain membership. This is a new and small organization—the National Farmers Organization. It has advertised that the "NFO insures your income instead of your car," [89] thereby implicitly critcizing the business activities of the

87. See Mildred K. Stoltz, *This is Yours—The Montana Farmers Union and Its Cooperative Associates* (Minneapolis: Lund Press, n.d.); Harold V. Knight, *Grass Roots—The Story of the North Dakota Farmers Union* (Jamestown, N.D.: North Dakota Farmers Union, 1947); Ross B. Talbot, "Agrarian Politics in the Northern Plains," unpub. diss., University of Chicago.

88. National Federation of Grange Mutual Insurance Companies, *Journal of Proceedings, Twenty-Sixth Annual Convention,* Sept. 12, 1960; letter of Aug. 2, 1961 from Sherman K. Ives, Secretary of the National Federation of Grange Mutual Insurance Companies, to author. On the importance of cooperatives to Grange membership in the early 1870's, see George Cerny, "Cooperation in the Midwest in the Granger Era, 1869–75," *Agricultural History,* XXXVII (October 1963), 187–205. For membership statistics on all major farm organizations, see Robert L. Tontz, "Membership of General Farmers' Organizations, United States, 1874–1960," *Agricultural History,* XXXVIII (July 1964), 143–156.

89. *NFO Reporter,* I (November 1956), 3. See also George Brandsberg, *The Two Sides in NFO's Battle* (Ames, Iowa: Iowa State University Press, 1964).

Farm Bureau. But it has had a great deal of trouble getting members, and this policy may be changing. Significantly, the National Farmers Organization has so far failed in its "holding actions," or strikes, to withhold farm products from the market. The failure of these strikes was exactly what the theory of latent groups would have led one to expect. Should the National Farmers Organization some day succeed, without using violence or other selective incentives, in maintaining farm prices by getting farmers to withhold some of their output from the market, that would tend to refute the theory offered here.

G. "NONECONOMIC" LOBBIES

The by-product theory of pressure groups seems to explain the lobbying organizations that represent agriculture, as well as those that represent labor and the professions. And, in connection with the "special interest" theory of small lobbying groups, it helps explain the organizations that represent business interests. The theories developed in this study thus appear to account for the main economic pressure-group organizations.

Although most of the lobbies in Washington, and all of the strongest lobbies, have economic objectives, there are also some lobbies with social, political, religious, or philanthropic objectives. Would the theories developed in this book apply to any of these types of lobbies? Logically, the theory can cover all types of lobbies. The theory is general in the sense that it is not logically limited to any special case. It can be applied whenever there are rational individuals interested in a common goal. As Chapter II explained, the theory of large groups, at least, is not even limited to situations where there is self-interested behavior, or where only monetary or material interests are at stake. Accordingly the generality of the theory is clear; on the other hand it is true that this theory, like any other theory, is less helpful in some cases than in others. It would take too long here to examine in detail any of these lobbies with "noneconomic" interests. But it is evident that the theory sheds new light on some essentially social and political organizations, such as veterans' organizations,[90] and that it is not especially useful in studying some

90. The veterans' organizations are not primarily economic organizations, or even political. Their main functions are social, and they attract most of their members because of the social benefits they provide. The neon signs in many American cities attest to the fact that the local chapters of the veterans' organizations have created

other noneconomic lobbies. The theory is not at all sufficient where philanthropic lobbies, that is, lobbies that voice concern about some group other than the group that supports the lobby, or religious lobbies, are concerned.[91] In philanthropic and religious lobbies the relationships between the purposes and interests of the individual member, and the purposes and interests of the organization, may be so rich and obscure that a theory of the sort developed here cannot provide much insight.[92]

---

countless clubs, taverns, and dance halls. These are, in general, open only to members and their guests. The veteran gets not only the physical facilities of a club, but also comradeship and recognition for his wartime service by joining a veterans' organization. Anyone who has seen an American Legion convention kows that the Legionnaires do not spend all of their time in solemn discussions of the evils of the United Nations, or even debating the levels of veterans' benefits. They also have parades and diverse other recreational and social activities. In addition, the American Legion offers group insurance benefits to members. All of these social and other benefits go only to those who join: they provide selective incentives. Any veterans' bonus or other benefit that the lobbies of the American Legion or the Veterans of Foreign Wars pressure the government into providing will by contrast go to any veteran, whether he has joined a veterans' organization or not. The political power of the veterans' lobbies is accordingly a by-product of the social and economic services provided by the veterans' organizations.

91. Many theorists simply assume that all individual behavior, whatever the context, is rational, in the sense in which that word is used in economic models. Whenever a person acts, it is assumed that he acted rationally to further some "interest" he had, even if the action was philanthropic, for that means that the individual got more "utility" (or, better, reached a higher indifference curve) by acting in a philanthropic way than by acting in any other way. All of the situations analyzed so far in this book require no such comprehensive and questionable definition of rationality. But the application of this theory to *some* noneconomic organizations might require such a comprehensive definition. A charitable organization could best be analyzed if the theory were interpreted in this way; the individual who made a modest contribution to a large nationally organized charity would under this interpretation do so, not from any mistaken belief that his contribution would noticeably augment the resources of the charity, but rather because he got an *individual, noncollective* satisfaction in the form of a feeling of personal moral worth, or because of a desire for respectability or praise. Although in this way the theory can be applied even to charities, in such a context it does not seem especially useful. For when all action—even charitable action—is defined or assumed to be rational, then this theory (or any other theory) becomes correct simply by virtue of its logical consistency, and is no longer capable of empirical refutation.

92. A religious organization that promised some ulitmate benefit, such as a favorable reincarnation, to the individuals who were faithful followers, and some punishment to persons who did not uphold the religious institution, would be consistent with the theory offered here. The pessimistic, "original sin" conception of human nature common to many religions is also consistent with the theory. It would be logically quite possible to explain some religious lobbies, then, as by-products of

The theory developed here is also not very useful for the analysis of groups that are characterized by a low degree of rationality, in the sense in which that word is used here. Take for example the occasional band of committed people who continue to work through their organizations for admittedly lost causes. Such a labor of love is not rational, at least from the economic perspective, for it is pointless to make sacrifices which by definition will be ineffective. To say a situation is "lost" or hopeless is in one sense equivalent to saying it is perfect, for in both cases efforts at improvement can bring no positive results. The existence of groups of individuals that work for "lost causes" therefore runs counter to the theory offered in this study (though the insignificance of such groups is of course consistent with the theory).[93]

Where nonrational or irrational behavior is the basis for a lobby, it would perhaps be better to turn to psychology or social psychology than to economics for a relevant theory. The beginnings of such a theory may already exist in the concept of "mass movements"[94]

---

organizations that provide selective incentives to potential members. The famous Anti-Saloon League, on this interpretation, would have been a by-product of the primary, religious function of the Protestant churches, which were its major source of support. Though logically correct, this approach does not seem very helpful, for it appears to neglect some central features of religious motivation. On the extent of lobbying by churches, see Luke Ebersole, *Church Lobbying in the Nation's Capital* (New York: Macmillan, 1951). On the Anti-Saloon League's relationship to the churches see Peter H. Odegard, *Pressure Politics* (New York: Columbia University Press, 1928).

93. There is probably less rationality, at least in the sense in which that word is used in economics, in noneconomic groups than in economic groups. The easily calculable relationships and the objective standards of success and failure in economic life probably develop the rational faculties to a greater degree than noneconomic activities do. The theory developed here would accordingly fit economic groups on the whole better than it would fit noneconomic groups. For a development of this point, see Joseph Schumpeter, *Capitalism, Socialism, and Democracy*, 4th ed. (London: George Allen & Unwin, 1954), pp. 122–123. See also Talcott Parsons, *Essays in Sociological Theory*, rev. ed. (Glencoe, Ill.: Free Press, 1954), pp. 50–69. On political irrationality, see Graham Wallas, *Human Nature in Politics* (Lincoln: University of Nebraska Press, 1962).

94. Mass movements are often utopian in character. Even large groups that work for a utopia could have a reason for acting as a group, even in terms of the theory offered here. Utopias are heavens on earth, in the eyes of their advocates; in other words, they are expected to bring benefits that are incalculably large or probably infinite. If the benefit that would come from establishing a utopia is infinite, it could be rational even for the member of a large group to contribute voluntarily to the achievement of the group goal (the utopia). A minute share of an infinite benefit,

(which, incidentally, are usually not very massive). The adherents of "mass movements" are usually explained in terms of their "aliena-tion" from society.[95] This alienation produces a psychological disturbance or disequilibrium. The support for "mass movements" can accordingly be explained mainly in psychological terms, though the psychological disturbances are in turn related to various charac-teristics of the social structure. A fanatic devotion to an ideology or leader is common in mass movements, and many of these movements are often said to be on the "lunatic fringe." [96] This sort of lobby is more common in periods of revolution and upheaval, and in unstable countries, than it is for stable, well-ordered, and apathetic societies that have seen the "end of ideology." [97]

There is to be sure always *some* ideologically oriented behavior in any society, and among even the most stable and well-adjusted groups. In the United States at present much of this behavior centers around the political parties. Yet it is striking how relatively minor the ideological sacrifices for the political parties in the United States are. Political scientists often comment upon the organizational weak-nesses of the political parties. American parties are usually important only as names and categories, not as formal organizations. As one well-known political scientist said, "the quadrennial creation of presi-dential parties is an exercise in improvisation." [98] This is not to deny

---

or a minuscule increase in the probability of such a benefit, could exceed an indi-vidual's share of the cost of the group endeavor. An incalculably large or infinite benefit could as it were make a "privileged group" out of a rather large group. Religious groups might also be analyzed in this way. But again, it is not clear that this is the best way of theorizing about either utopian or religious groups.

95. William Kornhauser, *The Politics of Mass Society* (Glencoe, Ill.: Free Press, 1959).

96. Eric Hoffer, *The True Believer* (New York: New American Library, 1958); Peter F. Drucker, *The End of Economic Man—A Study of the New Totalitarianism* (New York: John Day, 1939); Seymour Martin Lipset, *Political Man: The Social Bases of Politics* (Garden City, N.Y.: Doubleday, 1960).

97. Daniel Bell, *The End of Ideology* (Glencoe, Ill.: Free Press, 1960); see also Harold D. Lasswell, *Politics—Who Gets What, When, How* (New York: Whittlesey House, 1936). A detailed study of a community in Southern Italy, an area with a political culture profoundly different from that of the United States, suggests however that the theory offered here fits that culture very well: see Edward C. Banfield, *The Moral Basis of a Backward Society* (Glencoe, Ill.: Free Press, 1958).

98. David B. Truman, *The Governmental Process* (New York: Alfred A. Knopf, 1958), p. 532. The late V. O. Key argued that at the state party level the typical situation "is the almost complete absence of a functioning statewide organization. There may be informal cliques that operate by and large in the background. There

the decisive role that parties play in American politics. Even in two-party states the majority of the votes a candidate gets are apt to come from people who voted for him because of his party affiliation rather than his personal qualifications. In many states a candidate cannot feasibly get his name on the ballot unless he has the nomination of a major party. But despite the important role of the two major parties, they do not amount to much as formal organizations: they do not have many "members"—many who regularly attend precinct meetings or contribute to the party treasury (except for the political "machines" in some big cities). Nor do the political parties have large staffs, by comparison with, say, the labor unions.[99] Between 1924 and 1928, the Democratic party did not even maintain a national headquarters.[100] Yet a "very conservative estimate" by an authority put the number of organizations with *permanent* lobbies in Washington in the late twenties at "well over 500" (there are many more now).[101] That any one of a vast number of pressure groups, each representing a relatively small proportion of the American population, should amount to more as a formal organization than either of the great political parties, whose fortunes affect among other things the prospects of every pressure group, is surely a paradox.

One explanation is that political parties usually seek collective benefits: they strive for governmental policies which, as they say, will help all of the people (or at least a large number of them). Though most people feel they would be better off if their party were in power, they recognize that if their party is going to win, it will as likely win without them, and they will get the benefits in any case. The average American has about the same attitude towards his political party that Dr. Johnson said the English people had toward the exiled Stuarts in the eighteenth century. Johnson said that "if England were fairly polled, the present king would be sent away tonight, and his adherents hanged tomorrow." They would not,

---

may be local organizations that exert power. Yet organizations prepared to cope responsibly with statewide matters with a statewide view are the exception. Often party is in a sense a fiction." Quotation from Key's *American State Politics: An Introduction* (New York: Alfred A. Knopf, 1956), p. 271.

99. Perhaps one reason why political parties employ small staffs is that many of their professional workers and leaders are government officials or employees.

100. Arthur Schlesinger, Jr., *The Crisis of the Old Order* (Boston: Houghton Mifflin, 1957), p. 273.

101. Herring (note 37, above), p. 19.

however, "risk anything to restore the exiled family. They would not give twenty shillings to bring it about. But if a mere vote could do it, there would be twenty to one."[102] The point is that the average person will not be willing to make a significant sacrifice for the party he favors, since a victory for his party provides a collective good. He will not contribute to the party coffers or attend precinct meetings. There are on the other hand many people with personal political ambitions, and for them the party will provide noncollective benefits in the form of public office. Since 700,000 officials are *elected* in this country, the latter group is quite important. There are also many businessmen who contribute to the political parties in order to get individual access to officials when matters of importance to their own firms arise.

Political "machines," on the other hand, have massive organizational structures. But the political machines do *not* work for *collective*

102. The point Johnson mentioned shows on the cost side a parallel to the "unnoticed" or "imperceptible" benefits that have been discussed throughout this study, and this parallel is important to an explanation of voting. The action of the firm in the perfectly competitive market will have *some* effect on the market price, but this effect is so small the individual firm neglects it, or fails to perceive it altogether. The typical member of a labor union who will not pay his dues voluntarily, but who will without thought bear the "cost" of casting a vote for a union shop, is acting in the same way. So are the millions of people who do not contribute any time or money to their political party, but who nonetheless sometimes vote for it. So are those who vote on a sunny day, but not when it rains. The cost of voting and signing petitions is thus insignificant and imperceptible to many people, in something roughly like the same way that a competitive firm's effect on price is insignificant and imperceptible to it. The point is that there is a "threshold" above which costs and returns influence a person's action, and below which they do not. This "threshold" concept may also be explained by a physical analogy. Suppose a man's hand is placed in a vise and the vise is tightened. The man will feel pain, and as the vise is tightened further, he will feel more intense pain, and presumably try to free his hand. But while high pressure against a hand is painful and induces a reaction, a very low level of pressure will have no such effect. The small amount of pressure on the hand involved in a handshake will normally inflict no pain whatever, and will not lead to any reaction in any way similar to the reaction caused by the amount of pressure applied in the vise. The pressure must reach a certain level, or threshold, before any reaction occurs.

Some detailed empirical investigations into voting in one American community brought results that are consistent with the foregoing analysis. The investigators found that "the majority of the people vote, but in general they do not give evidence of sustained interest . . . even the party workers are not typically motivated by ideological concerns or plain civic duty." Bernard R. Berelson, Paul F. Lazarsfeld, and William N. McPhee, *Voting* (Chicago: University of Chicago Press, 1954), p. 307.

The fact that voting costs often fall below the threshold and are ignored suggests a way in which the Bentley-Truman "group theory" could be modified and corrected. If the lobbies or pressure groups that have been its major preoccupation were left

goods. A machine is at best interested in patronage, and at worse in outright graft. The workers who keep the precincts in line for a machine are usually interested in getting jobs in city hall. And each party hack knows he will not get a job if he does not aid the machine. Political machines are able to develop well-articulated organizational structures, then, because they strive mainly for benefits that accrue to particular individuals, rather than for the common interests of any large group.[103] It is surely significant that in the language of American party politics, "organization" is often used as a synonym for "political machine," and a "political machine" is assumed to be interested mainly in the individual benefits it can win for its members.

H. THE "FORGOTTEN GROUPS"—THOSE WHO SUFFER IN SILENCE

Now that the major economic pressure groups have been studied, and the relationship of the theories developed here to noneconomic groups and political parties has been sketched, only one major type of group remains to be considered. Unhappily, this is the type of group about which least is known, and about which very little can be said. The remaining type of group is the unorganized group—the group that has no lobby and takes no action. Groups of this kind fit the main argument of this book best of all. They illustrate its central point: that large or latent groups have no tendency voluntarily to act to further their common interests. This point was asserted in the Introduction, and it is with this point that the study must conclude. For the unorganized groups, the groups that have no lobbies and exert no pressure, are among the largest groups in the nation, and they have some of the most vital common interests.

Migrant farm laborers are a significant group with urgent common interests, and they have no lobby to voice their needs. The white-collar workers are a large group with common interests, but they have no organization to care for their interests. The taxpayers are a vast group with an obvious common interest, but in an important

---

out of the theory, and only voting was considered, the theory could be correct. I am indebted to Edward C. Banfield for calling this point to my attention, and for suggesting the Johnson quotation in the text. That quotation is from James Boswell, *The Life of Samuel Johnson* (London: Navarre Society Limited, 1924), II, 393–394.

103. The importance of big-city machines (and sometimes also rural courthouse cliques) suggests another source of such organizational substance as the state and national parties have. The state and national parties draw some organizational strength

sense they have yet to obtain representation. The consumers are at least as numerous as any other group in the society, but they have no organization to countervail the power of organized or monopolistic producers.[104] There are multitudes with an interest in peace, but they have no lobby to match those of the "special interests" that may on occasion have an interest in war. There are vast numbers who have a common interest in preventing inflation and depression, but they have no organizations to express that interest.

Nor can such groups be expected to organize or act simply because the gains from group action would exceed the costs. Why would the people of this (or any other) country organize politically to prevent inflation when they could serve their common interest in price stability just as well if they all spent less as individuals? Virtually no one would be so absurd as to expect that the individuals in an economic system would voluntarily curtail their spending to halt an inflation, however much they would, as a group, gain from doing this. Yet it is typically taken for granted that the same individuals in a political or social context will organize and act to further their collective interests. The rational individual in the economic system does not curtail his spending to prevent inflation (or increase it to prevent depression) because he knows, first, that his own efforts would not have a noticeable effect, and second, that he would get the benefits of any price stability that others achieved in any case.[105] For the same two reasons, the rational individual in the large group in a socio-political context will not be willing to make any sacrifices to achieve the objectives he shares with others. There is accordingly no presumption that large groups will organize to act in their com-

---

from the fact that they are partly federations of fairly small numbers of city machines and courthouse cliques. Harold Laski charged (with some exaggeration) that "political parties in the United States are not organizations to promote ideas but loose federations of machines for getting enough votes to enable the parties to lay their hands on the spoils." From "The American Political Scene: II. The Bankruptcy of Parties," *The Nation,* CLXIII (November 23, 1946), 583.

104. E. E. Schattschneider, *Politics, Pressures, and the Tariff* (New York: Prentice-Hall, 1935).

105. The point that the individuals in any economy have the power to prevent depression or inflation simply by spending more or less, but have as individuals no incentive to do so, came to my attention through William J. Baumol, *Welfare Economics and the Theory of the State* (Cambridge, Mass.: Harvard University Press, 1952), pp. 95–99. See also Abba P. Lerner, "On Generalizing the General Theory," *American Economic Review,* L (March 1960), 121–144, esp. 133.

mon interest. Only when groups are small, or when they are fortunate enough to have an independent source of selective incentives, will they organize or act to achieve their objectives.

The existence of large unorganized groups with common interests is therefore quite consistent with the basic argument of this study. But the large unorganized groups not only provide evidence for the basic argument of this study: they also suffer if it is true.

Appendix
(added in 1971)

As the Preface indicates, this Appendix provides a brief survey of the articles I have written (or co-authored) that are related to this book, and a discussion of an idea for related research that others have proposed.

The articles to be considered here are of two different types. Those of the type we shall consider first were published in journals intended for my fellow economists and are accordingly stated in the specialized language of economics. Though they may seem forbidding at first sight to readers outside of economics, they should in fact be meaningful to any interested reader who has followed the argument of this book. Moreover, if these papers are correct, they (like other writings on collective goods) will have applications in diverse areas of the social sciences. Thus I hope that not only economists, but those in some other fields as well, will find them of interest. The articles of the second type, to which we shall turn later, were written with audiences of varied disciplinary backgrounds in mind, so that any uses they may have should be immediately evident on all sides.

The first of the articles at issue is entitled "An Economic Theory of Alliances,"[1] and was written in collaboration with Richard Zeckhauser. It deals with the way in which members of a small group concerned with a collective good or externality should be expected to interact. It develops the argument that in most circumstances a small group interested in a collective good will provide a less than optimal supply of that good, and that there will also tend to be disproportionality in the sharing of the burdens of providing the good. The disproportionality is called the "exploitation of the great by the small" in this book. The book devotes only a few sentences to this disproportionality but the article develops a detailed model, applies it to real situations, and tests the predictions of the model against

1. *Review of Economics and Statistics*, XLVIII (August 1966), 266–279. This article is also reprinted, along with a part of this book, in Bruce Russett, ed., *Economic Theories of International Politics* (Chicago: Markham Publishing Company, 1968), pp. 25–50.

relevant data. Though the book also abstracts from "income effects," the article takes them fully into account.

The model elaborated in the article conflicts with Erik Lindahl's famous "voluntary theory of public exchange," and, to a lesser extent, with Leif Johansen's updated version of Lindahl's model,[2] and can be used to demonstrate some significant defects in the Lindahl-Johansen approach. The Lindahl and Johansen formulations are not explicitly criticized in the article, but they are touched upon in a fuller version of the study which was published as a separate monograph.[3] Though the applications and empirical tests in the article and the monograph relate only to international organizations and military alliances, the model can equally well be applied to other formal or informal groups containing limited numbers of members.

The theoretical literature on collective goods and externalities has tended to neglect not only the disproportionality of sacrifice explained in the study just described but also the degree of efficiency with which collective goods and externalities are generated or produced by different parties. Such differences in efficiency are often of decisive importance for public policy. In addition, the failure to take account of them has led some of the most skillful writers on the subject, particularly James Buchanan, Milton Kafoglis, and William Baumol, into logical confusion. That is demonstrated in "The Efficient Production of External Economies,"[4] which I also wrote with Richard Zeckhauser. Our argument is stated much more fully, and applied to a practical situation, in "Collective Goods, Comparative Advantage, and Alliance Efficiency."[5]

Another aspect of the theory of collective goods that seems to have been neglected in the literature is that involving what might be called their scope, domain, or clientele. Many writers implicitly assume that every collective good reaches everyone in the nation-state that provides it and no one outside that nation-state. In fact, some collective goods (such as pollution control in local airsheds, or neighborhood public parks) may have only a local impact, whereas others

2. Leif Johansen, "Some Notes on the Lindahl Theory of Determination of Public Expenditure," *International Economic Review,* IV (September 1963), 346–358.

3. *Economic Theory of Alliances* (Santa Monica, Calif.: The Rand Corporation, Rm 4297-ISA, 1966), esp. pp. 13–15.

4. *American Economic Review,* LX (June 1970), 512–217.

5. Roland N. McKean, ed., *Issues in Defense Economics,* Universities-National Bureau Conference Series, N. 20 (New York: Columbia University Press, 1967).

(such as the unpatentable benefits of pure research or the benefits of an international organization) can sometimes virtually cover the earth. It is generally understood among economists that a government cannot usually be expected to provide collective goods at anything approaching an optimal level when the benefits of a collective good it is expected to provide fall in significant proportion outside its boundaries, because the government will find it in its interest to ignore those benefits that are spillovers to other jurisdictions and accordingly produce less of the good than is optimal. I have argued in an article[6] on this subject that there is a similar but generally unrecognized problem when only a minority of the citizens in a jurisdiction would benefit from a collective good it could provide. If the jurisdiction is to provide collective goods to an optimal degree, it will provide those goods or projects that bring gains that are greater than their costs. But even a project that involves more gain than cost will leave more losers than gainers, if the gains go to a minority of those in the jurisdiction and the cost is covered through jurisdiction-wide taxes. When a collective good reaches only a minority of those in a jurisdiction, then, it will not (in the absence of some lucky bargaining) get majority support, and will be provided, if at all, only to a less than optimal degree.

If there are problems when a jurisdiction is *either* too small to encompass all of those who benefit from its services *or* so large that a good proportion of its citizens do not benefit from some collective good it is expected to provide, then there is a case for a separate jurisdiction or government for every collective good with a unique catchment area or domain. There is, in other words, a need for what I have called "The Principle of 'Fiscal Equivalence'."[7] The matter is, of course, far too complicated to justify policy conclusions on the basis of these considerations alone. Yet the arguments in the aforementioned article are sufficient to show that both the ideology that calls for thoroughgoing centralization of government and the ideology that calls for maximum possible decentralization of government are unsatisfactory, and that efficient government demands

---

6. "The Principle of 'Fiscal Equivalence': The Division of Responsibilities Among Different Levels of Government," *American Economic Review: Papers and Proceedings*, LIX (May 1969), 479–487, republished in a slightly altered form in *The Analysis and Evaluation of Public Expenditures: The PPB System*, vol. I, pp. 321–331, issued by the Joint Economic Committee, U.S. Congress, 91st Cong., 1st sess., 1969.

7. *Ibid.*

many jurisdictions and levels of government. The arguments in this paper also help provide a framework for the analysis of some current proposals for decentralization of various urban services in large cities with segregated ghetto populations.

The types of collective goods and externalities with which governments have to deal are not only diverse in their scope and locale, but are presumably also becoming more numerous and important over time. As population, urbanization, and congestion increase, external diseconomies almost certainly increase too. For example, the farmer in a sparsely settled area who is careless about disposing of his garbage, or who has a noisy household, or who decides to go off to work just when everyone else does, creates no problems for anyone else, whereas the same behavior in a crowded city imposes costs on others. As economic development proceeds and technology becomes more advanced, it is probably also true that education and research become relatively more important, and many types of education and research appear to provide significant benefits to the society in addition to those for which the educated person or researcher is rewarded financially. Thus external economies may (though this is not certain) also be increasing in importance. In any event, the percentage of national output spent by governments in developed countries, to deal with what are at least perceived to be externalities and public goods, has greatly increased. I have accordingly argued, in two semipopular articles,[8] that externalities and collective goods are evidently coming to have relatively greater importance in the United States (and perhaps other developed countries) as time goes on. If this argument is correct, it has three important implications that are relevant here.

First, it means that the number of problems requiring government action is increasing. This does not imply that the size of the public sector must soon grow beyond present levels, since governments may now do things that could better be left to the private sector. But it does mean that there has been a secular increase in what governments *need* to do, and that, if the apparent growth in the relative importance of externalities and collective goods continues, the burden that governments must ultimately bear will become even greater.

---

8. "The Plan and Purpose of a Social Report," *Public Interest* (Spring 1969), pp. 85–97, and "New Problems for Social Policy: The Rationale of Social Indicators and Social Reporting," *International Institute of Labour Studies Bulletin* (June 1970), pp. 18–40. These two articles cover approximately the same ground.

Second, an increase in the relative importance of collective goods and externalities means that the National Income and other measures of the National Product, though still extraordinarily useful, are becoming less satisfactory as measures of "welfare" or well-being. There is accordingly an increasing need for additional supplementary measures of "welfare" or "illfare," such as statistics on congestion, pollution levels, crime rates, health status, and so on. I have defined such measures of welfare or the "quality of life" as "social indicators." Most social indicators are measures of the volume or quantity (but not the money value) of an external economy (or diseconomy) or collective good (or bad). The uses of social indicators are explained in the two articles just cited, and illustrated in *Toward A Social Report,*[9] a government document for which I had immediate responsibility during a period of service in government.

Third, an increase in collective goods and externalities can add to the amount of divisiveness and conflict in a society. This can be the case, I argued in another article,[10] because diverse wants or values with respect to a collective good are a basis for conflict, whereas different wants with respect to individual or private goods are not. Everyone in the domain of a given collective good must put up with about the same level and type of collective good, whereas with different tastes for private goods each individual can consume whatever mix of goods he prefers. If this argument is correct, it follows that the explanation of social cohesion or harmony offered by many sociologists, most notably Talcott Parsons, is unsatisfactory.

The contrast between my argument about conflict and cohesion, which was developed with the aid of the tools of economic theory, and the literature of the Parsonian type in sociology and political science, prompted me to make some more general points in the same article about the relationship between the economist's approach and that used in some other parts of social science. I argued that it is not primarily the *objects* of inquiry, but mainly the method and assumptions, that distinguish economics from the other social sciences. The

9. U.S. Department of Health, Education, and Welfare, *Toward A Social Report* (Washington, D.C.: Government Printing Office, Superintendent of Documents, 1969).
10. "Economics, Sociology, and the Best of All Possible Worlds," *Public Interest* (Summer 1968), pp. 96–118, republished with some additional material as "The Relationship of Economics to the Other Social Sciences" in Seymour Martin Lipset, ed., *Politics and the Social Sciences* (New York: Oxford University Press, 1969), pp. 137–162.

economist's approach has been successfully applied not only to the workings of markets in modern Western societies, but also to fundamentally different societies and economic systems, and to problems of government, politics, and social status as well. Microeconomic theory is indeed relevant whenever behavior is purposive and there are not enough resources to achieve all purposes. Parsonian sociology is similarly general in its concerns, and often emphasizes the importance of its conclusions for the economic development of societies. The fact that modern economics and Parsonian sociology can be used to deal with some of the same problems, yet involve different methods and assumptions, makes it possible to show the contrast between the two approaches in practice. This leads to some fresh perspectives on some practical problems and at the same time exposes some methodological weaknesses in well-known works that have not always been evident before.[11]

The contrast between the modern economic and Parsonian sociological approaches has been developed, in a related and much fuller way, in a book by Brian Barry, a most lucid British writer. Barry's book on *Sociologists, Economists, and Democracy*[12] compares a number of writers in the Parsonian sociological tradition with Anthony Down's *Economic Theory of Democracy*[13] and with my *Logic of Collective Action*. Though Barry and I differ at several points, he finds a contrast in the methods and assumptions of the two approaches, and a level of generality in them, that is roughly consistent with what I observed.

There are many examples of concepts developed in one discipline that have been usefully applied to classical problems of another discipline. I would like to deal with one such example here, not merely because it illustrates the point that has just been made, but principally because it brings us to an approach to further research along the lines of this book that other writers have suggested.

This proposed approach emphasizes the role of the "entrepreneur." When Joseph Schumpeter developed the notion of the entrepreneur, he focused upon the businessman who did pioneering things as a

---

11. See either version of the article cited in the preceding footnote, and also "An Analytic Framework for Social Reporting and Policy Analysis," *Annals of the American Academy of Political and Social Science*, CCCLXXXVIII (March 1970), 112–126.

12. Published both in New York and London by Collier-Macmillan in 1970.

13. New York: Harper and Brothers.

producer or seller of individual or private goods. Some recent writers, in discussions of the difficulty of providing collective goods for unorganized groups, have introduced the idea of the entrepreneur who might help a group obtain a collective good it lacked. One aspect of this notion was outlined by the economist Richard Wagner in his review article on this book,[14] and other aspects have been independently developed and elaborated by Robert Salisbury[15] and by Norman Frohlich and Joe Oppenheimer,[16] and in a substantial book by the latter two writers and Oran Young.[17] One could discuss the logical errors and invalid conclusions[18] of this literature, but mistakes are commonplace in new areas of inquiry, and the more important task is to identify and underline the useful insight in these writings. One could also dwell upon the substantial differences among the works at issue, but this is again less significant than the fact that they all emphasize the role of the entrepreneur or leader who helps to organize efforts to provide collective good and tend to call him a "political entrepreneur."

14. "Pressure Groups and Political Entrepreneurs: A Review Article," *Papers on Non-Market Decision Making,* 1966, pp. 161–170. In this generous and stimulating article, Wagner emphasizes the point that, with appropriate democratic institutions and political leaders or entrepreneurs anxious to win votes, a large group may be able to obtain some consideration from the government even if the group is completely unorganized. So long as members of the group vote, political leaders may propose measures in the group's interest in order to win its votes. Thus consumers or farm laborers, for example, may get laws passed in their interest even without any powerful pressure group to lobby for them. This point is certainly correct. It is also perfectly compatible with the argument of the present book, which attempts to explain why some groups have the advantage of being organized and others do not, but does not go into the way a democratic political system can give some degree of representation to unorganized groups. The most casual observation of modern democracies, and particularly of the special interest legislation they have passed, makes clear that it matters a good deal whether a group is organized or not. The differences in the degree of organization among groups often lead to inefficiency as well as inequity. But Wagner is, of course, correct in emphasizing that even totally unorganized groups can have some impact on political decisions.

15. "An Exchange Theory of Interest Groups," *Midwest Journal of Political Science,* XIII (February 1969), 1–32.

16. "I Get By with a Little Help from My Friends," *World Politics* (October 1970), pp. 104–120.

17. *Political Leadership and Collective Goods* (Princeton: Princeton University Press, 1971).

18. The work of Norman Frohlich, Joe Oppenheimer, and Oran Young on this subject is in my opinion distinguished both by its stimulating and helpful qualities and also by some significant errors. The latter are most significant in the *World Politics* article cited above, but part of the responsibility for these rests with me and with other pre-publication critics for untimely or incorrect comments.

As I see it, an analysis of the role of the entrepreneur concerned with collected goods should begin with the special difficulty of providing such goods. The present book has hopefully shown that most groups cannot provide themselves with optimal amounts of a collective good, if any at all, in the absence of what the book calls "selective incentives." Those groups that can must be small enough for their members to have an incentive to bargain with one another. But it by no means follows that even the smallest groups will through the bargaining of their members necessarily obtain an optimal supply of a collective good. If the costs of bargaining are ignored, they will have an incentive to continue bargaining until they do achieve optimality. But individuals in the group will often also have an incentive to "hold out" for a time for a better bargain. Individual bargainers will often even have an incentive to threaten *never* to participate unless their terms are met, and a need to carry out the threat to maintain their credibility. In any event, the costs of bargaining cannot be ignored. The act of bargaining takes time. More importantly, the members of a group lose something every day that passes without their having an optimal supply of a collective good, and must in a world of positive interest rates discount the benefits of any optimal outcome in the future. Finally, the incentive the members of a small group would have to continue bargaining until in the long run they reach optimality may have little importance anyway, since in a changing world what is required for optimality will change from time to time, and then the bargaining may have to start all over again. For all of these reasons it will often be the case that even small groups will not have an optimal supply of a collective good, if any at all.

This means that a leader or entrepreneur, who is generally trusted (or feared), or who can guess who is bluffing in the bargaining, or who can simply save bargaining time, can sometimes work out an arrangement that is better for all concerned than any outcome that could emerge without entrepreneurial leadership or organization. If the entrepreneur senses that the outcome will be more efficient if each member of the group pays a share of the marginal cost of additional units of the collective good equal to his share of the benefits of each additional unit, and others do not sense this, the leader will (as is evident from pages 30 and 31 above) be able to suggest arrangements which can leave everyone in the group better off. If the situation before the entrepreneur arises or intervenes is not optimal, it follows that the entrepreneur may also get something for himself out of the gains he brings about. Because of this gain, and the liking some people have for being leaders, politicians, or promoters, there is often an ample supply of political entrepreneurs. There is no certainty, and often not even a presumption, that an entrepreneur will sometimes be able to work out an arrangement that is agreeable to the parties concerned, and sometimes the difficulty and expense of striking the needed bargains will be too great for an entrepreneur to succeed, or even want to try.

When the group in need of a collective good is sufficiently large (i.e., is a "latent group"), an entrepreneur cannot possibly provide an optimal supply of the good through bargains or voluntary cost-sharing agreements with those in the group; indeed, he normally[19] cannot in this way supply any of the good at all. As this book shows, no individual would have an incentive to contribute anything to the attainment of the collective good, whether through an entrepreneur or not, since an individual in such a large group would get only an infinitesimal share of any gain that resulted from his contribution. Thus either coercion or some reward that can be given only to those who contribute to the group effort (i.e., a "selective incentive") is needed to satisfy a large or latent group's need for a collective good. Because the departure from optimality is so large, and the number of people involved is so great, the gains that can be made from organizing a large group in need of a collective good are often enormous. Thus entrepreneurs will strive mightily to organize large groups. Many of the entrepreneurial efforts in this area, as in markets for private goods, will come to naught. But in some cases, as the sixth chapter of the present book indicates, imaginative entrepreneurs will be able to find or create selective incentives that can support a sizeable and stable organization providing a collective good to a large group. The successful entrepreneur in the large group case, then, is above all an innovator with selective incentives. Since large groups are often part of larger coalitions, and may contain many subgroups

---

19. For the one logically possible exception when there is rational behavior, see the long footnote on pages 48 and 49 of this book. I may be wrong, but the logical possibility outlined there seems to me to occur so rarely in practice, if it happens at all, that it is hardly worth mentioning. I have called attention to this footnote again now because it anticipates one line of argument in some commentaries on this book.

within themselves, the entrepreneur in the large group will often also be a maker of bargains, just as he is in the case where there is only the small group.

In short, the incorporation of the concept of entrepreneurship in the provision of collective goods into the model developed in this book does not contradict its logic or invalidate its conclusions, but rather enriches the argument, and makes it a better tool for the study of organization leadership and change. Here, as is usually the case in science, the contributions of different authors are cumulative.

Index